1 Chronicles

Cyril J. Barber, D.Litt., D.Min., D.D., has authored more than thirty books including commentaries on Judges, Ruth, 1 and 2 Samuel, 1 and 2 Kings, 1 and 2 Chronicles, Nehemiah, and Habakkuk and Zephaniah. He taught for twenty-five years on the faculties of the Trinity Evangelical Divinity School, Talbot Theological Seminary/Biola University, and the Simon Greenleaf University (now a part of the Trinity International University). Now retired, he lives in Hacienda Heights, California, with his wife Aldyth.

1 Chronicles

*The Faithfulness of God to His Word
Illustrated in the Lives of the
People of Judah*

Cyril J. Barber

CHRISTIAN FOCUS

© Cyril J. Barber 2004

ISBN 1 85792 935 7

Published in 2004
by
Christian Focus Publications,
Geanies House, Fearn, Ross-shire,
IV20 1TW, Scotland

www.christianfocus.com

Cover design by Alister Macinnes

Printed and bound by
Mackays of Chatham

Contents

Introduction

This is a devotional commentary on the First Book of Chronicles; I have also written, for this series, a commentary on the Second Book of Chronicles. Both commentaries are intended for lay people and leaders of lay Bible study groups (and perhaps pastors who, after they have done research in scholarly expositions, may find a fresh perspective in these pages).

The Book of Chronicles was written to encourage the Israelites who had returned to Judah after seventy years of captivity in Babylon. They had returned to their homeland with high hopes. On seeing the devastation of their cities and homes their spirits were crushed. The Temple was in ruins and their fields were uncultivated. And perhaps uppermost in their minds was the nagging fear that God had forsaken them.

In responding to these fears the Chronicler assured them of God's faithfulness to His word. But how much did they know of their history and of the covenants God had made with His people? Was their zeal purely patriotic, or were they aware of their spiritual heritage? To inspire hope in the hearts of the returned exiles the Chronicler quickly surveyed the history of the Israelites before dealing at length with the covenant God had made with David.

Bible commentaries generally fall into three broad groups (though each group is subject to subdivision and overlap). These are: exegetical, expository, and devotional. *Exegetical* commentaries are scholarly works that focus primarily on the grammar and syntax of the original text. Examples of such works are E. L. Curtis and A. A. Madsen's *A Critical and Exegetical Commentary on the Books of Chronicles* in the International Critical Commentary series, and J. M. Myers' *1 Chronicles* and *2 Chronicles* in the Anchor Bible. *Expositional* studies build on the work of the exegete using the insights gained from such study to expound the biblical writer's theme or purpose. Examples include J. G. McConville's *I and II Chronicles* in the Daily Study

Bible series, the recent volumes by M. J. Selman entitled *1 Chronicles* and *2 Chronicles* in the Tyndale Old Testament Commentaries series, and J. A. Thompson's excellent *1, 2 Chronicles* in the New American Commentary series. **Devotional** commentaries build upon the contributions of the exegete and the expositor, and seek to apply the teaching of the Word of God to the life of the believer. A recent example is M. Wilcock's *The Message of Chronicles*.[1]

Readers of commentaries need to be aware of the biases of commentators. The different points of view are best represented by marks on a horizontal continuum. Liberal and moderately liberal contributions are placed to the left of center and conservative works to the right. Liberal theologians are prone to find discrepancies in the Bible, and contemporary students of religious history have identified them with different negative schools of biblical interpretation. Conservative students of God's Word are more inclined to defend the Bible's accuracy. In the past, conservatives have often exhibited a shallowness in their thinking, paid little or no attention to exegetical matters, worked solely from an English translation, ignored problems, concentrated on the application of truth to the life of the believer, and have often resorted to typology or allegorism. To no one's surprise but their own, they have made little or no lasting impact. And the reason? Their works have given evidence of superficiality, inaccuracy in explaining the nuances of the text, and do not possess the quality of content that would lift them above the ephemeral.

Realizing this danger, I have tried to be thorough in my research. I have read widely, though I have not quoted from all the works I have consulted. Footnotes have been purposeful, for I have not wanted useful information to detract from the explanation of the biblical text – something that a discussion of critical issues is prone to do. However, having already contributed commentaries on the Book(s) of Samuel and the Book(s) of Kings, I have *not* duplicated here references to the works I consulted while preparing these earlier volumes.

Throughout this book I have provided my own translation of the Hebrew text. This does not mean that I lack appreciation for modern translations. I have provided my own translation (which I admit is a literal one) to bring out as clearly as possible the emphases of the original. The reader, with his or her own preferred translation in hand, can then compare the two. In addition, because very few writers have discussed "David's Mighty Men" I have devoted a few chapters to them.

A lay person may find the opening and closing chapters of First Chronicles a drawback. I have purposely treated these sections *briefly* so as not to bore my readers. A more extensive discussion can be obtained from any number of scholarly works.

At this point a word needs to be said about biblical references. Citations of Scripture in parentheses without mention of the book of the Bible are from 1 or 2 Chronicles (e.g., 20:4). Where references to both 1 and 2 Chronicles occur in the discussion, I have used Roman numerals (e.g., I:4:10 or II:12:8) to differentiate between these two books. Other books of the Bible are cited in full (e.g., Psalm 11:3). Quotations from non-canonical sources like the Apocrypha are identified accordingly (e.g., Apocrypha. Ecclesiasticus 25:6).

What's in a name?

A question naturally arises, "How did the Book of Chronicles get its name? Other books are called 'Joshua' or 'Judges' or 'the Books of Samuel' or 'the Books of Kings'." The name "Chronicles" seems inconsistent.

The Old Testament books were known to the ancient Hebrews by their opening line. Genesis, for example, was known by its first word *Beresit*, "In the beginning," and Exodus as *Weelleh shemot*, "And these are the names of." The Book of Chronicles was called *Dibere hayyamim*, "The annals of the days" or "The words of the days." When the Hebrew Old Testament was translated into Greek, the text of Chronicles was divided into two books. The reason? The Hebrew text was printed without vowels. Greek required vowels and this added significantly to the length of each book. At this time the Books of Chronicles were given the dubious title *Paraleipomenon*, "Things Omitted." Such a title conveyed the impression that the Books of Chronicles comprised addenda to the Books of Samuel and the Books of Kings. This caused them to be relegated to a subordinate position and it became easy to neglect them. It was not until the time of Jerome (4th century AD) that the title *Chronicon totius divinae historiae*, "A Chronicle of the Whole of Sacred History," was suggested. In the course of time Jerome's suggestion was adopted, and it has come to be preferred to either the Hebrew or the Greek titles.

Who wrote Chronicles?

It is important for us, whenever we take up a study of a book of the Bible, to find out all we can about the author, when he wrote his book, for whom, and why. These issues can be boring (and, in the hands of some writers, tedious to the point of curing the worst cases of insomnia). I shall attempt to make them easy to understand and, hopefully, interesting.

The question, "Who wrote the Book of Chronicles?" has puzzled many people. Though the work is anonymous, Jewish tradition from the earliest times has claimed that the compiler of this *selective* history was Ezra.[2] The evidence is not conclusive, but Ezra remains the most likely author. He was a lineal descendant of Phineas, the grandson of Aaron (Ezra 7:1-5), and through his diligent study of the Scriptures he had become a skilled interpreter of the Word of God (Ezra 7:6, 12). It is specifically stated that he "had set his heart to seek the law of Yahweh, and to do [it], and to teach in Israel [His] statutes and judgments" (Ezra 7:10). A careful reading of the Books of Chronicles indicates that only a person of such commitment, and possessed of such knowledge, could have compiled this historical record.

Ezra had been born in exile. While living in Babylonia he gained the favor of King Artaxerxes and, in 458 BC, he was given permission to lead a group of exiles back to Judah. His ministry in Jerusalem overlapped the governorship of Nehemiah, who was sent to the "Land Beyond the River [Euphrates]" by Artaxerxes in 445 BC.

The priests in Jerusalem were lax in their observance of the Law, and certain ceremonies (e.g., Passover) had not been performed for many years. The Levites, however, were more devout, and they became the ones whom Ezra used to teach God's Word to the people.

In addition to being a devoted student of the Scriptures, Ezra was also a man of integrity. On his arrival in Jerusalem he was installed as chief judge with power to settle all disputes arising from the practice of the religion of his people.

All of this is very commendable, but if Ezra did indeed provide a history from the beginning of time to his own era, what sources did he have to draw on? There is data in the Book of Chronicles that indicates that the writer had access to a large library that contained many works of antiquity including the histories of the kingdoms of Israel and Judah. Now it just so happens that in the Apocrypha we are told that Nehemiah, the governor of Judah during the time of Ezra, had a large collection of books that he turned into a "national" library.

The same things are reported in the records and the memoirs of Nehemiah, and also that he founded a library and collected the books about the kings and prophets, and the writings of David, and letters of kings about votive offerings (Apocrypha. 2 Maccabees 2:13).

We are pleased to note, therefore, that Ezra had access to material that he cited in the Book(s) of Chronicles. This data included "The Book of the Kings of Judah and Israel," the "Story of the Book of the Kings," the "Words of Uzziah composed by Isaiah," the "Words of Shemaiah the Prophet, and of Iddo the Seer," a "Midrash of the Prophet Iddo," the "Words of Jehu the son of Hanani," the "Words of Hozai," and the "Book of Nahum the Prophet." And in the Temple (that had been rebuilt in 516 BC) he had available to him the genealogical records of the different tribes and their families that had been kept for millennia.

Of interest in this discussion is the fact that 2 Chronicles ends with reference being made to the decree of Cyrus, king of Persia, allowing all Jews to return to Judah (2 Chronicles 36:22-23) and the Book of Ezra begins with the same information (Ezra 1:1-4). Ezra-Nehemiah was obviously intended to continue Ezra's history to his own day. And so, lest someone pick up and read "volume 2" (i.e., the Books of Ezra-Nehemiah) without first reading "volume 1" (i.e., 1 and 2 Chronicles that in his day was one book), he repeated the same event. And, inasmuch as no one seriously disputes Ezra's authorship of the book that bears his name, there is no real reason why we should doubt that he also gave us the Books of Chronicles. Because there is no absolute proof that Ezra was not the author of Chronicles (though we believe he was), we will refer to him as "the chronicler".[3]

When was Chronicles written?
If Ezra was indeed the author of the Books of Chronicles, then we must be able to assign a date for its composition within his lifetime. The evidence of 2 Chronicles 36:22-23 places the last recorded event at 538 BC. These books, therefore, must have been written after that date. Some writers have raised an objection to Ezra's authorship by pointing to 1 Chronicles 3:19-24 and claiming that it records six generations of Zerubbabel's family. Allowing 20 to 30 years for each generation, it would have been impossible for Ezra to have knowledge of them all.[4] The books, they claim, could not have been finished before 400 BC. Such evidence, if it were true, would be incompatible with Ezra's authorship.

But we must question whether those who dispute Ezra's authorship have not read into the text the kind of information they want to find in order to support their theories. Zerubbabel is of importance because he was a descendant of King David. The way in which his children are recorded implies that they were brothers and sister, not six successive generations.[5] There is no reason, therefore, why the Books of Chronicles could not have been completed before 400 BC.

What is the theme of Chonicles?

The Books of Chronicles contain a history that is highly selective.[6] Obviously everything that had happened from the dawn of time could not be included. Nor could all of the events of each era (from the time of the Patriarchs to the kings) be contained in a single book. Ezra, as a capable historian, singled out certain events that were important to those for whom his work was intended. He was not a historian in our western sense of the word. To him Israel's history was pregnant with spiritual and moral lessons. These he presented in a way that would edify and encourage his readers.[7]

Ezra's readers had returned from captivity in Babylonia to find the city of Jerusalem in ruins. They had tried repeatedly to rebuild its walls, only to be hindered by those who lived in the northern province of Samaria. For the Jews to live in a city without a protecting wall was to endure the reproach of all the people who lived about them. They were also an easy target for whoever wanted to plunder their possessions. Each time they suffered from a predatory raid they were left clinging to life and eking out a meager existence. And these experiences caused them to feel forsaken by the Lord who in times past had protected them. It was natural, therefore, for the Jews to question God's continued involvement in their national life. Were they still His chosen people? Could they still rely on Him for His help? With no king of David's line sitting on his throne, what had become of the Davidic covenant? To be sure, David's descendants were living among them, but had God's promise of an enduring dynasty been abrogated by their disobedience?

Ezra wrote to assure the people of God's faithfulness to His Word. He explained to them the reason for the exile and assured them of the Lord's continued involvement in their lives.[8] He also sought to encourage them in the pursuit of godliness in spite of their circumstances. While the monarchy might no longer be in effect, the theocracy was. The Lord still had His representatives (administrative/judicial, priestly/spiritual, and prophetic) whose task it was to rule on His behalf. By living in obedience to His Word (something their ancestors had failed to do), they could honor Him and be the recipients of His blessing.

The theme of the Books of Chronicles, therefore, is the continued faithfulness of God to His Word; and the way in which His people could enjoy His blessing was to obey and serve Him.[9]

When was Chronicles placed in the canon?

The term "canon" comes from the Greek *kanon* which means a "straight rod, ruler." In the course of time the word came to be applied to literature and intimated that a person's writings conformed to a specific rule or standard. In the case of the Scriptures, the words "canon" and "canonicity" apply to those books that bear the marks of divine inspiration (2 Timothy 3:16). In the Old Testament the usage of the word "canon" is restricted to the 39 books that the Jewish community considered to be inspired. It does not include the books of the Apocrypha, even though these writings are included in some Bibles.

The Old Testament canon was divided into sections: *The Law* (Genesis–Deuteronomy); *The Former Prophets* (Joshua–2 Kings); *The Latter Prophets* (Isaiah–Malachi); the *Writings* (including both poetic and wisdom books – Psalms, Proverbs, Job, including Rolls [Song of Solomon, Ruth, Lamentations, Ecclesiastes, and Esther]); and concluded with the historical books (written after the close of the Law and the Former Prophets) – viz., Daniel, Ezra-Nehemiah, and 1 and 2 Chronicles. The first part of the canon closed after Moses finished writing Deuteronomy. The second part likewise closed when Jeremiah had finished penning the history of the kings of Israel and Judah. When the writings that comprised the third part of the canon were completed, this part of the canon was likewise closed. And information not included in the other sections, but which the Jews desired to preserve because of its intrinsic quality, namely, *The Writings*, was closed with the addition of the single scroll containing Chronicles.[10]

OUTLINE

An outline of the contents of the Books of Chronicles will reveal the scope of the material we shall cover.

I. THE ROYAL LINE OF DAVID (1:1–9:44)
  A. The Genealogy from Adam to Abraham (1:1-27)
  B. The Genealogy from Abraham to Jacob (1:28-54)
  C. The Genealogy from Jacob to David (2:1-55)
  D. The Genealogy from David to the Captivity (3:1-24)
  E. The Genealogy of the Twelve Tribes (4:1–8:40)
  F. The Genealogy of the Returned Remnant (9:1-34)
  G. The Genealogy of Israel's First King (9:35-44)

II. THE REIGN OF DAVID (10:1–29:30)
  A. The Enthronement of David (10:1–12:40)
    1. The Death of King Saul (10:1-14)
    2. The Anointing of King David (11:1-3)
    3. The Conquest of Jerusalem (11:4-9)
    4. David's Mighty Men (11:10–12:22)
    5. The Men of Israel Who Came to Hebron to Make David King (12:23-40)

  B. The Enthronement of the Ark (13:1–17:27)
    1. Improper Transportation of the Ark (13:1-14)
    2. Digression: God's Blessings (14:1-17)
    3. Proper Transportation of the Ark (15:1-29)
    4. Celebration in Jerusalem (16:1-43)
    5. Institution of the Davidic Covenant (17:1-27)

  C. David's Military Victories (18:1–20:8)

  D. David's Preparation and Organization of Yahweh's Worship (21:1–27:34)

  E. David's Last Days (28:1–29:30)
    1. Final Exhortations (28:1-10)
    2. Final Provision for the Temple (28:11–29:9)

3. Final Prayer and Thanksgiving (29:10-19)
4. Coronation of Solomon (29:20-25)
5. David's Death (29:26-30)

III. THE HISTORY OF KING SOLOMON (2 Chronicles 1:1–9:31)

A. Solomon's Wealth and Wisdom (1:1-17)
B. His Building and Dedication of the Temple (2:1–7:22)
C. His Various Activities and Death (8:1–9:31)

IV. THE HISTORY OF THE KINGS OF JUDAH (10:1–36:23)

A. From Rehoboam to Zedekiah (10:1–36:21)
B. The Edict of Cyrus (36:22-23).

Other matters will be treated in the exposition of the text.

In closing, I would like to thank Mrs. Kevin (Jan) Hussey for her kindness in reading through the manuscript and making many suggestions for its improvement. Her labor of love is greatly appreciated!

1 Chronicles

Dedicated to

Maurice Bickley
A Faithful Servant of Jesus Christ

1

An Unexpected Oasis
(1 Chronicles 1:1–9:44)

People journeying to southern California either by car or by airplane have to cross hundreds of miles of barren desert. And those traveling east from California to Arizona or Nevada or places beyond have to do the same. People fortunate enough to look down on the desolate waste from the air-conditioned comfort of a plane can see in all directions. For the most part the barrenness of the landscape is broken only by hills that are devoid of growth. Only occasionally does one see a cluster of trees and the reflection of the sun's rays on the placid surface of a small lake. Otherwise there is a monotonous sameness that is depressing.

In like manner, the reader of the First Book of Chronicles faces nine chapters of genealogies. It is an almost uninterrupted record of "begats" and those who were begotten. To the Jewish reader, however, these chapters are like taking a walk among the graves of the honored dead who lie buried in a vast national cemetery, for they are all his or her relatives.

These chapters can be outlined as follows:

The Royal Line of King David (1:1–9:44)

The Genealogy from Adam to Abraham (1:1-27)
The Genealogy from Abraham to Jacob (1:28-54)
The Genealogy from Jacob to David (2:1-55)
The Genealogy from David to the Return of the Exiles (3:1-24)

The Genealogies of the Twelve Tribes (4:1–8:40)
The Genealogy of the Returned Exiles (9:1-34)

The Genealogy of King Saul (9:35-44)

For those of us who are Gentiles and find these genealogical tables boring, there is an unexpected blessing. It is to be found in 1 Chronicles 4:9-10. There we come upon a small "oasis." All of a sudden the seemingly endless chronological record[1] is interrupted to make mention of a man named Jabez. He appears unexpectedly and without any reference to his father.

> And Jabez [was] more honorable than his brothers. And his mother called his name Jabez, saying, "Because I bore [him] in sorrow." And Jabez called on the God of Israel, saying, "Oh that (lit. if)You would bless me indeed and make my border larger, and [that] Your hand would be with me, and [that] You would keep me from evil that it may not grieve me!"
> And God gave what he asked.

The name *Jabez* comes from the same root as the word for "pain" or "sorrow," and we might just as easily translate verse 9 as "And Sorrowful [was] more honorable than his brothers. And his mother called him 'Sorrowful," saying, 'Because I bore him in sorrow.'"

We may not think this a very appropriate name for someone to carry through life, but Jabez' story has been of encouragement to all who suffer pain and have had to endure adversity. The scant information about him may be summarized as follows:

Introduction (4:9*a*)
His Mother's Lament (4:9*b*)
His Ardent Prayer (4:10*a*)
The Lord's Response (4:10*b*)

Introduction (4:9a)
The words that introduce Jabez to us describe him as an honorable man. This indicates that over time his character had been tested in the furnace of affliction and he had been refined by the process. In other words, he had not succumbed to the vicissitudes of life, but had triumphed over the difficulties he faced. And he had done so without giving way before adversity or compromising his beliefs.

How significant was the life of this seemingly insignificant individual? When Jerome translated the Bible into Latin in the 4th century AD, he asked some rabbis if there was a connection between the man named Jabez and the place near Bethlehem called Jabez (1 Chronicles 2:55; after all, it is unusual to call the place where people live "the Village of Sorrow" or "Pain Town"). Their response was affirmative.[1] They explained that Jabez, after much diligent study of the Bible, had risen to become a doctor of the Law. He gathered about him scribes who made copies of the Scriptures so that God's people living in the towns and villages of Judah might have their own scrolls of His Word. From these scrolls the elders could read to the people the stories of the Lord's dealings with those generations that had preceded them.

We have no means of knowing if the rabbis were correct in their understanding of Jabez' contribution to the spiritual life of God's people. We do know that the word translated "honorable" is *kabod*,[2] meaning, "to be heavy." This does not mean that Jabez was overweight. The word is used figuratively of a person's reputation. When people spoke of him, it was with respect. He was a man of integrity. His word could be trusted. He was just and equitable in his business dealings. And, in his social contacts with others, he would not be a party to slander or gossip. We are not surprised to note, therefore, that he became an influential man in his community.

Because the text contrasts Jabez with his brothers, there exists the possibility that he was the youngest in the family. If he had been the oldest son, there would have been no need to even mention his younger brothers, for the firstborn was automatically given respect. This respect diminished with each son until the last to be born was deemed to be the one of least importance (cf. what is said of David in 1 Samuel 16:1-13).

His Mother's Lament (4:9b)

Next we read about Jabez' mother. But why, at the time of her son's birth, did she give him the name "Sorrowful"? Did his name refer to the pain of childbirth[3] or to something else?

21

We do not wish for one instant to minimize the pain associated with the birth of a child (cf. Genesis 3:16), and it is possible that Jabez' delivery was particularly difficult, but it is most unusual for a mother to give her son such a name (cf. Christ's words in John 16:21). It seems preferable to conclude that Jabez' mother gave him the name "Sorrowful" because of the kind of things she believed would be true of his life.

This has led others to conclude that when Jabez was born his mother saw that he was deformed in some way. Many who have borne some physical limitation know what it is like to be the object of practical jokes or the butt of callused humor. And all too often they suffer rejection at the hands of their peers. Those in this kind of situation have drawn comfort from Jabez' life and experiences. His triumph over adversity has encouraged them to persevere through the difficulties they face.

Helen Keller is an example of such perseverance. Soon after she was born she suffered from a high fever. The fever did not last for very long, but it left her blind and deaf. This caused her mother considerable anguish and she may have wondered what would become of her daughter. Refusing to be mastered by adversity, Helen taught herself Braille and read everything she could find. Later she met a teacher named Anne Sullivan who, with much patience, taught Helen how to speak. In the course of time Helen graduated from Radcliffe College (now a part of Harvard University). She then began to travel with Anne Sullivan and gave lectures all over the world pleading for those who shared her disabilities to be given a chance to become useful citizens.[4]

There is a third explanation, however, that carries considerable weight. With no mention being made of Jabez' father, the biblical writer may well be implying that his father was dead. If this is the case, then Jabez' mother may have lamented the loss of the love of her life and the fact that her son would have to grow to manhood without the involvement, modeling and instruction of a father. But this raises the question, When did her husband die? And why was it necessary for Jabez to pray that the Lord would enlarge the size of his farm?

As we read these verses, it is quite possible that Jabez' father had been killed by a band of Amalekites who had chosen to raid the part of the Negev (or Southland) where this family lived. These wily nomads made a habit of sweeping down on some unsuspecting farm or village, killing anyone who opposed them, and driving off the sheep and cattle. If Jabez' father had been killed by these raiders from the desert in the first few days of his wife's pregnancy, she may have found herself a widow before she knew that she was carrying another child. Within a day or two of her husband's death the land he possessed would have been divided among his sons. There was no such thing as probate in those days (with courts taking a year or two to disburse a deceased person's assets), and the allocation of the land among her husband's sons would have taken place almost immediately. All that was needed was for the division of the property to be rehearsed in front of the elders of the village who acted as witnesses.

If this reconstruction is accurate, then the estate of Jabez' father could have been settled before Jabez' mother knew that she was pregnant. And it would have been eight-plus months before the family would have known if the child she was carrying was a boy or a girl. And once it was known that she had borne a son, it would still have been twelve years before he would have been treated as an adult and be able to make transactions accordingly. By that time each of his older brothers would have developed his inheritance, and it is unlikely that they would willingly give up what each intended to give to his own children when he died.

The grief of Jabez' mother at the birth of her youngest son may have been occasioned by the fact that Jabez would have no inheritance within the tribe of Judah. In other words, he would be *persona non grata* – a person without standing in the community, and no family in their tribe would give their daughter to him in marriage for he would not be able to support a wife and children.

The early fears of Jabez' mother would have been reinforced

over and over again as she overheard conversations in the market place or at the village well, or saw her son face unjust criticism or opposition. There is no pain like the pain of rejection (with the loneliness that often accompanies it), and Jabez' mother probably anticipated the pain she believed her son would experience. And so, to try and alleviate his suffering, she may have approached Jabez' older brothers with the request that he be given some land to call his own.

His Ardent Prayer (4:10a)

If the land Jabez' father had possessed was again subdivided, with Jabez being given a very small portion, then it would explain why on attaining manhood he needed to enlarge the size of his inheritance. On the other hand, Jabez may have acquired a small parcel as a result of thrift and hard work. However he came by it, it was inadequate for his needs – certainly insufficient to raise a crop of either wheat or barley, and far too small for sheep or cattle to graze on. The need for him to enlarge the size of his farm, therefore, was obvious. And so he prayed to the Lord:

> "Oh that You would bless me indeed and make my border larger, and [that] Your hand would be with me, and [that] You would keep me from evil, that it may not hurt me!"

It is often in our extremity that we turn to the Lord and seek His help. But wasn't Jabez' prayer selfish? And what about the way it begins (in the Hebrew text the first word is *'im*, "if," implying a conditional element, "If you will do such-and-such ... then I'll do such-and-such." But his prayer lacks the expected conclusion and so the *'im* is better translated "Oh ...").

As to Jabez' prayer, let us note first of all that he prayed to the God of Israel. He petitioned the One who had entered into a covenant with Abraham and promised him the land of Canaan for a possession (Genesis 12:1-3; 15:18-21; etc.). And so, in contrast to many of the people of Judah, who had already begun worshiping idols, Jabez began by acknowledging his reliance upon the only true God. His prayer, therefore, was for the Lord to fulfill His revealed will.

But how did Jabez learn of God's promise? He had evidently been taught about the Lord (either by his mother or some godly person in the village where he lived), and what he had been taught he took to heart. He also believed that inasmuch as the Lord had graciously answered the prayers of Abraham, Isaac and Jacob, and Moses, Aaron and Joshua, so He would answer the prayer of one of the least of His followers. And so he prayed in faith, and the Lord answered him.

It is as we read God's Word that we learn of His past involvement in the lives of His people, and this serves to encourage us to bring our petitions before Him, trusting Him to help us resolve the difficulties we face (cf. Psalm 46:1; Hebrews 4:16; 1 Peter 5:7).

We hear a lot today about being in the will of God and praying according to His will. However, unless we know what God has chosen to reveal in His Word, how will we ever know if we are praying according to His will?

Years before Jabez had been born, and after the Israelites had come out of Egypt and were camped on the western bank of the River Jordan, the Lord had spoken to Joshua, and said:

> "...arise, go over this Jordan [river], you, and all this people, into the land that I will give them, even to the children of Israel. Every place that the sole of your foot shall tread upon, to you I have given it ..." (Joshua 1:2-3).

At first God's people set out enthusiastically to take possession of the land, but after a while they became discouraged and slackened in their commitment. Then they began living among the Canaanites and Amorites, and a decade later it was necessary for Joshua to remind the Israelites that "there remains much land to be possessed" (Joshua 13:1). It is also tragic to note that, after all of the Lord's warnings, His people had also begun worshiping pagan deities, and by the time of Jabez those who remained true to the Lord were a small, struggling minority. When Jabez prayed to the "God of Israel" he was demonstrating his faith in the One who had delivered His people from Egyptian bondage and promised them the land. His prayer, therefore, was in the will of God!

Years later the apostle John would write words of encouragement to us:

> Beloved, if our heart does not condemn us, we have boldness toward God; and whatsoever we ask we receive of Him, because we keep His commandments and do those things that are pleasing in His sight (1 John 3:21-22).

What a comfort to know that the Lord still hears and answers our prayers!

Before we go on with Jabez' prayer, we need to consider the importance of requesting God's blessing *before* we engage in any new undertaking. Without His help, we labor in vain (Psalms 94:17; 127:1). We need to have guidance from the start, not pray for His blessing on our plans after we have made them. Jabez realized his limitations. He knew of his need for divine strength and wisdom, and that is why he also prayed "and that Your hand might be with me." When God's "hand" is with us, guiding and protecting and enabling us, we can accomplish things that otherwise might be impossible.

But this is not all. Having faced opposition and borne reproach and rejection all of his life, Jabez also prayed that the Lord would break the cycle of evil, and so he prayed "and that You would keep me from evil, that it not cause me sorrow." The apostle Paul also knew from bitter experience the pain of opposition from Alexander the coppersmith, and he handed him over to the Lord for Him to deal with him as He saw fit (2 Timothy 4:14). In this way he was kept from nursing grudges or harboring any ill will.

The Lord's Response (4:10b)

We have already noted that Jabez' prayer began as a vow (though the conditional element was never added [cf. Genesis 28:20-22; Judges 11:30-31]). God, in grace, answered him without requiring that Jabez do anything for Him. And he still answers prayer today, not because He must, but because He wants to (cf. John 14:12-14; 16:24). And so, with the ease of one recounting a simple cause-and-effect relationship, the writer adds, "So God granted him what he requested."

The fulfillment of Jabez' prayer was orchestrated by God as He brought together a fortuitous combination of circumstances. Jabez worked and God worked, and God blessed Jabez' efforts and enabled him to achieve what many probably believed to be impossible.

The Benefit of Adversity

What abiding lessons can we learn from this story?

Most of us are not numbered among the movers and shakers of this world. We are insignificant people, and few of us will be remembered after we are dead. The story of Jabez – an honorable man – should serve to encourage us to lead lives of practical righteousness, to be true to our word, and over time to develop a reputation for integrity.

But Jabez' life also serves to encourage us to pray. A person who doesn't pray is like a tree without roots. E. M. Bounds wrote:

Prayer is the easiest and the hardest of all things; the simplest and the sublimest; the weakest and the most powerful; its results lie outside the range of human possibilities – they are limited only by the omnipotence of God. *Few Christians have anything but a vague idea of the power of prayer; fewer still have any experience of that power.* The Church seems almost wholly unaware of the power God puts into her hand; this spiritual carte blanche on the infinite resources of God's wisdom and power is rarely, if ever, used – never used to the full measure of honoring God. It is astounding how poor the use, how little the benefits. Prayer is our most formidable weapon, but the one in which we are the least skilled, the most averse to its use.[5]

One of the heroes of the Christian church, though now long-forgotten, was John Hyde.[6] The son of a Presbyterian pastor, John intended to follow in his father's footsteps. However, after completing both college and seminary, he joined a group of missionaries bound for India. Once there, he was assigned the Punjab region as the place of his ministry. Hyde quickly learned several of the local languages and became well known as one of rural India's most powerful preachers.

After several years of ministry, Hyde became dissatisfied with the results of his evangelistic efforts and turned increasingly to prayer. So intense did his prayers become that he would often spend forty or more hours on his knees, missing meals and unaware of his bodily needs. Such prayers eventually occupied much of his time and he became known as "Praying Hyde." The results of his intercession were soon evident. Numbers of Indians – that increased each year – came to know Christ.

Such is the power of prayer! Jabez prayed and the Lord heard him and granted his request.

2

Saul's Nemesis
(1 Chronicles 10:1-14)

The ancient Greeks were astute observers of human nature. They noticed that actions have consequences, and because they were also very religious they propounded the idea that there was a goddess who administered just retribution. They named her "Nemesis." According to Hesiod,[1] Nemesis hated every transgression of the bounds of moderation. According to one tradition she was given the name "She whom none can escape."[2] Though Nemesis is the figment of fertile human imagination, the reality observed by the early Greeks is true to life. Actions have consequences. What we sow we inevitably reap.

The chronology of 1 Chronicles 1:1–9:44 is intended to show *The Royal Line of King David*. David, however, was not Israel's first king and the chronicler found it necessary to explain how the way was cleared for him to ascend the throne. This chapter, therefore, follows the genealogy of King Saul (9:35-44) and tells of his death.

The Death of King Saul (10:1-14)

The End of the House of Saul (10:1-7)
The Desecration of Saul's Body (10:8-12)
The Cause of Saul's Death (10:13-14)

The Death of King Saul (10:1-14)

With 10:1 we observe a change in the writer's methodology. He moves from compressing extensive eras of biblical history into genealogies to a recounting of select events. He passes over Saul's reign of more than 30 years in Gibeah, ignores the reign of his son, Ish-bosheth (11:1-3), and appears to be in a hurry to tell of God's chosen king, David.[3] And so, though this chapter is not about David, it does prepare the way for David's enthronement as king over all the people of Israel. It also shows the deplorable state into which the kingdom had fallen under Saul's poor leadership.

The End of the House of Saul (10:1-7)

> And the Philistines fought against Israel; and the men of Israel fled from the face of the Philistines, and fell wounded on Mount Gilboa. And the Philistines pursued after Saul and after his sons, and the Philistines struck Jonathan, and Abinadab, and Malchishua, the sons of Saul. And the battle [was] heavy on (i.e., went against) Saul, and the archers found him, and he was wounded with the bow (i.e., by the archers).

The Philistines were Israel's arch-enemies. They had settled along the southern coastal plain with the Mediterranean Sea on the west and the Judean highlands on the east. Mount Carmel formed the northern most limit of Philistia, while the Brook of Egypt, south of Gaza, provided the southern border (though this changed continually, sometimes belonging to the Philistines and sometimes to Israelites). In the course of time the Philistine population became concentrated in and around five major cities known as the "Philistine Pentapolis." These cities were Gaza, Ashkelon, Gath, Ashdod, and Ekron.[4]

According to the prophet Amos (Amos 9:7), the Philistines, in the second millennium BC, came to Canaan from Caphtor (most likely another name for Crete). Minoan Crete controlled much of the Aegean and its culture spread throughout the Mediterranean world. However, around 1450 BC a period of decline set in and the Minoans no longer exercised as much influence as formerly.

After settling in Canaan, the Philistines seem to have quickly adopted Canaanite religious practices. As their population grew they needed more and more land, and so began the battles between the Philistines and the people of Israel. The superior military strength of the Philistines enabled them to dominate the southern tribes of Israel (especially Dan and Judah) and make frequent inroads into Israelite territory. On the occasion of Saul's death the Philistines controlled the Valley of the Jezreel.[5]

Saul and the Israelites had fought many battles against the Philistines, and though invariably outnumbered, by God's grace, they had been successful. Now, however, the five lords of the Philistines had combined their armies. They camped in the valley along the Hill of Moreh,[6] while Saul and his army bivouacked beside the fountain of Jezreel (1 Samuel 29:1) with Mount Gilboa at their backs.

When the battle was joined, the men of Israel were unable to hold their own. The Philistine chariots proved too much for them, and the Israelite army was compelled to retreat up the slopes of Mount Gilboa[7] where the chariots could not follow. It was then that the archers took over. And when the Israelites had been thinned out by the bowmen, the Philistine infantry charged up the slopes killing those who had not fled from the battlefield.

Saul's sons had joined him in the battle, and, though they took their stand against the enemy and no doubt tried to rally the fleeing Israelites, they were soon killed. Saul was easily identifiable by his height (1 Samuel 10:23-24) and the coronet on his head, and he became an easy mark for the archers. Time and again he was wounded, and it soon became obvious that he could not escape. Turning to his armor bearer he said,

> "Draw your sword and pierce me through with it, lest these uncircumcised ones come and abuse me." But his armor bearer was not willing, for he was very afraid; so Saul took the (i.e., his) sword and fell on it. And [when] his armor bearer saw that Saul was dead, he also fell on the (i.e., his) sword and died. So Saul died and his three sons, and his entire house; they died together.

But to what do Saul's words, *"lest these uncircumcised ... abuse me,"* refer? It was the custom in those days for captured

31

monarchs to be subject to torture, mutilation and sexual humiliation; and the Philistines were adept at this sort of violence. Dr. J. M. Myers wrote, "The prospect was so horrifying that suicide was not regarded as reprehensible under such circumstances. The fact that suicide is otherwise practically unknown in the whole of biblical history throws into stark relief the frightful prospect facing Saul should he fall [alive] into the hands of the Philistines."[8]

Saul's suicide has not stopped some preachers from criticizing him. What they ignore is the decision of other great men who have found themselves in a similar position. For example, when the Philippines fell to the Japanese during World War II, and the help promised General Douglas MacArthur did not materialize, MacArthur believed that he would die on the island of Corregidor. He kept a derringer in his back pocket and, as he looked across the narrow channel to Bataan, confided to an associate, "They will never take me alive."[9]

It is unwise for us to judge the conduct of a person such as King Saul (or Douglas MacArthur, or anyone else for that matter), for we do not know the kind of pressures they faced.

Dr. Dorothy Zeligs, in *Psychoanalysis and the Bible*,[10] is more objective than those who decry Saul's action. She deals at length with his conflict with authority figures and pursuit of a personal agenda. She concludes by stating that his death was the natural outcome of a life of continuous alienation. (Dr. Zeligs omits, however, all thought of God's punishment of Saul for his persistent self-will, cf. 10:14.)

Saul's death on the slopes of Mount Gilboa serves to accentuate his failures. He stands out on the pages of Holy Scripture as an example of self-serving disobedience. The chronicler presumes that his readers are familiar with the Book of Samuel and spares them the sordid details of Saul's wasted life. Instead he presents him as an example of what can happen to a great man whose self-orientation is opposed to a God-orientation.[11] The climax of Saul's life of failure is shown in verse 7: "And when all the men of Israel who were in the valley saw that they (i.e., those on Mount Gilboa) had fled, and that Saul and his sons were dead, they forsook their cities and fled; and the Philistines came and lived in them."

The rout was complete. The Philistines came and lived in the towns and villages scattered throughout the valley, and their presence effectively deprived the tribes of Issachar and Zebulun (whose territory lay in the Valley of Jezreel) of their land. It also deprived the tribes of Asher, Naphtali and Dan[12] (whose land lay north of the valley) of any help that might come from the south.[13] Israel suffered further loss because the east-west trade route ran along the Valley of Jezreel and brought considerable wealth to Israel. With this valley in the hands of the enemy, the Philistines now benefited from taxes and tariffs imposed on travelers and merchant caravans.[14]

The Desecration of Saul's Body (10:8-12)
Saul's fears of being abused by the Philistines were justified. Though he was dead, this did not stop the Philistines from desecrating his body.

> And it happened, on the next day, that the Philistines came to strip the wounded (i.e., take the spoils of war); and they found Saul and his sons fallen on Mount Gilboa, and they stripped him, and carried [away] his head and his weapons. And the Philistines sent [messengers] into the land all around to proclaim the news to their idols and the people; and they put his (i.e., Saul's) weapons [in] the house of their gods; and his skull they fastened [in] the house of Dagon.

Stripping the bodies of the dead was a normal procedure in these ancient times. Whatever valuables each soldier could find were regarded as compensation for his service.

At the command of the five lords of the Philistines, runners took the news of the victory to the cities of the Pentapolis, and within hours of the Philistine triumph the people of Philistia were celebrating the triumph of the army. They also took Saul's head and his armor to place in their different temples. Their actions provide tacit admission that their idols – made out of wood and stone and lavishly overlaid with silver and gold – had no knowledge of what had taken place. If they were really gods, they would not have needed to be told of the victory. Saul's head was impaled on a stake (or some such object) and placed in the temple of Dagon,[15] while his body (and the bodies of his sons) was fastened to the wall of the city of Beth-Shean[16] (cf. 1 Samuel 31:10).

With verses 11 and 12 the gloom that pervades this chapter gives way as a single ray of sunlight begins to filter through the mists of defeat. These verses illustrate for us the fact that kindness begets kindness. Thirty-plus years earlier Saul's first act as Israel's new king had been to bring relief to the people of Jabesh-gilead, east of the River Jordan.[17] The people of Gilead had been threatened with mutilation by Nahash the king of Ammonites (1 Samuel 11). Saul's kindness had not been forgotten. Now, valiant men from across the river came by night and removed the bodies of Saul and his sons, and by early morning the Philistines knew that their triumph had been short-lived.

And all Jabesh-gilead heard all that the Philistines had done to Saul; then every man of valor arose, and they carried the body of Saul, and the bodies of his sons, and brought them to Jabesh, and buried their bones under the oak in Jabesh; and fasted seven days (1 Chronicles 10:11-12).

Those valiant men most likely crossed the River Jordan at night, ascended the slope that leads up to Beth-Shean, reconnoitered the city, and when everyone was sleeping soundly, removed the corpses from the city wall. Then, carrying the bodies of the slain members of the royal family, they disappeared into the darkness, re-crossed the River Jordan and made their way to a safe place in Gilead. There they burned the bodies lest the Philistines attempt to retake them and further desecrate them. This done, they buried the bones of Saul and his sons beneath an oak tree, leaving the grave unmarked.[18] It was an act of reciprocation for what Saul had done for them. And having become ceremonially defiled, they fast for seven days.

The Cause of Saul's Death (10:13-14)

The chronicler now gives his readers the reasons for Saul's death.

> So Saul died for his (*ma'al*) trespass that he had trespassed against Yahweh, against the word of the Lord and also for asking of a medium to inquire [by her or it]; and did not inquire of Yahweh; so He killed him and turned the kingdom over to David the son of Jesse.

Three trespasses are cited: Saul was unfaithful to God and followed his own judgment rather than wait for Samuel to come and offer the appropriate sacrifice; he disregarded God's word through Samuel and did not utterly destroy the Amalekites; and he failed to seek God properly in his hour of need.

It is only as we reflect on Saul's life that we see how his external orientation[19] brought about his downfall. Saul was unaware of his weaknesses because his entire vision was taken up with what he wanted. The result was that the real issues – the spiritual issues that determine the course of each person's life – were obscured by a host of attendant circumstances. He was successful in his battles, but only because the Lord gave him these victories. But he ceased to enjoy the things God gave him as his self-orientation dominated more and more of his thinking. A mental and emotional decline set in, and as the years passed he became increasingly paranoid. His rash acts alienated the people over whom he ruled, and in the end only the tribe of Benjamin stood by him (though some of the bravest of them had defected to David's side).

In surveying Saul's life we see unmistakably that actions have consequences. In the end it was not Nemesis, but God who called Saul to account for his misdeeds. "He killed him and turned the kingdom over to David."

One of the bitterest lessons we learn in life is that our sins affect others. A man phoned me one day. He was crying. I asked,

"How may I be of service to you?"

"By giving me an honest answer," was his reply.

"What is your question?" I asked.

"If a Christian commits suicide, does he go to heaven?"

I wanted to keep him talking and so responded, "I'll give you an honest answer if you will be kind enough to tell me the reason why you're asking it."

By way of reply he told me that he was married to a wonderful Christian woman and had two terrific daughters both of whom had accepted Christ as their Savior.

"We had a terrific marriage," he said.

"Had ...?" I queried.

"Until last night."

"What happened last night?"

With this his sobbing became uncontrollable. I waited for him to gain his composure. When he was again in control of his emotions, I very quietly repeated my earlier question: "What happened last night?"

With this his sobbing started all over again. In between his tears he said, "I committed adultery last night with a woman with whom I work. We had to work late. When we were finished, I offered to drive her home. We talked in the car for quite a while, and then she asked me in. And then it happened."

This man's remorse was real. He was consumed by guilt and shame. All he could think of was the disgrace he had brought on himself and his family. In his present state of mind suicide seemed the only option. I asked him about the effect his death would have on his wife and daughters.

We talked for a long time. It is fair to say that he found himself caught in the maelstrom of his sin. The first issue concerned his relationship with the Lord. It involved confession and the need to consciously receive forgiveness and cleansing. The next issue was how to minimize the consequences of his sin to those whom he loved. And then there was the need to talk with the woman in his office, take responsibility for what had happened, and establish parameters so that this incident would never be repeated.

Saul's sins involved his sons and the people of Israel. His wrongdoing brought the nation to their lowest level since entering the land of Canaan 425 years earlier. Yet in spite of his example, people of every age think they can sin with impunity. And for a time (as with King Saul) they appear to escape punishment. In the end, however, their sins catch up with them (Numbers 32:23).

Closing Thoughts

"What," we may ask, "did the people for whom the Book of Chronicles was first written learn from this account of Saul's death?" Without question, they, as well as all subsequent generations, learned from Saul's life what happens to a person who deliberately disobeys God in order to follow some personal agenda. He or she begins to forfeit the blessing and protection of the Lord, and unless there is genuine repentance (with restoration to a place of blessing), God's punishment will inevitably follow. Before the punishment, however, the Lord in His great grace reproves us. If, however, we ignore His chastening, then we leave Him with no alternative but to deal with us as He sees fit.

It is interesting to note that the word used in 10:13 to describe Saul's actions is *ma'al*.[20] It is variously translated as "trespass, commit a trespass, act unfaithfully." The majority of the occurrences of *ma'al* occur in the Books of Chronicles (with Ezekiel using the word only seven times and Daniel only once) – indicating that God's inspired penman wanted to draw attention to the reason for Saul's and the nation's downfall. *Ma'al* is significant because it draws attention to the breaking of a covenant or the violation of some religious law. It looks at a conscious act of treachery against God (cf. Leviticus 6:2; Numbers 5:6; Joshua 22:31; etc.). All of this serves to underscore how God viewed Saul's selfish acts.

It is true that, viewed from the perspective of history, Saul is a tragic figure. And it is also true that he appears weak and irresolute. But more is at stake than the feeble blundering of a fickle individual. The chronicler lays his unerring finger on the real reason for Saul's demise: *disobedience to the known will of God*. There is no such thing as neutrality where God is concerned. And let us not overlook the fact that the sins of the Lord's people encourage the ungodly in their ungodliness (cf. 2 Samuel 12:14). When Saul's sins finally overtook him, God's people became a reproach and the Philistines boasted of their victory in the temples of their gods.

This kind of situation led Blaise Pascal to write in his *Pensées*: "There is nothing on earth that shows the wretchedness of man [like] ... the weakness of man without God." In the end, after the Lord had departed from Saul, his irresolute nature caused him to consult a witch who lived at Endor[21] (1 Samuel 28:7ff.). He had failed to seek the Lord's face with a truly penitent heart, and when the Lord did not answer him he instituted "Plan B" (cf. Jeremiah 2:26-28) – consultation with a medium so that he could speak to Samuel who had died several years earlier. To do this he had to travel behind enemy lines to the little village of Endor. His actions illustrate for us both his basic disposition ("I'll approach God as best I can") and his desperation ("I need to know what will happen to me." Cf. Isaiah 8:19-20). If Saul had confessed his numerous acts of willful disobedience and offered the appropriate sacrifices, the Lord would have graciously forgiven him. Instead, Saul persisted in his hardness of heart and eventually died in his sins.

We need to note the chronicler's emphasis as he described Saul's death. It was not attributed to the Philistines or even to himself. The text explicitly states that "He [the Lord] slew him." Saul died for his numerous violations of God's revealed will, and when the cup of his iniquity was full, He, the supreme Judge of all, called him to account for his wrongdoing.

This is a theme seldom preached on today. People like to hear positive, uplifting words spoken from the pulpit. And to a degree this is understandable. A preacher, however, has the responsibility to remind his congregation of their accountability to a holy and righteous God (cf. Hebrews 9:27). Happy are those who, in this present day of grace, live in obedience to His revealed will. They will have no regrets when they are called to appear before the Judgment Seat of Christ (1 Corinthians 3:15-15; 2 Corinthians 5:10).

Finally ... God's Word Fulfilled
(1 Chronicles 11:1-9)

Aesop, the Greek author of numerous fables, told a story of some frogs that lived in a lake. They had grown tired of their carefree life – swimming about all day and sunning themselves on lily pads – and concluded that what they needed was a king to rule over them. They believed that having someone to give purpose and direction to their lives would lift the burden of having to make decisions. So great was their desire for a leader that they prayed to Jupiter, the supreme god of their pantheon, and asked him to send them a king. Jupiter, being in a good mood, threw a log into the water, saying, "There is a king for you."

Awed by the splash and the size of their new monarch, the frogs watched their king with fear and trembling. He was very big, but he didn't say much. Instead he drifted about the lake as if inspecting his new realm. In time the frogs tried to attract his attention. One jumped on to his back as if to speak to him. The problem was he didn't know which end to approach first. Soon others followed.

It was not long before the frogs in this lake tired of such an impersonal leader and petitioned Jupiter for another king. To comply with their request, he sent them a stork. The stork looked imposing enough as he strode methodically along the bank of the lake on his long legs, but he didn't protect them, as a king should. He tossed them about and even gobbled them up.[1]

Israel's Desire for a King

Earlier in their history, when the people of Israel had desired a king, the Lord had given them Saul (1 Samuel 8:4-9; 10:1, 17-24). But Saul had lacked direction. He was also disobedient to the revealed will of God, and in the end he consulted a spiritist (i.e., medium) – something no Israelite should ever do, for it was forbidden by law (Deuteronomy 18:10-22)! All of this angered the Lord, and in the end He took Saul away.

Unlike the frogs in Aesop's story, the Israelites had been instructed by the Lord to appoint as their leader a fellow-Israelite, one like themselves (Deuteronomy 17:15). Either through ignorance of God's Word or self-will they relied on their own wisdom. The result was failure and misfortune. Now, however, when their needs drive them to seek for another leader, they select one from among themselves who came from the tribe of Judah (cf. Genesis 49:10).

Chapters 10:1–29:30 deal with *The Reign of King David.* Within this broad section, 10:1–12:40 treats his accession, choice of a new capital, and then lists those who helped him. Here is the outline we will follow:

The Anointing of King David (11:1-3)

I. *The Enthronement of King David (11:1-3)*
II. *The Choice of a New Capital (11:4-9)*
    A. The Selection of a New Capital (11:4-5)
    B. The Appointment of a New General (11:6)
    C. The Fortification of the City (11:7-8)
    D. The Evidence of God's Blessing (11:9)
III. *The Administration of the Kingdom (11:10–12:40)*
    A. The Mighty Men Who Helped Establish the Kingdom (11:10-47)
    B. The Men Who Defected to David During His Outlaw Years (12:1-22)
        1. Those Who Joined David in Ziklag (12:1-7)
        2. The Gadites Who Joined David in the Stronghold (12:8-15)
        3. The Men from Benjamin and Judah who Joined David in the Stronghold (12:16-18)
        4. The Men from Manasseh who Defected to David (12:19-21)
        5. Summary (12:22)
    C. The Leaders Who Came to Hebron to Make David King Over Israel (12:23-40)

As we have seen, this chapter places in stark contrast the leadership styles of Saul and David. The failure of King Saul illustrates for all time the importance of a leader living in subjection to the Word of the Lord. Leadership is serious business. There is no room for partial obedience. The centrality of the Word of God has always been the hallmark of godly leadership.

Both Saul and David had been confronted by choices. Each had had placed before him the right way and the wrong way (cf. Deuteronomy 30:15, 19). Their decisions illustrate the fact that, in the final analysis, there are only two kinds of people: Those who say to the Lord, "Your will be done," and those to whom the Lord says, "Have it your way."

This principle transcends time, reaching even to our own day, and is as relevant now as it was then.

The Enthronement of King David (11:1-3)

> And all Israel was gathered to David at Hebron, saying, "Behold, you we [are] your bone and your flesh; and yesterday and three days ago (i.e., in time past), even when Saul was king, you [were] he (i.e., the one) who led out and brought in Israel; and Yahweh your God said to you, 'You shall feed (i.e., shepherd) My people Israel, and you shall be prince over My people Israel.' " So all the elders of Israel came to the king, even to Hebron; and David cut (i.e., made) a covenant with them in Hebron before Yahweh; and they anointed David king over Israel, according to the word of Yahweh through Samuel.

With these verses the chronicler continued his interpretation of Israel's history by jumping forward to the anointing of David as king over all Israel. To do so he omitted all of 2 Samuel 1–4 dealing with David's seven and a half year reign in Hebron[2] (2 Samuel 5:5) and picked up the story when the tribes of Israel came to make him their king.

Hebron was a city known in ancient times as Kiriath-arba. It had been built at an elevation of 3040 feet on the southern end of the central mountain ridge running north-to-south through Israel. It was located 19 miles south southwest of Jerusalem and overlooked a fertile valley to the west that was unusually well supplied with springs and wells. The city itself was a place dear to the heart of every Israelite. Abraham had lived near Hebron most of his life in Canaan, and it was there, close to the oaks of Mamre, where he had offered a sacrifice to the Lord. Sarah had died in Hebron, and both she and Abraham had been buried in the cave of Machpelah close by. Jacob had buried Leah in this same cave, and his own remains had been laid to rest next to hers.

It was during his successful reign in Hebron that David became more and more aware of God's blessing (2 Samuel 5:10). Belatedly an assembly of 280,000 men converged on the city intent on asking him to become their new king. All the northern tribes were represented (12:23-40), as well as those from the south. In petitioning David the leaders of the northern tribes acknowledged that he was one of them (11:1*b*). They also reminded him of his past service to the nation and how, even when Saul was king, he had been the one who had led the tribes to victory (11:2*a*). Then, as an afterthought, they reminded him that Yahweh had marked him out as the one who would shepherd His people (11:2*b*).

But why refer to God's known will after ignoring it for the past seven and a half years during which time the people in the north were perfectly willing to wage a civil war against those in the south?

The answer may lie in the fact that, as a result of their own choices, they had been brought to the nadir of their national existence. They were desperate. They realized that as twelve autonomous tribes they lacked unity. Division rather than concord had characterized their actions. As a result, it had been comparatively easy for their enemies to gain the upper hand. And perhaps they had also learned from painful experience what happens to those who disobey the Word of the Lord. To show David that they were not entirely devoid of spiritual values, they tacked on to their invitation the words: "and Yahweh *your God* said to you, 'You shall feed My people Israel ...'" (11:2, emphasis added).

We frequently find that when people of the world (and this is particularly true of politicians at all levels!) want Christians to do something for them (i.e., for their benefit), they will make a show of piety by mentioning God. The place they give Him in their negotiations, however, shows very clearly where their priorities lie.

Sensing their spiritual ambivalence, David made a covenant with them before the Lord (11:3). He probably pledged himself to rule justly and in accordance with the principles already laid down in Scripture (cf. 1 Samuel 10:25; see also Deuteronomy 17:14-20), and they pledged themselves to obey him as God's representative. And so, though David was to be their king, his rule was to be regulated by divine statute; and they, as the people of God, were to submit to his authority. Both parties, therefore, recognized Yahweh as the nation's Suzerain.

All this led the great Scottish preacher, Dr. William M. Taylor, to point out that God's sovereignty is the one great fundamental difference between the administration of Saul and that of David. Saul accepted the monarchy, designing to make it as absolute and autocratic as that of other kings; but David counted himself only as an under-shepherd, and desired to regulate his conduct as a ruler by the commands of God. The people's perception of this feature in his character gave them great confidence in him, and, we may be sure, formed one reason for their joy on this memorable occasion, as it witnessed by the fact that as soon as the anointing was over, they began a feast that lasted for three days (12:39-40).[3]

Of significance to the people who first had the Book of Chronicles read to them (as well as to us!) is the fact that, after a long delay, God's promise to David through Samuel was fulfilled (1 Samuel 16:13). The trials of David's early years had been bitter (cf. Psalm 18), but David's response to them had always shown his submission to the will of God. Now, in his prime, he finally sat ensconced on the throne of a united Israel.

The Choice of a New Capital (11:4-9)

In contrast to Saul's reactive posture (i.e., returning to his hometown of Gibeah after being crowned king), David was proactive. He took the initiative. The words "And went" are prominent in the text.

> And David and all Israel went [to] Jerusalem – it is Jebus – and there [were] the Jebusites, the dwellers of the land. And the inhabitants of Jebus said to David, "You shall not come in (lit. to) here"; but David captured the fortress of Zion – it [is] the city of David.[4] And David said, "Whoever strikes the Jebusites first shall become head and captain [of the army]; and Joab the son of Zeruiah went up first and became the head. And David lived in the fortress; therefore it is called the city of David. And he built the city all around from the Millo[5] even to the area around; and Joab revived (i.e., repaired) the rest of the city. And David went, going and increasing (i.e., became greater and greater), for Yahweh of Hosts [was] with him.

The late Bernard L. Montgomery, in his fine book *The Path to Leadership*, has pointed out that "the capacity and the will to rally men and women to a common purpose, and the character which will inspire confidence" are the essentials of leadership. In another place he explains that "unless a leader is a man who can be looked up to, whose personal judgment is trusted, and who can inspire and warm the hearts of those he leads – gaining their trust and confidence, and explaining what is needed in language which can be understood" – he will not succeed.[6]

In David's case we note first the emphasis on "*all* Israel." It would have been natural for David to rely mainly on the men who had been with him for many years. Instead, he united all the Israelites in a common venture. But who would serve as their head? Joab had been the leader of David's army while he lived in Hebron. It might have been thought expedient to give the command to him. Instead, David gave everyone the same advantage: "And David said, 'Whoever first strikes the Jebusites shall become head and captain'" (11:6). There was to be no favoritism or nepotism in his administration.

So it is that in verses 4-8 we note (1) the capture of the city of Jebus (11:4-5), (2) David's appointment of a new general (11:6), and (3) the fortification of the nation's new capital (11:7-8). This section of Scripture then concludes with evidence of God's blessing on David (11:9).

The selection of a new capital (11:4-5). The most pressing need facing David as he assumed rulership of a united Israel was a new capital. Hebron was too far to the south and in other respects unsuitable for a nation that stretched from Beersheba in the south to Dan in the north.[7]

On the border of Benjamin and Judah stood the ancient fortress of the Jebusites. It had been built on a cluster of hills and was surrounded by deep valleys on three sides that made the city well nigh impregnable. To capture this fortress would be a worthy undertaking, and with the large army that now gathered around him it would be the kind of task that would build *esprit de corps* and give each soldier something to talk about when he returned home to his wife and family. It was also sound policy, for this would place his capital city in a more central position.[8]

Whether David asked the Lord for directions or was led by the Holy Spirit to attack Jebus, we do not know. It is quite possible that God had intimated to him years earlier that Jerusalem was the place where He intended to place His name (cf. 1 Samuel 17:54). Whatever David's motivation, he drew up his forces on the northern side of the city – the only one not defended by deep valleys. The Jebusites, confident of their city's impregnability, mocked him from behind its walls. Such bravado was common in those days, and their derision has been preserved for us. They said in effect, "You shall not come to (i.e., in) here. We're so well defended that even the blind and the lame can keep you at bay" (11:5). But David captured the fortress of Zion, and it became known as the city of David.

The question, of course, must be asked, "If the Jebusites were so confident of their ability to defend their city, how was David able to take it?" Josephus tells us that the Jebusites actually placed the blind and the lame on the wall as further evidence of their confidence.[9]

The appointment of a new general (11:6). The capture of Jebus is intimately connected with a challenge David made to all his men. He stated that whoever was the first to enter Jebus would become the commander of the army (11:6a). Joab, who had always been conspicuous for his acts of bravery, was the first to enter the city, and he was rewarded with the generalship of the army.

It would appear from research done by Colonel (later Sir) Charles Warren that there was a sloping shaft[10] that enabled the citizens of Jebus, during a siege, to draw water from a pool fed by the Gihon Spring. By climbing up this shaft, Joab, followed by other soldiers, was able to enter Jebus unobserved. The result was that the city was captured in a single night. And Joab became David's general.

The fortification of the city (11:7-8). This stronghold became David's new residence. To secure the city on its only vulnerable side, he extended the fortifications of "*the* Millo,"[11] and gave Joab oversight of the repair of the rest of the city. As word of what David had done spread, his fame increased and the residents of the heretofore disaffected northern tribes gave willing obedience to him.

The evidence of God's blessing (11:9). Under God's gracious hand David had been successful and a measure of prosperity began to return to Israel. Foreign nations sent their envoys to Jerusalem with their congratulations, and the Phoenicians, who had recently helped the Philistines in their wars, found it expedient to reverse their previous policy and entered into a trade alliance with Israel. And so the chronicler concludes this portion of his history by saying, "David became greater and greater, for Yahweh of Hosts was with him."

Truths We Tend to Forget

Two matters come to the fore as we consider this passage: God's Promise and David's Choice.

God's Promise

Twenty years earlier Samuel, at the Lord's direction, had anointed David king over Israel (1 Samuel 16:13). At that time Saul was Israel's king and David had to wait patiently for the time when the Lord would fulfill His word. At first David became a part of Saul's court, serving as a musician to help relieve the king's depression, and then as the general of Saul's army. During this time he gained valuable leadership experience.

On one occasion, when Saul and his army were returning from battle the king heard the young women singing a song of triumph. The refrain was

"Saul has slain his thousands,
And David his ten thousands"
(1 Samuel 18:7).

On hearing this Saul became very angry, and said: "They have ascribed to David ten thousands, but to me they have ascribed [only] thousands. Now what more can he have but the kingdom?" And he eyed David with suspicion from that day on (1 Samuel 18:8-9). As Saul's jealousy and paranoia increased, it became too dangerous for David to continue living in Gibeah, and he had to flee the city. And thus began his "outlaw" years (1 Samuel 19:1–26:25). At first he sought safety with Samuel, but eventually he was forced to leave the land of Israel and find sanctuary in Philistia. With every step he took it seemed as if the throne that had been promised him was being left farther and farther behind. What was he to make of God's promise? Had the Lord forgotten him? Could it be that Samuel's anointing of him in Bethlehem had been a colossal mistake?

David's experience as an outlaw spanned a period of between

ten and thirteen years, and saw him continually hounded by King Saul. So precarious was his existence that, on one occasion, he confided in Jonathan that there was scarcely one step between him and death (1 Samuel 20:3).

It is difficult for us to believe in God's promises when our life is a continuous series of misfortunes. It is during these "desert experiences" that our faith is tested. And it is through adversity that we mature.

In the course of time David, who had gathered about him a large band of warriors, settled in Ziklag. A measure of peace prevailed. Each man could spend time with his wife and children, and those under David's command were happy. To David, however, the throne of Israel seemed very far away.

Then, as if without warning, the Philistines decided to launch a united attack on Israel. As we found in 1 Chronicles 10, Saul and his sons were killed in the battle. When David learned of what had happened he inquired of the Lord if he should leave Ziklag and live in one of the cities of Judah. The Lord indicated that he should. He then asked which city? And the Lord directed him to Hebron (2 Samuel 2:1).

It came about that soon after his arrival in Hebron, as the news of Saul's death spread, the elders of Judah came and anointed David king over the tribe of Judah. Was this the fulfillment of God's plan? Had he been mistaken in thinking that he would reign over a united Israel? In God's plan for David, he would serve a seven-and-a-half year "apprenticeship" in Hebron (2 Samuel 2:4). But what is clear to us with the benefit of 20×20 hindsight was not as clear to David.

During the time David reigned in Hebron, Saul's surviving son, a man named Ish-bosheth (also called Eshbaal in 1 Chronicles 8:33), reigned in the kingdom east of the River Jordan. He made his capital the city of Mahanaim (2 Samuel 2:8-11), and a period of civil war followed. The Lord was with David, however, and though he did not know it he was steadily gaining in strength while Ish-bosheth was becoming weaker and weaker.

Then, for a brief period it seemed as if God's promise might

soon be fulfilled, for Abner, Saul's general, came to see D
promising to unite the tribes under David's rule. Abner, however,
was treacherously assassinated by Joab, and plans to unite north
and south had to be put on hold (2 Samuel 3:1-29). And once
again David may have felt that being king over all the tribes of
Israel was as far off as it had ever been.

David was just beginning to enjoy the peace that accompanied
the end of the civil war when a vast number of soldiers were
seen coming toward Hebron. What could this mean?

We do not know if David and the people of Hebron were
taken by surprise when this large delegation came to Hebron.
We do know that the elders of the northern tribes entered into
negotiation with David and ended by crowning him king. And
so God's word, that had seemed as if it would never be fulfilled,
came to pass.

We live in an impatient age. We want what we want
immediately if not sooner. Patience is no longer deemed to be a
virtue. And the discipline that accompanies the delayed
fulfillment of God's promise often leads us to doubt His goodness
and the reliability of His promises. God, however, is not in a
hurry. The work of grace being done in our hearts takes time
and is more important to Him than all the gifts He can give us.
The encouragement we derive from David's experiences is that
God's promises are sure, and each one will be fulfilled in
accordance with His perfect will.[12]

David's Choice
Verses 4-9 describe for us David's choice of a new capital. How
long Jerusalem had been in his mind as the place of his future
operations is not known. We do know that David was always
careful to seek God's will before taking any deliberate action
(cf. 2 Samuel 2:1; 5:19, 23). Why then is there no mention of
consulting the Lord about his plans for a new capital?

On several occasions in the past the Lord had intimated that
when He gave His people possession of the land of Canaan, He
would choose a place for His name (cf. Deuteronomy 12:11;

ghly probable that Samuel had taught David ... may even have told David that Jerusalem was ... where God would put His name. If so, David ... knew this and that is why, after he had killed ... ad cut off the giant's head and taken it to Jerusalem (1 Sa... 17:54). It was designed to show to the Jebusites that, inasmuch as his God had given him victory over the Philistine champion, He would also give him the victory over them.

This would confirm the principle found throughout the Scriptures that *obedience precedes blessing*. And inasmuch as David consistently obeyed God's Word we are not surprised that he became greater and greater, for the Lord was with him.

Those who know their Bible best can affirm the truth of this observation that whenever God led a person (e.g., Moses, Nehemiah, Paul) to do something, the methods, materials, and specific directions were always provided. All God's servant had to do was obey. In our day we find that enthusiasm has all-to-often replaced obedience. However, as C. H. Spurgeon remarked on one occasion, "Faith and obedience are bound up in the same bundle. He who obeys God, trusts God; and he who trusts God, obeys Him."

4

David's Mighty Men (1)
(1 Chronicles 11:10)

A recent survey has shown that young Americans cannot name a single personal hero. In our TV-loving era their role models are invariably those captured on film and paraded before the public looking more handsome and macho or beautiful and seductive than they really are. And the parts these individuals play taps into the felt desires of our young people and meets their human needs. In reality, the private life of these "stars" is often far removed from the role they play on television.

So where may we find *bona fide* heroes?

One potential source of information comes from the Congress of the United States. It has to do with the Medal of Honor awarded by the Congress. First given in 1861, the Medal of Honor is the highest award that can be given to anyone in the armed forces. Often referred to as the "Blue Max", it is only bestowed on those who have exhibited unusual bravery and have gone above and beyond the call of duty in the service of their country.

One recipient of the Medal of Honor was Audie Murphy.[1] He came from a very poor home and enlisted in the army so that he could support his younger brothers and sisters. These were the dark days of World War II, and it wasn't long before he was sent overseas as a member of Company B, 15th Infantry Regiment, 3rd Infantry Division. As one by one those in command of Company B were killed, Murphy took on more and more responsibility. He had been unable to finish high school and always felt he was unworthy of promotions that were given him.

On one occasion, during the bitterest fighting in France, two American tank destroyers rumbled up beside Murphy's platoon. Just then six German tanks emerged from the tree line opposite them followed by about 250 infantry. The German tanks unleashed a barrage of shells that ripped through Murphy's position. A round from the German tanks disabled one American destroyer and the other slid into a ditch with its guns uselessly pointing at the ground. From behind the lines the order was given to retreat.

The first salvo from one of the German tanks had killed one of the machine gun teams. Murphy, who didn't understand the meaning of "retreat", took over their position and began firing at the enemy. The German tanks continued their attack and at one time were so close the men in them could be seen clearly. At this point Murphy grabbed a phone and called for artillery backup while he continued to decimate the enemy's infantry. He kept up his attack until his machine gun ran out of ammunition. Undaunted he grabbed a carbine and continued fighting his lone war. His aim was so accurate that the Germans began falling back. Though wounded in the leg, Murphy continued fighting until the last of the German tanks and infantry had left the field. Then he limped back to camp.

Though he didn't think his efforts were worthy of notice, he was later informed that he had single-handedly won a significant battle. And when word of what he had done reached the United States, Congress awarded him the Medal of Honor. By war's end he had received more decorations that any other person in the history of the armed forces.

David, too, had his men who were worthy of a medal of honor. Information about them has to be pieced together.[2] The primary Scriptures are 2 Samuel 23 and 1 Chronicles 11. These men of renown are grouped together. There is *The First Triad* known as "The Three" (11:10-14; cf. 2 Samuel 23:8-12). The record of their heroic deeds is followed by a digression telling of *three of David's friends* (11:15-19; 2 Samuel 23:13-17). Then mention is made of a *Second Triad* (11:20-25; 2 Samuel 23:18-23); and finally we are given a list of David's "*Mighty Warriors*" (11:26-47; 2 Samuel 23:24-39).

But there is more to David's mighty men than a rehearsal of their names. God was at work behind the scenes, and the section of Scripture that begins with 11:10 and ends with 12:40 lets us see how the Lord orchestrated all things so that the events of David's "outlaw" years, followed by his kingship in Hebron, were climaxed by his coronation over all Israel (note 11:10 and 12:38). Through the efforts of these "mighty men," the Lord brought to pass His purpose for His people.

Some, however, may remain unconvinced. They will ask, "What possible relevance can these records have for us today?" In answering their question we shall do well to remind ourselves of the words of the apostle Paul: "For whatever things were written previously, were written for our teaching, in order that through patience and the comfort of the Scriptures we may have hope" (Romans 15:4). God the Holy Spirit did not include these brief biographies in the sacred writings to fill space. He had a purpose, and, as we shall see, the life of each of these men is instructive. Furthermore, Dr. William G. Blaikie has pointed out that a study of their lives helps us "understand the human instrumentality by which David achieved so brilliant a success", and the portions of Scripture devoted to them "enable us to gain a clearer grasp of the kind of men by whom [David] was helped [in attaining the kingdom], and the kind of spirit by which they were animated, [as well as] their intense personal devotion to [him]."[3]

It is significant that Joab is *not* listed among David's mighty men. He was a fearless general, and we would expect his name to be mentioned first. Joab, however, was as unscrupulous as he was brave, and as ruthless as he was self-seeking. His murder of Abner, Saul's general (2 Samuel 3:6-37), and his assassination of Absalom, David's son (2 Samuel 18:5, 14-15), had prejudiced David against him. And so, though today he would have been regarded as a "five-star" general, his lack of character caused his name to be omitted from the list. Instead, David's commanders-in-chief were "the Three" – Jashobeam, Eleazar, and Shammah.

First of the Three

> And these [were] the heads of the warriors who [were] to (i.e., with) David, who made themselves strong with him in his kingdom, with all Israel, to cause him to reign, as (i.e., according) to the word of Yahweh, over Israel. And these [are] the number of the warriors who [were] to (i.e., with) David: Jashobeam, the son of a Hachmonite, head of the thirty; he lifted his spear against three hundred at one time, and killed [them] (11:10-11).

Information about Jashobeam is sparse. We first learn of him during the time Saul sat on the throne of Israel. There was growing disenchantment with Saul's leadership and many were deserting him to join forces with David.

> These [were among] those coming (i.e., who came) to David in Ziklag, while [he was] held back (i.e., banned, a fugitive, an outlaw) from the face of Saul the son of Kish; and they [were] among the warriors – helpers in the war, armed with bow[s] [using both] right and left hands, with stones, and with arrows, [and] with the bow[s] – of the brothers of Saul, of Benjamin... (12:1-2).

Included in their number was Jashobeam. He is described as a Tachmonite in 2 Samuel 23:8 (where his full name is given as Josheb-Basshebeth) and a Hachmonite in 11:11. The solution to this apparent discrepancy is easy to explain. In Hebrew letters "T" and "H" are so similar that a scribe, working from a worn manuscript, could easily mistake one letter for the other. Then, as copies were made from his manuscript, the error would be perpetuated.

Jashobeam was a descendant of Korah (12:6), whose ancestors had settled in one of the cities in northern Judah where a man named Hachmon (or Tachmon) had at one time wielded considerable power and influence. Eventually his name was given to the territory in which he and his descendants lived (27:32) and, in keeping with Semitic custom, people who lived there were spoken of as his "sons."

The area in which Jashobeam grew to manhood was originally

included within the tribe of Judah, but when Saul became king the citizens found it preferable to identify themselves with Israel's king and as a result their town and the surrounding area was included within the tribe of Benjamin. Growing up as a Benjamite, Jashobeam early learned to use a bow and arrow. He also became expert at throwing stones (weighing up to a pound in weight) from a sling with either hand (cf. 12:2). At a young age he qualified for inclusion in Saul's army and in the course of time became a part of the king's "elite corps." From this time onwards he was numbered among Saul's "kinsmen." As a part of Saul's army Jashobeam would have fought against the warlike Philistines. These people were trained for war from infancy. The gods whom they worshiped were cruel and rapacious, and the people became like them. The Philistine army also had within its ranks men of giant stature. They struck terror into the hearts of the Israelite militia (20:4, 6, 8; cf. 1 Samuel 17:4-10). It was only by God's grace that the Israelites were able to maintain their independence.

Growing Disillusionment

As one of Saul's "kinsmen" it is fair to conclude that Jashobeam was a trusted soldier. He probably worked closely with the king, enjoying the prominence that came with his position. In the course of time, however, he became an unhappy witness to the king's lapses into paranoid delusion. This was particularly evident in Saul's frequent pursuit of David. On these occasions the kingdom was left undefended. And so, while Jashobeam may initially have been prepared to excuse these lapses on account of the king's recurring "sickness" (1 Samuel 16:15; 19:1*a*, 20ff.; 22:1-2, 6; 24:2ff.; 26:2ff.; 27:1), with the slaughter of the priests of Nob (1 Samuel 22:11-19) he came to the conclusion that Saul's cause was not worth fighting for. And in company with other "kinsmen" of King Saul, he came to realize that God's hand was on David.

This was brought home to Jashobeam in two different ways: (1) David's numerous miraculous escapes from Saul, and (2)

David's magnanimous sparing of Saul's life (1 Samuel 24; 26). The righteousness of David's actions stood in marked contrast to Saul's hostile acts. All of this resulted in a growing realization that David was God's anointed; and this new understanding was given fresh impetus when he realized that some of his closest friends shared his views. We do not know who first began speaking of defecting to David, but we do know that after careful consideration several came to the conclusion that they could no longer serve Saul.

Defection?

One day Jashobeam quietly left Saul's camp. Others, perhaps in pairs, met at a secret rendezvous. In all, twenty-two of Saul's "kinsmen" crossed the rugged hills of Benjamin, traversed the hot, sultry Valley of Aijalon,[4] and came to David in Ziklag (12:1-7).[5]

Ziklag is about twenty-two miles south of Gath. At one time it had been included in the borders of the tribe of Judah. Now, however, it was controlled by the Philistines; and Achish, king of Gath, had given it to David as a mark of his favor.

When Jashobeam and his comrades arrived in Ziklag they found the town filled with other defectors and their families. It did not take them long to look the place over and send for their wives and children. And, content that they had made the right decision, they settled down to enjoy the good things God provided for them.

While from a military standpoint the number of David's men was not great, their skills were unmatched.

A Compromising Situation

Late one evening a runner arrived from Gath. He brought news from King Achish. David, with his six hundred warriors, was to join the Philistine army in their battle against the army of Israel under King Saul.[6] Their specific task was to protect the king of Gath.

While many of David's men were disenchanted with Saul

and his leadership, it is doubtful if any of them relished the idea of taking up arms against their own people. Jashobeam had twice witnessed David spare Saul's life. What would he do now? He could not refuse to the command of his suzerain. And so, compelled by one of those unfortunate circumstances, David and his men had no option but to march northward toward Aphek[7] breathing the dust of the Philistines who marched in front of them.

Once the combined Philistine army was assembled at Aphek, the lords of the Philistines assembled on some knoll overlooking the valley where the battle was to take place. As their armies marched past them in review, they noticed Hebrews bringing up the rear behind the men from Gath. "What are these Hebrews doing here?" they demanded of Achish.

Achish gave a perfectly logical and reasonable explanation for the presence of David and his men, but the other lords of the Philistine Pentapolis were unconvinced. They became angry. "Make the man go back to his place," they demanded (1 Samuel 29:2-4).

With reluctance Achish called David to his tent and told him of the decision. David protested his innocence, but it was with an inner sigh of relief that he and his men began their journey home. And they made good time so that by the end of the second day they were in the vicinity of Beth-shemesh.[8] Once again they camped out in the open fields, determined to make an early start the next morning. If we place ourselves in the position of David and his men, we can easily imagine the longing of each one as his thoughts turned to his wife and children, the warm embraces and loving kisses he would receive, and the good meal and sound sleep amid comfortable surroundings that he would enjoy.

As the darkness finally began to give way to the gray light of dawn, and the rising sun dispelled the shadows of the night, the men stirred, gathered their things together, and set out for home. They ate what food they had in their pouches as they walked along the dusty path, for they were eager to place the last leg of their journey behind them. By mid-morning they were still on the maritime plain, but only a few miles from the level plateau on which Ziklag stands.

When Ziklag finally came into view it was strangely silent. No one roused the residents with the news that they were back. Instead they saw faint traces of smoke drifting listlessly into the air. Their hearts sank as they realized what must have happened. When they had been summoned away to join the Philistine forces, the Amalekites – those wily nomads of the desert – must have been informed of their departure. Seizing the opportunity, they rallied together the different clans that made up their tribe, and in large numbers and with incredible speed raided the Negev (or Southland). One city after another was captured and looted. Everything was taken: women and children, cattle, possessions. Nothing remained (1 Samuel 30:1-4).

Seeking Counsel from the Lord

Jashobeam may have been standing quite close to David when he heard him issue an order for Abiathar, the priest, to be brought to him. As soon as Abiathar appeared, he asked him to seek counsel from the Lord: Should they pursue the Amalekites? The Lord answered, Yes.

The story of David's pursuit is recounted in 1 Samuel 30. What is of interest to us is a possible explanation of an apparent discrepancy in the biblical text. In 2 Samuel 23 we are told that Jashobeam was responsible for killing eight hundred of the enemy at one time (2 Samuel 23:8), whereas in 1 Chronicles 11:11 we are informed that he "lifted up his spear against three hundred whom he killed at one time." Is this an error or can the apparent discrepancy be explained?

The context of the latter passage seems to imply that the three hundred were Philistines, for mention is made in the preceding verse of those who gave David strong support in his kingdom, to make him king according to the word of the Lord through Samuel (cf. the wars of 2 Samuel 5:17-20 and 22-25). If this is so, then the eight hundred whom he killed at one time may very well have been Amalekites whom David and his men finally overtook following the destruction of Ziklag.

After a forced march through the desert, David and his four hundred men came across the Amalekite camp. There were so many of them that they were spread over all the land. The Israelites observed them eating and drinking and engaging in merry-making on account of the great spoil they had taken from the land of the Philistines and from the land of Judah (cf. 1 Samuel 30:16). With the element of surprise on their side, David and his men attacked the Amalekites. The battle began at twilight and lasted until the evening of the next day. Some indication of the vast numbers of the Amalekites may be deduced from the fact that only 4,000 were able to escape.

The Lord was good to David and his men. On account of His gracious providence, they recovered everything that had been taken from them (1 Samuel 30:18-20).

Strong Support

On David's return to Ziklag, he learned of the death of Saul and his sons (2 Samuel 1:1-7). He sent some of the spoils taken from the Amalekites to the elders of Judah (1 Samuel 30:26-31). Sometime later he inquired of the Lord, "Shall I go up to one of the cities of Judah?" The Lord said, "Go up." David again asked for direction: "Which city shall I go to?" "Hebron" was the Lord's answer. So David and his fighting men and their families journeyed to the district of Hebron. Some found homes within the city and others lived in the surrounding towns and villages (2 Samuel 2:1-3). And there, in the course of time, the elders of Judah came and crowned David king (2 Samuel 2:4). Then, seven and a half years later, representatives from the northern tribes came to Hebron and made David king over all Israel (11:1-3).

As David proceeded to organize his kingdom, twelve individuals, who had previously demonstrated their "strong support" of him, were appointed to positions of administrative responsibility (27:1-15). The special task of these leaders was to raise money and food for the maintenance of the realm, and to protect Israel's borders. The first of these leaders was

Jashobeam. Dr. O. R. Corvin describes him as "a man who gained his honor, not by right of birth, nor by semi-deified ancestry, but by actual courage, daring, and skill .... He could sit in the seat of authority or lead honored warriors ..."[9] with equal ability. He did not ask for advancement, but when responsibility was given him he discharged it in a thorough and acceptable manner. David never had to check up on him, for his trust in Jashobeam's integrity, loyalty, courage, perseverance, and versatility was unquestioned. It is no wonder, therefore, that Jashobeam took his place at the head of David's mighty men.

Five Smooth Stones

Five well-rounded principles of success can be deduced from Jashobeam's life.

Integrity

The first characteristic that stands out like a polished stone is Jashobeam's integrity. Initially Jashobeam had been in the service of King Saul. When he found that he could no longer serve Saul without compromising his beliefs, he left. He chose instead to identify himself with a man who at that time was *persona non grata* in the kingdom. It was a costly move for it necessitated turning his back on his rank and the prestige that he had earned while in Saul's army.

All too often integrity is compromised for the sake of temporary gain – a sense of security or a few moments of pleasure. Those who truly seek to honor the Lord realize that each act, each decision, and in fact everything they do is subject to His scrutiny. Only those whose lives are marked by integrity can be trusted.

Integrity is essential to sound leadership. Each leader must be able to earn the respect of his subordinates. And because power corrupts, it is all too easy for advancement to lead a person to seek selfish advantages and use questionable means to secure his personal ends. Only a commitment to principles of righteousness and honesty can insure that a person in high office remains true to the confidence placed in him. Jashobeam was such a man. In time he emerged from the ranks of David's militia to become the chief of the king's trusted supporters. And the more responsibility given to him, the more he discharged his duties with self-effacing thoroughness.

Loyalty

The second characteristic of Jashobeam's success was his loyalty. Although loyalty is hard to define, it is easy to detect. It is one of life's greatest virtues, and it achieves its highest ends when linked with integrity and followed through with a commitment to a person whose cause is just. His loyalty to David grew as trust developed and confidence was established, and David never had to question Jashobeam's commitment to him. Through all the difficult years at Ziklag, the unpopular march with the Philistines to Aphek, the return to find their homes plundered by the Amalekites, and the long forced march through the desert to recover what had been stolen from them, Jashobeam never wavered. He met each challenge with confidence, never compromised on a single principle, and was eventually rewarded by being numbered among David's chief advisors. In the end he became the head of the mighty men.

While integrity and loyalty are notable traits, courage is essential if a person is to be successful.

Courage

It is possible for a virtuous person to possess inherently the qualities of success, and yet fail because he or she does not have courage enough to take reasonable, calculated risks. Trials will come. Some may appear to be overwhelming. Only those who have the courage to face them will eventually emerge as victors. Courage, however, is *not* a synonym for recklessness, for recklessness involves a lack of prudence, is careless of the consequences of one's actions, and often results in rash and thoughtless conduct.

On numerous occasions Jashobeam faced situations that called for courage. On one occasion he slew eight hundred armed men (quite likely Amalekites who had kidnapped his wife and children), and on another occasion (possibly in a battle against Israel's enemies, the Philistines) he alone killed three hundred. These acts called for courage. At no time, however, was he reckless. He knew his strengths and weaknesses, and had the patience to wait for the right opportunity.

Theodore Roosevelt's comment about courage is worth remembering. He said: "Far better it is to dare mighty things, to win glorious triumphs ... than to take rank with those poor spirits who neither enjoy nor suffer much, because they live in the gray twilight that knows not victory nor defeat."

The person in the office who puts values and principles above security and popularity displays courage. To live out one's convictions in the midst of a culture obsessed by materialism is to demonstrate courage. To follow biblical values and spiritual principles in the face of strong opposition or accepted social mores or ridicule is to demonstrate courage. The young person in high school who turns down an invitation to take a drink or "get high" on drugs is acting with courage. Only cowards join in. They find it easy to "go with the flow." As strong as the desire for acceptance and affirmation may be, all of us can exhibit the same kind of courage as Jashobeam as we take a stand for what we believe to be right.

Euripides, a Greek poet of the 5th century BC, believed that courage could be taught. If so, then it is learned from the example of great men and women of the past, as well as those of our acquaintance who name the name of Christ and hold positions of responsibility in church and school, office or factory, home or hospital. Integrity is vitally important if the truth is to be served; loyalty must be demonstrated if our cause is to be advanced; and courage is essential if opportunities are to be seized when they present themselves. These notable traits must also be linked with perseverance if we are to be successful and triumph over the forces that are arrayed against us.

Perseverance

From our story it soon becomes evident that Jashobeam was able to sustain remarkable perseverance. He did not rise from obscurity to prominence overnight. Instead, as we look at his life we find that he persevered in the service of King Saul until he was numbered among Saul's elite guard (i.e., Saul's "kinsmen"). When he found that his beliefs, values and goals were irreconcilable with those of King Saul's, he left and joined David in exile. In doing so he relinquished the rank he had attained in Saul's army, and as a part of David's militia he was compelled to work his way up from the bottom. In doing so he demonstrated those qualities of perseverance that ultimately led to him becoming the chief among David's mighty men. Even then many years passed before he was accorded that title.

While it is easy to commend perseverance by reminding ourselves of the over-worked cliché that "a great oak is merely a little nut that held its ground", much more is demanded of us in the real world. A story that has been of great encouragement to me concerns a man named John Creasey. He became one of the world's most prolific and successful mystery writers. His versatility was astounding. During the course of his lifetime he authored 560 books that sold more than 60 million copies in 23 different languages. It is easy to look at his virtuosity and admire his greatness, but a point that is most often overlooked has to do with the fact that he collected 743 rejection slips from publishers before he managed to get a single word into print. In the end his perseverance was rewarded.

Versatility

One final point. As we review the life of Jashobeam, we find that there was an important characteristic that lay latent in his success: Versatility. As occasion required he could be a great warrior or an efficient administrator. When David set up his kingdom, he commissioned twelve men to oversee those who, in lieu of paying taxes, would support his administration one month a year. This was no small assignment, for Jashobeam was responsible for overseeing 24,000 people.

The ability to switch roles and be both a task-oriented and a social-emotional (or relational) leader, is very important. It is common in business circles to talk about "Type A" and "Type B" personalities, or "Theory X" and "Theory Y" styles of leadership. Few, however, can combine these traits and make the necessary changes that are essential to success. An example of a person who could be both task oriented and relational is Nehemiah.[10] And Jashobeam exhibited a similar versatility. While he did not occupy a prominent place in the inspired record, the fact remains that the principles of integrity, loyalty, courage, perseverance, and versatility that we see in his life are essential if a person is to keep pace with the changes that progress and different circumstances demand.

5

David's Mighty Men (2)
(1 Chronicles 11:12-14)

There are some notable landmarks in history around which all future events revolve. Thomas Archer described some of them in his book *Decisive Events in History*. These included the Battle of Marathon, the Fall of Jerusalem to Titus, the Norman Conquest of England, the First Crusade, the signing of the Magna Carta, Martin Luther's nailing of his "Ninety-five Theses" to the door of the Castle Church in Wittenberg, and the defeat of the Spanish Armada. To these could be added Alexander the Great's defeat of Darius at the battle of Arbela, the Apostle Paul's crossing over the Aegean Sea from Troy to Philippi (an event that began the evangelization of Europe), the conversion of Constantine, and many others.

As we examine these events, we are given glimpses of courage and perseverance that leave us deeply impressed at what others did so that we might enjoy the freedom and privileges that are ours. We are also overawed as we contemplate the hidden hand of God behind the scenes. To our deep regret, however, one date in the annals of the Christian church seems to have been forgotten.[1] It is known to us as "The Disruption of 1843."

Some time ago, while I was rummaging through a second-hand bookstore in Scotland, I came across an old work that bore the title *Disruption Worthies: A Memorial of 1843*, edited by James A. Wylie. It contains biographical sketches of the great men of that time who, for conscience sake, and in order to preserve the "peace, liberty and purity" of the church, relinquished their pulpits (and with that decision, their livelihoods) rather than go along with the British Parliament's attempt to bring these churches under its political control. In time these men banded together and gave strong support to the formation of the Free Church of Scotland. They were the champions of orthodoxy of the time, and they are familiar to us today as a result of the books they wrote.

Less well known are the men of another time and a different disruption. They, however, have their names enshrined in a more enduring "memorial". They are the men who left their homes and means of a livelihood and rallied around David, giving him strong support in the establishment of his kingdom. Among these "worthies" is a man named Eleazar.

> And after him (*viz.*, Jashobeam)[was] Eleazar the son of Dodo, the son of Ahohi, [one] of the three mighty men with David [in Pas-dammim] when they taunted the Philistines [who] had gathered there to battle; and the men of Israel went up [possibly from the cave of Adullam to do battle]; and he (i.e., Eleazar) arose and struck the Philistines until his hand was weary, and his hand clung to his sword; and Yahweh worked a great deliverance on that day, and the people returned after him only to plunder [the slain] (2 Samuel 23:9-10; cf. 1 Chronicles11:12-14).

As we take a closer look at this man, we notice three important things about him:

- The Importance of a Godly Heritage
- The Evidence of Remarkable Courage; and
- The Significance of His Victory

The Importance of a Godly Heritage (11:9)
Eleazar's name means "God has helped", and it points to something in the experience of his parents that illustrates the focal point of their lives and of the home they established. Apparently, in naming their son, they did so in grateful recognition of the way in which the Lord had helped them. The precise circumstance that led to giving their son the name of "Eleazar" is not known to us. We may be certain, however, that when they named their son it was to honor Him who had shown His goodness to them.

Parents try to instill their own beliefs and values in their children. Their children, however, do not always live up to the expectations of their parents. That is why it is important for us to begin the training of our children as early as possible – while the "cement" of their personalities is still wet. The longer we delay their spiritual nurture, the more difficult it is to cultivate an awareness of spiritual realities.

The principle of people living in Bible times giving a special name to their child or children is easy to verify. Sarah, for example, waited for ninety years before she was able to conceive. When she gave birth to a son, she was so filled with joy that she called him "Isaac," meaning "Laughter," exclaiming "God has made laughter for me; everyone who hears will laugh with me" (Genesis 21:6). And when Joseph, after his many sufferings, became prime minister of Egypt, he called his firstborn "Manasseh" meaning "Forgetting," saying "God has made me forget all my trouble" (Genesis 41:51). Then, when his second son was born, he called him "Gershom" meaning "Fruitful," saying, "God has made me fruitful in the land of my affliction" (Genesis 41:52). And so we could go on.

Names are important. Some years ago I had the privilege of visiting Dr. Paul Tournier in Switzerland. His book, *The Naming of Persons*,[2] had recently been released. In it he stated how important names are and then showed how some children, on account of their names, suffer discrimination at the hands of their peers. Others, however, have names that are readily remembered and esteemed. They do not face the same difficulties as those whose names are hard to recall or conjure up some negative connotation.

Earlier, in his book *The Strong and the Weak*, Dr. Tournier had written, "To put a label on someone is inevitably to contribute to making him conform to the label, especially if the person is at the impressionable age of childhood."[3] And in *The Meaning of Persons* he gave his rationale: "The power of suggestion exercised by the labels we are given is considerable. This is particularly the case in childhood. But the same is true throughout our lives."[4]

There can be little doubt that Eleazar's life was molded by the attitude of his parents. What he perceived in them, and the influence they exerted upon him, permeated every part of his being. His physical, psychological and spiritual life bore the imprint of their Godward relationship,[5] and he grew to manhood with a deep trust in the Lord as the One who keeps His covenant with His people and fulfills His Word to all who are in a right relationship with Him.

While we are inclined to develop religious "goose bumps" when we recall the influence of Susannah Wesley on her children, or think of the impact of James Hudson Taylor on his children, or recall the influence men and women of God have had upon our own lives, it was Dr. Urie Bronfenbrenner of Cornell University who reminded us that "The family transmits the values on which civilization supposedly is built, such as respect for law, personal integrity and some degree of selflessness, plus the ability to forego immediate gratification in return for anticipated future rewards."[6]

The undermining of social structures by state imposed legislation, and the ready availability of pornographic literature in bookstores and on the Internet, has contributed to the demise of family values. And these factors cannot be ignored. As Dr. Bronfenbrenner told his audience:

> "I would suggest that the United States can no longer afford to be methodical ... in its technological advances and so sloppy, neglectful, cautious and fatalistic in its social programs. We want so much to 'make it' for ourselves that we have almost stopped being a society that cares for others. We seem to be hesitant about making a commitment to anyone or anything, including our own flesh and blood."[7]

The information we glean from the biblical record is fully in keeping with Dr. Bronfenbrenner's observation, and it is illustrated for us in the life of Eleazar. He benefited from training by godly parents, and the ideals they instilled in him molded his thinking. The time in which he lived posed difficulties for all honest people, and the Philistines were a constant threat to the peace and security of the nation of Israel. And it is precisely that threat that brings us to the continuing saga of David's "mighty men" and the place of Eleazar within their ranks.

The Evidence of Remarkable Courage (11:10a)

The Valley of Elah,[8] also known as Pas-dammim, provided the Philistine army with direct access to central Israel. Identified today as the *Wadi-es-Sant* ("Valley of the Acacia"), it was well protected by the Philistine fortress of Azekah. Pas-dammim was the same valley where, on an earlier occasion, David had killed Goliath (1 Samuel 17). And it was here, at the time of our story, that the Israelites came down from the safety of the hills to try and prevent the Philistines from stealing their harvest.

The great Scottish preacher, Dr. William G. Blaikie, wrote:

> ... the dangers to which [David] was exposed in his military life, were manifold and sometimes overwhelming, and [on occasion] all but fatal; and thus enable us to see how wonderful were the deliverances he experienced .... The language applied to David, "David and his men went down," would lead us to believe that the incident happened at an early period, when the Philistines were very powerful ... and it was a mark of great courage to "go down" and attack them [on level] ground.[9]

Following the Israelites' initial engagement with the Philistines, the text of 11:13*b* tells us that the Israelites "fled" before their enemies. It was while his countrymen were engaged in a hasty and undignified withdrawal that Eleazar found himself fighting alone. He fought so hard that the hand holding his sword grew "weary." He then suffered from a painful muscle spasm[10] so that when the fighting was over he could not release his sword. It was left for others to help pry open his fingers and massage the stiffened muscles so that the pain was eventually eased.

All of this lays emphasis on the fact that the price of success is effort. The ingredients of success are developed through hard work, training, a willingness to take calculated risks, and a determination to see things through to their conclusion.

I have had a lifelong admiration for Winston Churchill. In his early years he was rambunctious and caused his parents and schoolteachers considerable grief. He was sent to Harrow, a prestigious school, but proved to be a poor student. In fact, his teachers were glad to see him leave. Many years later, however, after he had risen to prominence as a politician and military strategist, the faculty of Harrow issued a cautious invitation for him to return and address the student body. He did so. After the principal had given a long and loquacious introduction in which he tried to ease any tension that might have lingered, Churchill rose to his feet and approached the podium. In ponderous tones that had become well known to the people of England during World War II, he said:

> "Never give in, never give in, never, never, never, never – in nothing, great or small, large or petty – never give in except to convictions of honour and good sense."[11]

And he sat down. The students, who had expected a protracted and possibly boring oration, were stunned. They had expected his speech to be filled with high-sounding words and clever phrases. Now they sat in awed silence as Churchill's words sank in, for in those dark days all in Britain wondered just how soon Hitler might launch an invasion of their tiny island.

Eleazar never gave in through all that long day of fighting. Hot, tired, and thirsty, he fought on; and years later, when David established his kingdom, this brave man was rewarded with increased responsibility (27:4).

The Significance of His Victory (11:10b)

The Bible tells us that the rest of the Israelites returned to the scene of the battle only after the fighting had ceased. There they claimed the spoils of war. The actions of these Israelites illustrate an important principle. Great men and women of the Christian church have won notable victories for us, and we now enjoy the fruits of their labors. For example, Athanasius boldly combated the Arian heresy that had swept most of Christendom into its false embrace. Whereas Arius and his followers had attacked the person of Christ, claiming that He was not co-eternal with the Father, Athanasius proved that He was fully God and fully man. And what of Martin Luther? At a time when the church had been caught up in all sorts of errors, he boldly championed the doctrine of justification by faith alone. Nor should we forget J. Gresham Machen who, while on the faculty of Princeton Theological Seminary, took issue with the encroachment of theological liberalism and was subsequently defrocked. He never wavered in his convictions, however, and in the course of his lifetime wrote several important apologetic works that still are in use today.

And there were others, Wycliffe and Coverdale and Tyndale (to name only three), who at great personal risk translated the Bible into the language of the people. It is on account of their efforts that we possess copies of God's Word today. However, in our forgetful age, we seldom give thought to those who labored to bring it to us. We, therefore, are in the same position as those Israelites who benefited from the victory Eleazar had won.

Four Important Truths

The Hand of God in Human Events
We should not leave this story without seeing the hand of God behind the events that took place. Both in 2 Samuel 23 and 1 Chronicles 11 we read that "the Lord brought about a great victory that day."

There are many commentators who are quick to tell us that these words are an editorial gloss inserted in the text by some pious scribe who was intent upon seizing any and every opportunity to give a spiritual emphasis to Israel's hard-fought victories. Don't believe it. What we are reminded of in this brief statement is that God uses people to achieve His purpose. We all allow the things of time and sense to shape our world of reality. Part of our growth toward maturity requires that we enlarge our understanding to include in our worldview the things that cannot be seen. I am not implying that we should become superstitious mystics who supposedly discern the will of God in the barking of a dog or the formation of clouds or a sunrise. Those who engage in such activities find that their lives are eventually controlled by fanciful subjectivity. What I am advocating is the kind of mature reflection that leads to an increased understanding of God's goodness and lovingkindness.

The Importance of a Godly Heritage

We have all sat in testimony meetings and heard the stories of those who have been won to Christ from lives of crime, drugs, immorality, and a variety of other vices. Their testimonies have stirred our hearts. We are happy to hear of the way the power of God has shattered the shackles of sin. What we unwittingly forget is the place and importance of the Christian home. Our children may feel that unless they can tell of something terrible that they have done, they will not receive the recognition or hear the gasps of surprise that are so readily given those who have been saved from the abyss of self-destruction.

Eleazar reminds us that it is in the home and from one's parents that character is formed. It is through our daily honoring the Lord that we transmit sound beliefs, values, and goals to our children. There is no substitute for a godly heritage and we err if we fail to place proper emphasis on godly instruction received in the home.

As we look back over the past, we find that some of the most noble men and women came from Christian homes. Amy Carmichael, for example, descended from a long line of God-fearing people. She was the oldest of seven children. Her father was a physician who reared his children on the Bible. As Amy grew up it was the most natural thing in the world for her to surrender her life to Christ. Following this event she volunteered to go to India as a missionary where she spent fifty-five years of unbroken service.[12]

F. B. Meyer was brought to Christ at his mother's knee. He

dedicated himself to the Lord while still a child. Then, after preparing for the ministry, he held several notable pastorates and wrote books that continue to bless God's people.[13]

The list of those who were reared in Christian homes, who have given significant service to the cause of Christ, could be extended *ad infinitum.* The important fact is this: There is no substitute for godly parents who honor the Lord and set their children an example by the things they say and do.

The Need for Preparation

It is possible that some young adults (who are in agreement with what has been written thus far) may be eager to go out and engage the enemy. On account of their youthful inexperience, however, they may overlook the importance of proper preparation.

Hollywood has placed us in its debt for the movie made of Alvin York. York was drafted into the infantry and sent to France. In the course of time he found himself engaged in the battle of Meuse-Argonne. His platoon ran into a storm of German machine-gun fire and ten of his comrades were killed within a few minutes. York suddenly found himself in command. He waved his seven men forward, and they quickly captured a machine gun crew. York then advanced alone to see what lay ahead. He took several steps and then flattened himself on the ground as 35 machine guns opened fire, some only 25 yards away.

Alvin York seemed trapped. It was then that his training as a mountain man in Tennessee came in handy. He had often won prizes for his marksmanship at "turkey-shoots." He knew that for those behind their machine guns to aim at his position they had to raise their heads. So he patiently waited for someone in one of the gun emplacements to raise his head. When he did, York fired. So accurate was his aim that before long a German major emerged with a white flag and an offer of surrender. York agreed and ninety Germans came out with their hands up. York shouted to his seven men to disarm them. Then, as the Americans began to move their captives to the rear, York realized another problem. The battle lines had moved and they were now behind enemy lines. What was worse, a trench of German soldiers lay directly in front of them. Pushing his pistol into the major's back he ordered him to march up to the trench and demand that the occupants surrender. They did.

When York's activities for the day were tallied it was found that he had silenced thirty-five machine gun emplacements and taken 132 prisoners.[14]

We admire such bravery and resourcefulness, but we should not allow ourselves to lose sight of the fact that this was only possible because Alvin York had diligently practiced marksmanship in the mountains of Tennessee. There is no substitute for thorough preparation, particularly where the ministry is concerned. And though attaining some mastery of Greek and Hebrew, biblical studies, systematic theology and church history requires hard work, no person should consider taking on a pastorate without such training.

The Need for Courage

When the British Parliament wanted to tax the people in the American Colonies without granting them fair representation, Granville Sharp took action on their behalf. Sentiment in England ran high and was overwhelmingly in favor of the position adopted by its leaders. Sharp was denounced for his views, lost his government position, and was so stigmatized that he was not able to find any other form of employment.

This experience of adversity did not prevent Granville Sharp from espousing another seemingly "lost" cause. Many of his friends owned slaves. He spoke out on behalf of those who had lost their freedom and were exploited against their will. Once again the tide of public opinion threatened to engulf him. He persevered, however, and eventually won a case (which he had to argue in court himself because no lawyer would take it on). It set a precedent for the emancipation of slaves in England, and similar action was soon taken in the United States.

Though suffering one injustice upon another, Granville

Sharp's courage enabled him to persevere through obstacles that would have caused a person of lesser character to turn and seek anonymity in the shadows of some cottage at the end of a country road.

In more recent times there have been men of courage such as Clarence Edward Macartney. When Harry Emerson Fosdick preached his (*in*)famous sermon, "Will the Fundamentalists Win?" it was Dr. Macartney who took issue with him and boldly defended the evangelical cause. At that time it was not known how many learned men on the faculties of church-sponsored universities and seminaries would stand with him. We now know that most were so committed to theological "modernism" that they took sides against Dr. Macartney. The battle that was fought in the pulpits and lecture rooms was waged at great cost. Rhetoric ran high and reputations were ruined. Nonetheless, in our evangelical circles today, we owe a great debt to men such as Clarence Edward Macartney, for without their timely intervention the truth of God's Word might have perished from the land.[15]

These conflicts are now a part of history. Does this mean that there are no more battles to be fought? Today, we face problems that are equally as great. Tension surrounds the "Right to Life" movement; confusion permeates the "legalization of drugs" debate; and masses of red tape confront those who would try to protect our young people from the evils of pornography. The need of the hour is for a person such as Eleazar or Granville Sharp or Clarence Edward Macartney who will take a stand for what is right and persevere until the victory has been won.

6

David's Mighty Men (3)
(1 Chronicles 11:14)

A little to the north of the rugged, yet breathtakingly beautiful coastline of Big Sur, and slightly to the south of San Francisco, is the rustic comeliness of the Monterey Peninsula. Each year thousands of visitors pay the toll and take the seventeen-mile drive to the picturesque village of Carmel. As they do so, they pass the fabled Pebble Beach golf course, and stop at the rugged headland to see the "Lone Cypress."

With its features sculptured by the wind, and its roots penetrating into the cracked rock, this cypress tree seems to symbolize a courage and determination to survive that creates in observers a sense of awe. It is as if this cypress tree's lone stand against the worst weather that nature's changing moods can produce evokes our admiration.[1]

On visiting the "Lone Cypress" recently, I was reminded of one of David's mighty men. His name is Shammah. The biblical record about him is very brief. It tells us only that a large raiding party of Philistines – much larger than normal – came to plunder and pillage his village. Perhaps the town where he lived was larger than most and on this account the number of raiders resembled an army. The biblical text tells us that the residents, perhaps taken by surprise, fled before the Philistine advance.[2] The biblical writer tells the story:

> And after him (*viz.*, Eleazar) [was] Shammah, the son of Agee, the Hararite: and the Philistines had gathered into a company (lit. army), and there was a plot full of lentils; and the people fled before the Philistines; and he set himself in the midst of the plot, and saved it and struck the Philistines; and Yahweh worked a great deliverance (2 Samuel 23:11-12).[3]

Though this is all we know about Shammah, we err if we fail to see Bible personalities as flesh-and-blood human beings with feelings and aspirations similar to our own. When we "clothe Shammah with flesh" (as one of my professors used to say), we are prompted to ask, What motivated him to fight single-handedly against so large a company of Philistines? And after the fighting was over, and those who had fled returned to take spoils from the slain, what might the attitude of the people of his village have been? How did the elders treat him, for though they were responsible for leading by example, they, too, had fled before the approach of the enemy?

In answering these questions some information can validly be inferred from other, similar incidents. It can then be added to our understanding of human nature.

The Response of the People

When we attempt to answer the question, "What was the response of the villagers to Shammah's victory?" we can only assume that they were glad to see him alive, and in all probability treated him as a hero. And to show their gratitude, they may even have celebrated his victory with a feast. Is all of this conjecture? No. In 1 Samuel 23 we read of a similar incident when David and his men brought relief to Keilah. They delivered the city and afterwards were treated like liberators. It would have been the height of ingratitude for those whom Shammah saved not to show their appreciation. Common people, however, are more inclined to express their gratitude, whereas their leaders may feel that to praise someone else diminishes their prestige.

The Issue of Power

Shammah was rightly regarded as a hero, and in time this same spirit of courage and resourcefulness caused him to be included in the inner circle of David's mighty men. There he took his place alongside Jashobeam and Eleazar in the first triad (2 Samuel 23:19b). He also gave strong support to David in the establishment of his kingdom, and later on David appointed him a commander over a division of 24,000 men. In this capacity he helped protect Israel's borders one month each year, while also raising support for the central administration (2 Samuel 23:11).[4]

People in influential positions often see a person such as Shammah as a threat to their own position of power. They will then try various strategies to neutralize a powerful person's potential influence. Drs. R. R. Carkhuff and B. G. Berenson describe for us an all-too-common unhealthy side of leadership – one which most of us have experienced at one time or another:

> ... society functions in its advanced stages for its own protection, preservation, and perpetuation.... It functions to control man's destructive impulses; [yet] always seeks its own survival and equilibrium.
>
> Society is organized most often to fix responsibility for those actions that threaten its continuation *in its present form.* This is not to say that society does not change. It does. However, it changes only through the efforts of those who live independently of society, those who sometimes run against the mainstream of society, and those who live always on or beyond the very tenuous and lonely margin of society. Whatever progress society makes, it makes by moving over to incorporate the strong words and actions of this marginal man. However, it does so only when the marginal man is potent, when he has somehow withstood the attempts to be neutralized, and has survived the attempts to destroy him. Society changes in order to neutralize the full effects of the potent man's words and actions. It does so in order to render the potent man less potent.
>
> Society is not organized to free man's creative potential, but rather to maintain or render man impotent, or maintain him with limited potency.[5]

This is a very important statement, and we should note the process whereby attempts are made to try and render a powerful person less powerful. As these psychologists have shown, the strategies used include neutralizing ... destroying ... or changing [the rules] in order to render the potent man less potent.[6] It is a tribute to David's leadership that he did not try to make powerful individuals less powerful. Instead, he set an example of healthy leadership, for he recognized the strengths of Jashobeam, Eleazar and Shammah, and appointed them his "joint chiefs of staff" without attempting to inhibit them (and by doing so reduce their potential).

History is replete with examples of governments and church bodies that have tried to neutralize a powerful man or woman. Of the great men and women of the sixteenth century, the most colorful was Martin Luther. He brought the church back to the fundamentals of the faith, *viz.*, a belief in the Holy Scriptures as the sole authority for the believer in all matters of faith and practice; justification by faith alone without the addition of good works; and the realization that every true child of God shares equally in the priesthood of all believers.

But Luther was not always a popular reformer. Earlier in his life there had come a time when, as with Shammah before him, he had to take a stand "in a field of lentils." The scene in this particular instance was the city of Worms, and the date January 1521. Those present were the religious and political leaders of Europe who did not want this young monk to "rock the boat." So they convened a special meeting with the specific purpose of making Martin Luther less potent. And if they failed, then Luther (who had already been branded a heretic) could always be assassinated by anyone who found him. And if this failed, he could be seized and burned at the stake.

Two years earlier (1519), in Leipzig, Luther's friend Andreas Bodenstein (better known as Carlstadt) had challenged to a debate the eminent Roman Catholic theologian, Dr. John Eck. When Carlstadt could not hold his ground against Dr. Eck, he asked Luther to take his place. In what followed, Luther called in question the general councils of the church (upon which Eck leaned for his authority), and offered in their place the Scriptures. The hierarchy present at the debate sensed the need to speedily crush Luther, and early in 1520 convened a heresy trial. By June the Pope had signed a Bull excommunicating Luther from the church's fellowship. The Bull also ordered that all of Luther's writings be burned.

During 1520 Luther was safely ensconced in Wittenberg where he kept himself busy writing his "tracts" (i.e., "position papers" which were in reality vigorous rebuttals of points of Catholic doctrine). By means of these tracts he gained wide popularity among the people, and thousands flocked to hear him preach. But by January 1521 he was summoned to appear before his superiors in the city of Worms. Frederick of Saxony and the Emperor promised him safe conduct, but similar assurances had been given John Huss, and these did not prevent him from being burned at the stake.

The proceedings began with Luther being accused by the Catholic hierarchy of heresy. Their goal was to rob him of his power and influence. Like Shammah in the field of lentils, so Martin Luther took his stand at the Diet of Worms and answered each accusation as it was put to him. Finally, after a long and vengeful tirade, the leading prosecutor ordered Luther to recant his writings. It was at this time that he gave expression to his memorable refusal: "Here I stand. I cannot do otherwise. God help me."

Luther was now in very grave danger. In the language of our day, an "open contract" had been issued whereby any person finding him could kill him; and by doing so, earn the church's blessing. Frederick, Luther's protector and friend, had to literally abduct Luther in order to save his life. He took him secretly to Warburg Castle near Eisenach. It was there, during ten months of seclusion, that Luther busied himself translating the Bible into the language of the people. He also wrote other tracts promoting the cause of reform.[7]

The people of Germany regarded Martin Luther as their champion. Others, however, were adamantly opposed to everything he did. In Germany and elsewhere the progress of reform was furthered, not by making Luther less influential, but by incorporating his strong words and actions into the social structure of his times.

The Issue of Motivation

As we return to Shammah, we are compelled to ask, What motivated him to take a stand against such a large body of Philistine soldiers?

In answering this question, let us first consider what Frederick Jackson Turner wrote about in *The Frontier in American History*. In this book he praised those values that he believed were characteristic of the American frontier, namely, a deeply ingrained sense of personal freedom, strong determination, rugged individualism, an inquisitive nature, and the ability to develop creative solutions to perplexing problems. Dr. Turner concluded his book by stating that, in his opinion, these values were in large measure lost when the frontier closed. And this loss, he affirms, signaled an end to the "American way of life."

There is a lot of truth to Frederick Turner's observation, and while it is easy to agree with him, we would do ourselves great injustice if we concluded that the spirit, which he so eloquently praises, is entirely dead. It is true that the contours of our contemporary society have been determined in large measure by social structures (with a corresponding high premium placed on conformity), but God's Word encourages us to think creatively, work diligently, and emulate the example of the great men and women of the past (cf. Hebrews 11).

As we turn to examine the heroic feat of a person such as Shammah, we find that there are three basic criteria that may motivate an individual to take risks in order to secure something worthwhile. These are a strong sense of right and wrong, a pressing need, and some external threat. And one or more of these criteria may be present at any given time. Upon further reflection, however, we also find that people who take risks may also be motivated by selfish gain, or altruism, or perform their courageous deeds out of conviction (i.e., a belief that what needs to be done is right). As we examine the biblical record we see two major areas of motivation illustrated in (a) the people who fled, and (b) Shammah who stayed behind.

We are familiar with the former. Illustrations of the latter are harder to find. One man who stood boldly against the evil forces arraigned against him was General Charles Gordon. General Gordon's name is familiar to those who visit Israel as the man who discovered "Gordon's Calvary" and "The Garden Tomb." The location of these sites was immediately recognized by most evangelicals as answering the biblical description of the places where Christ was crucified and buried.

Charles Gordon is also remembered as the governor of the Sudan, and the defender of the city of Khartoum.[8] He had been sent to the Sudan at the request of an inept and vacillating British government with instructions to do two seemingly impossible tasks: evacuate several thousand people from the area, and establish a stable, independent government.

A self-appointed and half-crazed Mahdi had called upon his Muslim followers to expel all white people from their land. The growing unrest, together with the raids made by the Mahdi on different towns, made Gordon's task well nigh impossible. And, to make matters worse, the military help that had been promised him never arrived. In spite of this, he accomplished the first task with unparalleled success. Khartoum, however, fell before he could bring to completion the establishment of a settled, secure government.

Like Shammah, Charles Gordon stood alone as he faced the changing forces of life. One of his biographers wrote:

Gordon's character was unique. Single-minded, modest, and retiring, he was fearless and outspoken when occasion required. Strong in will and prompt in action, and with a naturally hot temper, he was yet forgiving to a fault. Somewhat brusque in manner, his disposition was singularly sympathetic and attractive, winning all hearts.

Weakness and suffering at once enlisted his interest. Caring nothing for what was said of him, he was indifferent to praise and reward, and had a supreme contempt for money. His whole being was dominated by a Christlike faith, at once so real and so earnest that ... the object of his life was the entire surrender of himself to work out whatever he believed to be the will of God.[9]

When news of the fall of Khartoum reached England, and the people learned that Gordon had been killed, they were outraged. A day of national mourning was proclaimed. The outburst of popular grief could hardly have been paralleled. Gordon was held in high esteem by all who either knew him or knew of him. Only a few politicians were openly opposed to him. And the reason? They had tried by every means possible to neutralize his potency. When their sullen opposition did not work, they delayed sending him the supplies and personnel that had been promised. They believed that if he failed he would be compelled to return home in disgrace. They could then force him to retire. In the end, on account of their own bureaucratic intransigence, the cause was lost and many lives were sacrificed. To the consternation of his adversaries, Gordon dead became an even more powerful force than he had been when he was alive!

Someone once said, "Each human being is really three people: Who he thinks he is, who other people think he is, and who he really is." It often takes a crisis to bring to the fore the true character of an individual. In the case of Shammah, the hinge of destiny that revealed who he really was, was a Philistine invasion. Without premeditation, he took his stand in a field of lentils and defended it. The crisis revealed him to be a man of courage and perseverance, skill and determination.

Crises and difficulties beset all of us. How we respond to them reveals who we really are. We do well, therefore, to ask ourselves, What set a man like Shammah apart from those who fled from before the Philistines? And to this question may be added another general one: What causes any person to rise above his or her peers? The answers to these questions are not academic. They are supremely practical, for connected with them are the questions, Why did Louis Pasteur spend endless hours of research so that he could eventually control and then conquer disease? What drove an athlete like Roger Bannister toward the tape to become the first man in history to break the four-minute mile? What prompted a courageous woman like Mother Teresa to devote her life to the care of the destitute and dying in the slums of Calcutta? What caused an inventor like Thomas Edison to persevere through more than a thousand failed experiments before being able to give to the world the light bulb? What kept a writer like Algernon Swinburne at his desk eight hours a day and for as many years before becoming (as far as the world was concerned) "an overnight success"? What inner dynamic impelled Lowell Thomas to be the first white man in modern times to enter Afghanistan or bring back a report of the forbidden land of Tibet? And what inspires missionaries to brave life in a distant land without the benefit of hospitals and schools in order to take the gospel to those living in the darkness of sin and superstition?

The answer to all of the above is really very simple. It is to be found in what psychologists call the "locus of control". The locus of control can be either external or internal, and the Bible adds a further dimension to what psychologists have discovered (cf. Romans 8:5-8). Basically, we can either allow others to make decisions for us by permitting outside factors like public opinion or some form of pressure, censure or threats of one kind or another, to control our attitudes and actions, or we can take responsibility for our own conduct, believing that by exercising appropriate autonomy we can have a part in determining our future goals and the course of our life.

In people such as David and his mighty men, we find that they were activated by a strong internal God-consciousness (cf. Psalms 5:4-10; 49:5-9; 64:1-6; 72:12-15). That is why the Lord was able to work in them and accomplish great things through them. And as we, too, develop an inner Godward orientation or drive (e.g., by walking each day in reverential awe of God; cf. Proverbs 1:7; 8:13; 14:2, 26; 16:6*b*; 19:23; 28:6, *et cetera*), we are set free from the need to either please or placate others[10] (Proverbs 29:25). As the *process* continues, we gain strength while enjoying true liberty. The Lord can then work in us so that in the end, He can accomplish His will through us.

This spirit of freedom will enable us to stand boldly against the winds of adversity, while demonstrating a strong determination, a rugged individualism, and a solemn resolve to solve the problems that confront us. The "frontier spirit" that Frederick Jackson Turner described is not dead. It just needs the right kind of opportunity to manifest itself. Whereas Shammah's arena of activity was a field of lentils, the place of another's efforts can just as validly be a dusty laboratory full of test tubes and bottles smelling of formaldehyde; seemingly endless hours of training on a cinder track; the squalor of some far off corner of the world; a dimly lit office wrestling with one idea after another in order to solve some problem; writing at a desk with back aching and eyes burning, while trying to give expression to thoughts that lie deep within; or trudging through some swamp or jungle in order to bring the gospel to an unevangelized tribe. All who engage in such activities exhibit the same courage as Shammah. Without their dedication we would not enjoy peace and freedom, and the benefits of knowledge, travel, health and happiness that we often take for granted. So let us thank God for people such as Shammah!

7

The Marks of Friendship
(1 Chronicles 11:15-19)

If someone approached you and asked, "What do you believe could immeasurably and enduringly enrich your life?" how would you respond? If another asked, "In your opinion, what do you perceive to be the major cause of restlessness and discord, frustration and a sense of hopelessness in our society?" what would be your answer?

Some celebrities on a talk show were asked to define "friendship". They had obviously been told ahead of time that they would be asked this question, for they came prepared with a variety of observations:

"Friendship is like an antique. Its value increases with age."

"Friendship is the only cement strong enough to hold the world together."

"Friendship is usually a plant of slow growth."

"Genuine friendship is like sound health. Its value is seldom known until it is lost."

And one, less creative than the rest, merely quoted the familiar statement of Aristotle, "A friend is a single soul living in two bodies."

To Hugh Black, friendship was "the priceless art of seeing with the heart, rather than with the eyes."[1] And Ralph Waldo Emerson said that the true "ornament of a house are the friends who frequent it."[2]

History records many notable friendships: Hero and Leander, Achilles and Patroclus, David and Jonathan,[3] and Socrates and Theophrastus. The Apostle Paul also had his circle of friends.[4] And in more recent times we have the friendships of Goethe and Schiller, George Washington and Joseph Paul Lafayette, and Helen Keller and Anne Sullivan. They all stand out as examples of relationships that transcended the ordinary. Few, however, can compare with the friends of David. They rallied about him and supported him through the many trials and vicissitudes of his life.

The Pattern of Friendship

The writer of Chronicles, having introduced us to the inner circle of David's advisors (known as "The Three"), now provides us with a vignette of the devotion that was characteristic of his friends. Their bravery is illustrated in a venture undertaken at a time in David's life when he was an outlaw, and was constantly being harassed by King Saul.

> And three of the thirty heads (i.e., chief men) went down to the rock to David, to the cave of Adullam; and the camp of the Philistines was pitched in the valley of Rephaim. And David [was] then in the stronghold, and the garrison of the Philistines [was] in Bethlehem. And David longed [for water from the well of Bethlehem] and said, "Oh that someone would (lit., who will) give me a drink [of] water from the well of Bethlehem, that [is] by the gate?"
>
> And the three broke through the camp of the Philistines, and drew water from the well of Bethlehem that [is] by the gate, and carried [it] and brought [it] to David; but David was not willing to drink it, but poured it out before (lit., to) Yahweh, and said, "Be it far from me, O my God, to do this; shall I drink the blood of these men [who went] with (i.e., at the risk of) their lives? For with (i.e., at the risk of their) lives they have brought it."
>
> And he was unwilling to drink it.
>
> These things did the three mighty men.

The information given us by God's inspired penman is important. As Dr. William G. Blaikie has pointed out, "the description of the exploit of the mighty men ... is singular proof of [David's] great personal influence. He was so loved and honored that to gratify his wish, these three took their lives in their hands to obtain the water."[5]

The story of their heroic deed is well known. It is taught to children in Sunday school, and various lessons may be drawn from it. The incident is so beautifully told that it does not need elaboration. David's friends are not named because the essence of a healthy relationship is that it does not seek its own. The central thoughts, however, focus on *friendship*. We note...

- The Freedom Allowed (11:13)
- The Loyalty Shown (11:14)
- The Desire Expressed (11:15)
- The Deed Accomplished (11:16)
- The Love Acknowledged (11:17)

The Freedom Allowed

The fact that these men "came down" to David who was in the Cave of Adullam shows that they had the freedom to come and go as occasion required. No compulsion was laid on them. Some of David's men did have their wives and children with them, but not all. And all may have needed to return to their farms, as occasion required. The point illustrated for us is that the relationship of David and his men was non-possessive. He did not require them to be with him all the time.

From the shortage of water it is evident that what happened took place during the hot summer months when streams dried up and water was hard to find. In Israel, the drought ends in late November/early December with the "early rains." This is a time for the sowing of wheat and barley. This is followed by the winter rains that provide the necessary moisture for the germination of the seed. The "latter rains" of March/April are needed in order to bring the grain to a head (cf. Deuteronomy 11:17; 28:12, 24; 2 Chronicles 6:26-27; Psalm 84:6; Jeremiah 3:3; 5:24; etc.).

Two primary crops are harvested: wheat and barley. Barley requires a shorter growing season, and is therefore harvested first. Because of the unevenness of the terrain, not all crops ripen at the same time. Those that mature first are found in the deep, hot Jordan River valley, with barley generally being harvested in April/May and wheat in May/June.

These men came down to David when the hot summer months were well advanced. Seasonal streams in the different riverbeds would have already dried up, and it would be a major task for each man living with David to provide sufficient water for his household.[6] By the time of our story David and his men would have to draw water from springs at some distance from the cave. And to make matters worse, the difficulty of sustaining life was increased because the Philistines had overrun the land, taking possession of the Valley of Rephaim,[7] even penetrating as far inland as Bethlehem.[8]

David's men, therefore, came to him at a time of great danger.

The Loyalty Shown

In joining forces with David, these men demonstrated their willingness to share with him the hardships of his life. They ran the risk of being detected by Saul's spies, and had to dodge Philistine patrols. The love of these men for David led them to willingly share these trials with him.

The importance of their loyalty has been illustrated in an article that appeared in *Psychology Today*.[9] The writer pointed out that true friendship requires a unique form of human bonding. Unlike marriage or the ties that bind parents to children, the ties of friendship are not defined by law. And friendship is distinct from other social roles such as citizens to their country, employees to their company, or members of professional societies to a sponsoring organization.

Friendship has its own subjective rationale for its continuance. It enhances feelings of warmth, trust, love and affection between two people, and grows more out of free choice than necessity. Because friendship lies outside – or transcends – the structured roles and institutions of society, it is a topic that allows an exploration of the ways that people relate to others at times when they are most free.

When interviewed by *U. S. News and World Report*, Dr. Eugene Kennedy stated, "Friendship is the capacity to accept ourselves as we are and then to present ourselves to others in a way that they will also perceive as genuine and real." Dr. Kennedy went on to point out,

> There's a lot of talk in our culture about 'be yourself,' but frequently what that means is 'be your selfish self.' You know: Insist on your rights, don't let anybody stand in your way, get everything that's due to you and sue them if they won't yield to you. That isn't what it means to be yourself....
>
> To be yourself is to discover the qualities that you possess.... Friendship means having enough trust in others to act genuinely. Yet many people aren't on good enough terms with themselves and don't appreciate the simple things about their own character.... People [often] want the rewards of friendship without the hazards.... There's a death to self in every friendship.[10]

As we shall see, David's friends exhibited true loyalty and devotion.

The Desire Expressed

One day, perhaps during the heat of the afternoon, and while David was enjoying what coolness the cave provided, he said light-heartedly, "Who shall give me water to drink from the well of Bethlehem that [is] at the gate?" (11:17). He was jesting, of course, and it is certain that he never expected anyone to undertake such a hazardous task! His remark, however, showed his transparency. He felt free to share his innermost feelings.

Transparency is an important ingredient in friendship, but one that takes time to develop. C. Neil Strait wrote: "Every life needs a friend with whom he [or she] can share the blessings and burdens of living. Such friendships are cultivated through listening and caring."[11] David felt free to share his feelings, and his friends entered into the thoughts he expressed.

The Deed Accomplished

As the story continues it illustrates the fact that true friendship produces the kind of relationship that gives friends the opportunity to care for one another. Out of love and devotion to

David, his friends risked their lives for him. And they never thought that what they were doing was reckless or unnecessary. Traveling at night, they covered the miles between the cave of Adullam and Bethlehem, broke through the Philistine lines, and drew the water (the Hebrew text has "waters") from the well.[12] It is probable that at some point the Philistines became aware of their presence, and so David's friends had to fight their way past the Philistines before they could escape into the darkness and make their way back to the cave.

And they brought the water to David.

All of us stand in need of encouragement. David certainly did. His situation was precarious. The presence of the Philistines in the land weighed heavily on him. At such a time it is natural for us to reminisce about happier times. And when David expressed a wish, perhaps to divert attention away from their present predicament, his friends decided to cheer him up by surprising him with water from Bethlehem's well.

Friends – good friends – lighten our burdens, increase our joys, and dispel the gloom that accompanies disappointment while also rekindling hope and providing the kind of incentive that encourages us to try again.

How valuable were David's friends? David's successes may be attributed to the fact that those who rallied around him were possessed of a spirit of self-sacrifice that made it easy for his cause to become their own. We are not surprised to read, therefore, that they gave him strong support in establishing his kingdom.

But this story requires an ending, and "What," we may ask, "was David's response to their heroic deed?"

The Love Acknowledged
When David's friends returned to the cave and gave David the skin of water, he immediately became aware of their devotion and daring. He was overwhelmed by their kindness, and with deep gratitude in his heart he walked to the mouth of the cave and poured out the water before the Lord, saying: "Far be it

from me, by my God, to do this; shall I drink the blood of these men? For with their lives they have brought it" (11:19).

Friendships are often fractured by misunderstanding or a lack of communication. Such might have been true on this occasion. David, however, acknowledged the greatness of their deed and expressed his appreciation before the Lord. And this leads us to another aspect of real friendship: It is nourished through understanding. That which blocks the growth of friendship is selfishness, neglect, and a lack of concern. David, we find, esteemed the love of his friends as one of his most cherished possessions. He enjoyed their company, and knew that without their support the trials and hardships he faced would eventually prove to be intolerable. His recognition of their devotion was evidenced by his words as well as his actions.

Where Do We Fit In?

We began this chapter by asking two important questions: "What do you believe can immeasurably and enduringly enrich your life?" and "What do you perceive to be the major cause of the restlessness and discord, frustration and feeling of hopelessness that is evident in our society?"

The answer to the first question lies in our ability to form deep and lasting friendships. This involves the development of true affection. As our population continues to mushroom and our cities become larger, loneliness seems to be spreading like a medieval plague. Ironically, the lonely person isn't necessarily the man or woman living in solitude, though I know of many who are. People can experience a deep sense of isolation and loneliness in a crowd. It is probable that the cause of such loneliness is two-fold: (1) the pressures of modern city living, and (2) the mobility of many people that makes the development of lasting friendships very difficult.

Dr. Ignace Lepp, in *The Ways of Friendship,* believes that an *in*ability to develop deep, meaningful friendships lies, in part at least, with a lack of communication. In his book he points out that all of us derive satisfaction from *emotional* communication through the giving of ourselves in dialogue and other expressions of warmth and intimacy. It is this kind of human communication that enables us to share with another our hopes and needs, problems and disappointments, and find in our friend a listening ear, a wise counselor, and a source of continual encouragement.

Friendship expresses itself through sharing. And it stands to reason that if they cannot share their felt needs, they will also have difficulty expressing appreciation.

The answer to the second question points to a trend within our society that needs to be understood before it can be corrected. Because society tends to enforce conformity and mold the social character in a definable way, three basic personality types have emerged. These have been identified as *tradition-directed, inner-directed,* and *other-directed.*[13]

The *tradition-directed* person finds security in conformity. Such conformity is dictated to a large degree by power relations within the group to which the individual belongs. In such situations the prevailing culture controls behavior; and, while rules are not so complicated that the young cannot learn them, careful and rigid standards of etiquette govern their relationships. And because conformity is highly prized, the tradition-directed person is not encouraged to develop his or her capabilities, take initiative, or pursue new and different aspirations. There are many contemporary examples of people living tradition-directed lives (e.g., the Amish).

The second group is *inner-directed.* The inner-directed segment of society emerged with the Renaissance and Reformation, and flourished for more than three centuries. Now, however, inner-directed people have almost vanished. The few who are still inner-directed derive their motivation from inner principles implanted early in life. They are directed toward generalized, but inescapably destined goals. For the Christian, being inner-directed implies the development of a strong internal God-consciousness.

Third, those who are *other-directed* appear shallower in their relationships, superficially friendlier, but more uncertain of themselves and their values than those of an earlier generation. They are also more demanding of approval than those who are inner-directed. In addition, and to a large extent, they are conformists and take their cues from established power structures within society. They tend to become "people pleasers," and seem to evidence few discernable convictions. The goals toward which they move constantly shift because those who are the "leaders" are themselves motivated by externals (e.g., fashion, opinion, or a political party), have few internal convictions, and are therefore unsure of the goals they wish to achieve. As a consequence, their relationships become casual and superficial.

A Backward Glance

The development of lasting friendships involves maturity. While Aristotle believed youth to be the "golden period of friendship," he also lamented the fact that young people enter into and dissolve friendships very quickly.[14] Cicero, however, pointed to maturity as the basic prerequisite of a lasting relationship.[15] True maturity begins with the development of autonomy. Only as one becomes able to sustain friendships apart from one's family can friendships be cultivated that provide companionship, compatibility, and encouragement toward further growth.

While the ancient Greeks and Romans believed that mutual profit, pleasure, the development of virtue, and the enjoyment of one another's company were the primary goals of friendship, Christ demonstrated that the highest form of friendship is love for one another (John 15:12-13). He even went so far as to say that we should show goodwill toward those who could never repay us (Luke 6:32-35). *True love involves desiring the highest good in the one loved, even to the point of self-sacrifice.*

As we weigh carefully the friendships David was able to establish and sustain, we find that they were characterized by acceptance (12:1, 17), mutuality (1 Samuel 18:1), availability (2 Samuel 23:13), openness (2 Samuel 15:19-22), appropriate and complementary assertiveness (2 Samuel 21:15-17), the opportunity for personal growth (1 Chronicles 27:1-31), and confidentiality (12:33, 38).

True friendships are built upon shared beliefs, values and goals (John 13:34; 17:21). With acceptance, there is reciprocal loyalty (cf. Job 17:5; Psalm 122:8; Proverbs 16:28; 17:17; 18:24), the ignoring of generation gaps (2 Samuel 3:8; Proverbs 27:10), the expectation of consistency (*contra* 2 Samuel 16:16ff.), the exclusion of slander (Psalms 7:4; 15:3), the demonstration of devotion (2 Samuel 15:32ff.; Acts 24:23; 2 Timothy 1:16), and evidence of prayerful support (Job 42:8f.).

Sharing, giving, and serving are an integral part of friendship. The Bible makes mention of friends rejoicing in another's success, sharing each other's good fortune, and being present at festive occasions (Esther 5:10; Luke 15:6, 9, 29; John 3:29; Song of Solomon 5:1; Psalm 45:14). By the same token, friends also help bear our burdens (Judges 11:37f.; Job 2:11ff.; *contra* Job 19:19).

An unknown author shared his experience of friendship:

Friendship needs no studied phrases,
  Polished face, or winning wiles;
Friendship deals no lavish praises,
  Friendship dons no surface smiles.

Friendship follows nature's diction,
  Shuns the blandishments of art,
Boldly severs truth from fiction,
  Speaks the language of the heart.

Friendship favors no condition,
  Scorns a narrow-minded creed,
Lovingly fulfills its mission,
  Be it word or be it deed.

Friendship – pure, unselfish friendship,
  All through life's allotted span,
Nurtures, strengthens, widens, lengthens,
  Man's affinity with man.

To have friends is to have one of life's greatest gifts. To be a friend is to have a solemn and tender obligation to lovingly help and support the one whose companionship and confidence we cherish. Friendship gives us the opportunity to care for others, and to have them, in turn, care for us.

8

The Power Within
(1 Chronicles 11:20-21)

The *Oxford American English Dictionary* defines zeal as "enthusiasm, hearty and persistent effort." In the Bible we find zeal used in both a positive and a negative way. Positively, it may be described as a capacity or state of passionate commitment to a person or a cause that involves all the forces that motivate personality (e.g., interest, taste, initiative). Negatively, it is seen in jealousy, envy, self-seeking, competition, and contention.

Zeal is essential to success. Samuel Goldwyn, the filmmaker, once remarked that zeal "is the key, not only to the achievement of great things, but to the accomplishment of anything that is worthwhile." But people in the western world have not always appreciated a man or woman of zeal. There have been times in our history when any display of enthusiasm has been regarded as a lack of self-control. David Livingstone, in reflecting upon an entry in his journal describing how he had discovered some new rivers in Central Africa, penned the following comment: "I find I wrote when the emotions caused by the magnificent prospect of the new country might subject me to a charge of enthusiasm." Then he added, "I find, however, that nothing good or great has ever been accomplished in the world without it."[1]

Without appropriate zeal, no battles have ever been won, no Iliads written, no cathedrals built, no empires founded, no tribes reached with the gospel, no solutions sought for the enigmatic problems of life, and no breakthroughs made in science, medicine, or engineering. The secret of success lies in the zeal or enthusiasm that takes hold of us and uses our God-given abilities to accomplish a particular task. As the great novelist Edward Robert Bulwer-Lytton said in his *Last Days of Pompeii*, "Enthusiasm is the genius of sincerity, and truth accomplishes no victories without it."[2]

Zeal is like fire: it needs both feeding and watching. As we consider the life of Abishai, we see in a series of vignettes the strengths and weaknesses of zeal, its positive and negative effects, and how a competent leader such as David channeled and directed his activities.

In a Nutshell

Abishai was the oldest of the three sons of Zeruiah, David's sister (2:16).[3] As we review the events of his life, our first glimpse of him is when he accompanied David into Saul's military encampment on a daring venture (1 Samuel 26). Later, he was present with representatives from the southern tribes in the battle of the "Field of Daggers" near the pool of Gibeon. It was on that occasion, when the men of Judah pursued the army of Israel, that his brother Asahel was killed (2 Samuel 2:16-23). Then, in the first Ammonite war, when David's forces found themselves attacked from both sides, Joab divided the army into two divisions, placing one division under Abishai's leadership (2 Samuel 10:7-14). This may have been the time when he killed three hundred of the enemy in a single engagement. At the time of Absalom's rebellion, when a Benjamite named Shimei threw stones at David and cursed him, Abishai wanted to go and remove his head from his shoulders (2 Samuel 16:5-13), but David restrained him. And in the battle with Absalom that followed (2 Samuel 18:1-8), Abishai was again honored with a command. Then toward the end of David's life he distinguished himself again. This time he prevented a man of incredible stature from killing David (2 Samuel 21:15-17). For his bravery and zealous service Abishai was included in the "Role of Honor" of David's "Mighty Men" and made the commander of the thirty (2 Samuel 23:18-19).

Now, if Jashobeam, Eleazar and Shammar were the "four-star generals" in David's army, Abishai and those in the second triad may be regarded as his "three-star generals."

When we take a closer look at Abishai's life, we note …

His Loyalty, Courage and Zeal

Abishai probably joined David when David's movements were restricted on account of Saul's unrelenting harassment and persecution (1 Samuel 22–27). If this is the case, then he shared with David those trying and difficult years when, as an outlaw, David was hounded by the king and had no permanent home to call his own (note esp. 1 Samuel 23:14). As David's various hiding places became known, there were many occasions when there was scarcely a step between him and death (1 Samuel 20:3). Abishai probably endured with David these years of privation and hardship, uncertainty and fear.

While the biblical historian passes over this period of Abishai's life quickly, one important incident is related of him. When the Ziphites again betrayed David's whereabouts to Saul (1 Samuel 26), he and three thousand chosen men came looking for David. Saul and his army camped on the slope of the hill of Hachilah, overlooking the desert. His strategic position made it virtually impossible for David and his men to escape undetected.

David had been forewarned of Saul's approach, and while he could not escape, he took careful note of the layout of Saul's camp. That night, after the weariness of the day's march had taken its toll upon the sentries, David asked two of his men, Ahimelech the Hittite and Abishai, to accompany him down to Saul's camp. Abishai's response was quick and to the point: "I will go down with you," but Ahimelech was not as ready to forfeit his life.

In the darkness, the two men crept down toward the sleeping soldiers and made their way into the middle of the circle of men about the slumbering king. Standing over the body of the prostrate king, Abishai whispered to David, "On this day God has delivered your enemy into your hand, and now let me pin him [to the ground] with the spear. One thrust [is all I need], and I will not have to [strike him] a second time" (I Samuel 26:6).

The suggestion was a most reasonable one. David had suffered much at the hands of Saul. Earlier (1 Samuel 24) he had spared Saul's life in the hope that the king would realize that he was indeed loyal to the crown. David's magnanimous gesture, however, had not produced a lasting change, and now it appeared as if God had given to him a second opportunity to be rid of his implacable enemy. By killing Saul he would he free, and would be able to rally the tribes around his banner.

David, as a wise leader, curbed the zeal of his nephew. He was tactful, yet firm. He did not rebuke or upbraid Abishai. Instead, he appealed to spiritual values and gave the young man a valid reason for his refusal to allow him to end Saul's life. He explained that for Abishai to follow through with his plan was not in *his* own best interests. "Do not destroy him," he said, "for who can lay his hand on the Lord's anointed and be guiltless?" (1 Samuel 26:9).

Realizing the disappointment that Abishai probably felt, David took steps to compensate him for his zeal. Together they took Saul's spear[4] (which was stuck into the ground within easy reach and was a symbol of his *authority*) and his skin of water that also lay close by (and symbolized what Saul needed for *survival*). Then they crept silently out of the camp and made their way up the hill again.

When they were at a safe distance, David called out to Abner, chief officer of Saul's bodyguard, and with his voice ringing through the clear air, chided Abner for not taking better care of the king. This was enough to arouse all of the sleeping soldiers (I Samuel 26:13-25).

Saul also awoke, and recognizing David's voice, realized that David could easily have killed him. He readily admitted his error in persecuting his son-in-law. Unfortunately Saul's repentance was always short-lived,[5] and David, realizing that his life was in continual danger, left the territory of Ziph as soon as it was safe to do so.

Abishai's loyalty, courage, and zeal stand out in this incident. As with many other young men, he needed wise guidance so that his unique gifts and abilities might not be misspent. Happily for him, David was there to channel his activities in constructive ways.

His Passion for Revenge

In the course of time, the very thing David had predicted (I Samuel 26:10) took place. Saul was forced to take up arms against the Philistines (1 Samuel 29). As is now well known, the king was killed in battle, and David, showing great magnanimity, mourned for him in a fitting eulogy (2 Samuel 1:17-27).

It had been a little more than fifteen years earlier that David, having been anointed by Samuel (1 Samuel 16:13), had been promised the kingdom. With Saul dead, David now asked the Lord what he should do. God instructed him to go to Hebron; and there, in the course of time, he was anointed king over Judah. In the meantime Abner, Saul's general, made Saul's sole surviving son, Ish-bosheth, the titular king of the northern tribes (2 Samuel 2:10). In order to settle the issue of who had the right to rule the nation of Israel, Ish-bosheth or David, Abner and an elite corps met with Joab (the second son of Zeruiah) and representatives of Judah at a place called *Helkath Hazzurim*, the "Field of Daggers." They could not reach a satisfactory solution,[6] and a battle ensued. During the battle, Abner killed Asahel, Zeruiah's youngest son, and Joab and Abishai vowed to take revenge (2 Samuel 2:23-24).

The war between the house of Saul and the house of David lasted for a long time. David grew stronger and stronger, and in the end Abner, tiring of Ish-bosheth's weakness as a leader, went so far as to attempt to take the throne for himself (2 Samuel 3:7ff).[7] When difficulties arose with Ish-bosheth, Abner came to see David in Hebron with the intent of entering into a covenant that would help unite the tribes. An agreement was reached between the two men, but when Abner left to take word to the leaders of Israel, Joab sent a message after him requesting him to return (2 Samuel 3:26). When Abner did so, Joab took him aside from the gate as if to speak to him privately. He then stuck his knife into Abner's stomach and killed him. Apparently Abishai had collaborated with Joab in this, for the biblical text states, "So Joab *and* Abishai his brother killed Abner, because he had put their brother Asahel to death in the battle at Gibeon"

(2 Samuel 3:30, emphasis added). Their misguided passion delayed the uniting of the tribes under David, and serves to show us the kind of problems misguided zeal creates. 2 Samuel 3:31-39 reveals that Joab and Abishai were motivated by personal considerations and could not subordinate their desire for vengeance to the good of the kingdom.

His Commitment

Abishai must have learned an important lesson following this incident, for David never had to rebuke him again. In the course of time, however, another event took place that shows us Abishai's character.

In the Near East, the rights of the firstborn were carefully guarded. The oldest son enjoyed a special consecration to the Lord, and could only be redeemed by sacrifice (Exodus 34:19-20; Numbers 3:41, 46-47). He was also his father's heir who received a double portion of the inheritance. This was determined by the number of sons in the family, plus one. For example, if there were five sons living at the time of their father's death, then six shares or proportions were allocated. The firstborn received two of these shares, and this was called a "double portion of the inheritance." In addition, from his earliest days, he was treated with special honor by his father and by the members of his extended family. He was the one to whom the father committed certain tasks, and he was the one whom the family also recognized as their future leader. All of this is important as we consider Abishai's commitment to David.

In the course of time, the northern tribes joined forces with David, and David sought to make Jerusalem his capital (2 Samuel 5:6-12). The Jebusites who inhabited Jerusalem derided David on account of his seemingly weak army, and did not believe that he could take their city. David issued an invitation to his men: "Whoever is the first to enter the Jebusite stronghold will become my general." As we now know, Joab was the first, and from this time onwards he was elevated to a position above Abishai. The older brother now had to obey his younger sibling.

Abishai's commitment to David, however, remained unchanged. In spite of any personal disappointment he may have suffered, he served his king with unflagging zeal. His loyalty was never called in question, and regardless of what others may have thought or said, Abishai never deviated from the path of duty.

Abishai suffered a second personal disappointment as the roster of David's "mighty men" began to take shape. Jashobeam, Eleazar and Shammah were included in the inner circle of David's advisors and confidants. He was not. He came close, but the final honor was denied him, in spite of the fact that he "lifted up his spear against three hundred and killed them, and he had a name as well as the three; [and] was more *honored* than the thirty, and therefore became their commander; but he did not attain to the three" (2 Samuel 23:18-19, emphasis added). This must have been a great disappointment to him.

Within the heart of every man and woman there lies the desire to become great in one cause or another. It is this longing that spurs him or her on. Few of us, however, with the talent we possess could ever attain to greatness. And, as with Abishai, we face disappointments of one sort or another. With some it may be the failure to achieve recognition, while with others it may take the form of being passed over for promotion. In each case, however, discouragement is normal. It is how we handle these feelings that determines if we are people of honor or not. If we turn from a noble pursuit or our commitment to excellence or our quest for the truth to some lesser goal, then our zeal begins to falter, our enthusiasm wanes, and we eventually gravitate to lesser pursuits and become content with mediocrity.

In this we are reminded of the fact that greatness does not reside only in those who are nominated for the top positions. It is also a part of everyone who knows his or her strengths and weaknesses, and commits himself or herself to doing the very best he/she can, regardless of the situation in which they find themselves.

Abishai never faltered in his zeal. He never flagged in his

loyalty to David. He was made commander of "The Thirty" and performed those duties well, even though his younger brother, Joab, as David's general, enjoyed greater prominence and, for a time, received greater acclaim.

His Perseverance and Reliability

While Abishai stood in the shadow of both David and Joab, two incidents are recorded of him that show him to be a person upon whom others could rely. The first was the war with the Ammonites, and the second was the leadership position he assumed in the battle in the Wood of Ephraim.

War with the Ammonites. David's reign was marked by kindness. When Nahash, king of Ammon, died, and his son Hanun succeeded him, David sent ambassadors to Ammon to offer his condolences to Hanun. His sentiments, however, were rejected; his ambassadors were humiliated before the people; and David was forced to take up arms against the Ammonites.

Realizing that he had made a grave blunder, Hanun hired 33,000 mercenaries from three Aramean (Syrian) kingdoms. When David's army under Joab attacked the Ammonites, they did not know that the (Syrian) force was lying in wait for them. As they approached the gates of Hanun's capital, the Syrians closed in behind them and they were caught in a pincers movement. The Israelites were now fighting a war on two fronts.

To meet this new challenge, Joab divided up the army and placed one contingent under Abishai. He then turned to face the alliance of Aramean soldiers (2 Samuel 10:16-19). It was a fierce battle, but in the end they won the victory. Abishai's men were inferior in experience and skill to those under Joab's command, but throughout the day's hard fighting Abishai displayed great courage, and his zeal inspired his men to persevere until victory was secured.

Battle in the Wood of Ephraim. This was not the only time Abishai was selected for special command. On a later occasion, when Absalom sought to steal the throne from his father, David's small army was forced to do battle with those who had gathered about his popular son (2 Samuel 18:1-18). The location was the thick Wood of Ephraim.

In order to take advantage of the element of surprise, and also conceal how many men he had with him, David divided his army into three equal parts. One-third he assigned to Joab, and the other two segments were entrusted to Abishai and David's loyal follower, Ittai of Gath. The battle took place in the vicinity of Mahanaim (2 Samuel 17:24, 27). David knew that he could trust Abishai with the command of a battalion of men, and he was also confident that Abishai's zeal would spur those under him to great achievement. Absalom's losses were great, and in the melee the heir-apparent to the throne was killed.

This incident reminds us of the fact that in any venture, lasting success comes through planning and execution. It is the result of hard work, and those who are successful are not the ones who merely create good plans and come up with profound thoughts, but those who can act upon ideas and carry them through to their conclusion.

His Resourcefulness

The final episode in Abishai's colorful (though obscure) life took place when David was old. He had grown old in the service of his people. In 2 Samuel 21:15-22, God's inspired penman gives us a description of his last battle with the Philistines. During the fighting a Philistine named Ishbi-benob, a man of giant proportions, cut his way through the soldiers toward David. The weapons he carried were formidable. He had a spear whose head would penetrate any shield, and a new sword that instilled fear in the hearts of all who faced him. He attacked David, and would have killed him had not Abishai stepped in the way. Abishai warded off the blow that would have ended David's life, struck the Philistine and killed him.

The Philistine giant might have intimidated other men, but not Abishai. His zeal and dedication had prepared him to take on difficult tasks. He had also developed the ability to make decisions quickly. He knew intuitively that the real secret of success lay in expecting pressure and learning how to cope with it. He quickly sized up the situation and took prompt action. Instead of succumbing to doubt and indecision, he was the means of defeating a formidable adversary. His resourcefulness and courage saved David's life.

The Role of the Leader

As we look back over Abishai's life we come to realize that he owed much of his success to David. David was a unique leader of men, and he helped Abishai build upon his strengths so that his weaknesses gradually became insignificant. The kind of self-seeking that brought about the death of Abner was not repeated. Through David's leadership, Abishai developed the ability to work with others, cultivate togetherness, and clearly understand the demands of each new situation. He learned how to help people meet their personal goals, while at the same time fulfilling national ones. Cooperation (not compromise) and teamwork are still the ingredients of success.

Because of David's unique leadership ability, those who followed him were prepared to endure hardship and privation. They had confidence in his leadership, and as a result the obstacles they faced gave way before their united purpose. He inspired his men with the will to succeed, and it should not surprise us that they eventually subdued all who rose up against them. Impossibilities crumbled before David's godly guidance, and any discouragement they may have felt disappeared before his infectious optimism.

Our society has created in us a desire for quick and often dramatic solutions to difficult problems. We are accustomed to seeing the problems portrayed on television solved in sixty minutes. The most heroic feats are seemingly accomplished with relatively little effort. As a result, many of our young people have forgotten the meaning of the words, dedication, perseverance and zeal. And hard work is no longer regarded as a virtue.

Arturo Toscanini owed his great success to his diligence, commitment, and zeal. He began life as a musician, playing the cello in an orchestra. Because he couldn't see very well, he had to memorize the musical scores. One day the conductor became ill. Young Toscanini was the only member of that orchestra who knew the score. Although inexperienced, he conducted the entire piece to the amazement of the audience. At the conclusion, they stood and gave him a resounding ovation. And audiences continued to do so for the remainder of his life. Toscanini was enthusiastic about his work. Initially he wanted only to play the cello well. But when compelled to assume the role of a conductor, he brought the same zeal to this sphere of music.

Without zeal, there can be no lasting success. Tom Seaver of the New York Mets summed up success as follows: "You try for success by using four elements: hard work, dedication, concentration, and God-given natural talents. There is no other way." That's what Abishai did, and the same principles of success can be ours if we are willing to pay the price in hard work, dedication, perseverance, and zeal.

9

Success, Without Compromise or Regret
(1 Chronicles 11:22-25)

Conservationists play an important role in our society. They keep watch over our environment, monitor our laws, and seek to preserve our natural heritage. Whether it is the Big Horn Sheep or the Blue Whale that is placed on the "endangered species" list, or the California Condor or the Whooping Crane that is threatened with extinction, these men and women attempt to preserve for posterity the creatures God has created. Otherwise, future generations might only see these magnificent animals as stuffed exhibits in a museum.

Sociologists, historians and preachers also seek to preserve our heritage. They call attention to trends within our civilization and warn us of the dangers we face. For example, in much of the world there is a growing uneasiness over the shortage of people who possess the qualities of character that build confidence and inspire trust. In a word, there is a dearth of competent leaders.

While we all want to be successful, achieving our goals seems to be far more difficult now than it was fifteen or twenty or more years ago. There are few in positions of authority whose personal knowledge, practical wisdom, and commitment to serving the interests of others causes them to be looked up to and respected by those who know them. Happily there are a few who do show that they are prepared to stand against the rising tide of corruption, while striving to open up new frontiers for man's achievements.

Are Leaders An Endangered Species?
As we take a careful look at the modern scene, we find that the world in which we live is distracted, if not numbed, by the

conflicting views that are communicated to us via the media. The *Washington Post*, for example, published the following in its column "Letters to the Editor."

> America today has no heroes because as soon as anyone, alive or dead, threatens to rise above the norm of mediocrity we all seem to find so comfortable, less than divine characteristics are accentuated to the point where human foible is made to appear as inhuman monstrosity.... As one matures, however, it becomes obvious that the ideals represented by such figures as Jefferson (rather than their personal lives) make them deserving of our admiration and emulation.[1]

Those who have studied the social mores of the United States have noted that there is an absence of heroes in our culture today. And some of our leaders have proved to be both inept and corrupt. This has caused us to lose confidence in our national representatives. Now, we stand in need of the kind of intrepid, valiant, and fearless leadership that inspires confidence. But such men and women are hard to find. This absence of solid leadership has led to fragmentation and the kind of pluralism that now characterizes our nation.

But what will be the effect of the present wasteland on the attitudes and values of the rising generation? Studies have focused on the attitudes of three groups: children, teenagers, and young adults.

Children's Ideals

Ralph Schoenstein, writing in *Newsweek* magazine, commented on the dilemma facing young children. He wrote: "Last night Lori, my eight year old daughter, told me that she wants to grow up to sing like either Judy Garland or Michael Jackson." Apparently she had been impressed by Judy Garland after watching a rerun of *Wizard of Oz* and had seen reruns of some of Michael Jackson's concerts. What caused her to think of Michael Jackson was mystifying. "Try for Judy Garland," Schoenstein said. "A girl needs to be a great soprano to be Michael Jackson."

These two singers have become Lori's latest hero and heroine in spite of the fact that neither of them are candidates for commemorative stamps. But many children have *no* heroes or heroines at all, for there is a dearth of noble achievers for them to emulate.

To further ascertain the views of children of Lori's age, Schoenstein visited his daughter's class and asked the children whom they admired most. "Michael Jackson," said a small blond girl. "Michael Jackson, Spider-Man, and God," chimed in a boy. Ralph Schoenstein then continued: "In a day when parents seldom have noble achievers whom they yearn to emulate, it is not surprising that [great leaders of the past] have been replaced by contemporary folk singers or TV characters."

Youth's Heroes

Not to be outdone, *Life* magazine did a study of teenage attitudes. As expected, the researchers found the teen years to be rife with turmoil, personality and identity crises, and clashes with authority. Their idols were Madonna and Bruce Springsteen. When asked what they wanted to be when they grew up, most teens opted for one of the professions – either a doctor or a lawyer. A high percentage also said they wanted to be "stars" – in music, movies, or sports. By far the greatest number, however, simply said that they wanted to be rich.

When inquiry was made as to what these teens valued most, emphasis was placed upon externals. They said they "treasured their clothes, record collections, cars, and stereos" more than relationships or anything else.

Young Adults

In the course of time *U.S. News and World Report* commissioned a survey of the attitudes of young adults. They found that this age group expressed appreciation for people like Clint Eastwood, actor-comedian Eddie Murphy, and Steven Spielberg (who tied for popularity with Sally Fields). Others voted for Oprah Winfrey, Howard Stern, Harrison Ford or Meryl Streep. Of course, by the time this book is placed in the hands of readers, these heroes will have been replaced by others.

All of this caused Dr. Amitai Etzioni of George Washington University to point out that there is apparently a yearning for leadership that evidences qualities of character and stresses a "strong, go-it-alone, conquer-against-all-odds individuality."[2] But such individuals are hard to identify. Dr. Kenneth E. Clark of the University of Rochester has summarized this quest for people who can serve as models:

> Heroes stand for what is right. If someone is your hero, it's because that person does what you would like to see accomplished. But there is a prevailing attitude today that there are no right answers, which is a way of saying that there is no *right* and wrong. Our young people are unable to talk about right and wrong; they don't know the language of ethics and religion. If there is no agreement on what is right, then a consensus [of what is worthy of emulation] is impossible.[3]

As we turn to 1 Chronicles 11:22-25 we are given an example of a *successful* individual whose brief biography is worthy of serious consideration. His name is Benaiah. The description provided for us in God's Word is at once brief and revealing.

> Benaiah [was] the son of Jehoiada, the son of a valiant man of great deeds, from Kabzeel: He struck the two lion-like ones of Moab; and he went down and struck a lion in the midst of a (lit. the) pit on a snowy day. And he struck a (lit., the) man, an Egyptian, a man of great stature, five by the cubit (i.e., about 7'6" tall); and in the Egyptian's hand [was] a spear like the beam of weavers', and he went to him with a rod and wrenched the spear from the hand of the Egyptian, and slew him with his own spear. These [things] did Benaiah the son of Jehoiada, and he had a name among the three warriors. Behold, he was honored by the thirty, but he did not come (i.e., was not counted) with the [first] three. And David set him over his council (or bodyguard).

As we consider the biblical record, three valuable principles emerge, each of which has a bearing upon our quest for success:

- The Importance of Having Right Attitudes
- The Importance of Being Proactive
- The Importance of Handling Disappointments Properly

Benaiah joined David when he [David] was forced to live as an outlaw, and was being hunted constantly by his father-in-law, King Saul.

Standing Tall

The Importance of Having Right Attitudes

As we consider Benaiah's life, we notice first of all the importance of having the right attitudes. He came from a godly home. He had been born and reared in Kabzeel, a small village on the border between Judah and Edom (Joshua 15:21). Life was hard in this arid, semi-desert area, and Bedouin from the desert were constantly trying to overrun their village and drive off their flocks and herds. A man had to learn early in life how to defend his wife and children, and safeguard his livestock.

Benaiah's father was a priest (27:5), and his grandfather was a great and godly man. Together they set Benaiah an example of righteousness and dedication to duty that made a lasting impression on him. We can imagine the talk around the dinner table being both political and religious, and the thoughts implanted in young Benaiah's mind gave him a clear perspective on life. Israel was experiencing times of adversity under the poor leadership of King Saul, and some big decisions faced Benaiah as he reached manhood. There came a day when, placing commitment to what was right ahead of expediency, he left his home and joined forces with David, most likely in the cave of Adullam.

The key to Benaiah's decision lay in the training he had received in his home. It led to the development of internalized norms and standards that resulted in independent thought and action. And these attitudes characterized all he did.

As we reflect upon the importance of a godly home, we have

117

occasion to remind ourselves that only in such an environment can proper *beliefs*, *values*, and *goals* be cultivated. And the inculcation of these values in our children requires of us *involvement, modeling*, and *instruction* in their lives. As we read about what Benaiah did, and then reflect back upon the home from which he came, we realize how much of his success can be attributed to the attitudes and example set him by his father and grandfather.

It is in the home that character is formed; and depending on the kind of character developed, it can lead ultimately to success without compromise or regret.

The Importance of Being Proactive

As we take a closer look at the verses before us, we come across a second principle of success: the importance of being proactive.

It should not surprise us that, as Benaiah attained manhood, he became known for his own "mighty deeds." He did not become great all at once. There was a methodical growth that eventually was seen in significant acts of bravery. And these paved the way for the three notable feats that are described for us in the text. Each act illustrates the importance of taking the initiative, the ability to press home an advantage, and the know-how that accompanies calculated risks so that what we do eventually results in success.

The first remarkable act occurred when Benaiah struck down "two Ariels" of Moab. Our problem in interpreting the text is that we do not know who or what these "Ariels" were, and this limits our understanding of his deed.

The Authorized (King James) Version of the Bible follows the Greek translation of the Old Testament, the Septuagint, and regards these Ariels as being men of lion-like appearance who may even have worn lion skins to intimidate their adversaries.

A second view draws upon the usage of the word in other portions of Scripture (e.g., Ezekiel 43:15f.; Isaiah 29:1-2,7), and seems to imply some cultic practice. It may be that two lion-like statues in or near the temple area gave inspiration to the Moabites who were fighting against David's forces (cf. a similar incident when the Ark served to inspire the Israelites, 1 Samuel 4:59). If this is the correct interpretation, then, in spite of the danger to himself and the soldiers who would defend these religious symbols with their lives, Benaiah single-handedly broke them down and, in doing so, destroyed the confidence of the people so that victory for Israel was easier to win.

A third view, espoused by Dr. Ray Stedman, suggests that these "Ariels" were two military troops – elite corps of trained men – who had won fame as a result of their exploits.[4] He believed that Benaiah single-handedly took on these military units and defeated them.

Whatever view is chosen, the point brought before us is that Benaiah did not suddenly become a mighty man of valor. He had developed his skills over many years. He defeated these "Ariels" of Moab because he had disciplined himself and could draw on his skills when occasion required. He also had developed the strength needed for the task, and possessed the insight, courage and resourcefulness necessary for success. And for his bravery he won deserved fame.

A second illustration of Benaiah's ability occurred one wintry day. A lion, probably driven out of the hills by hunger, had approached a village. The snow lying on the ground had blurred visual distinctions, and the lion had fallen into a pit or well. It would have been easy for Benaiah to walk by and ignore the danger this trapped animal posed for the women and children of the village. Furthermore, no one was standing on the sidelines to cheer him on.

Disregarding any danger to himself, Benaiah jumped into the pit and single-handedly took on this hungry, frightened and angry "king of beasts." It was not an easy task. Lions strike fear into the heart of the bravest people. Clark, a friend of mine, while on a safari through Africa, was invited by a game warden to accompany him as he tracked down a pride of lions. These predators had been raiding some of the local villages, and needed to be moved to a different location. The task required careful planning, and it was necessary to first determine how many lions were involved.

"It is purely a routine matter," the game warden assured him.

Clark gladly accepted, and went along for the ride.

The jeep was parked some distance from the lions so as not to disturb them, and the men approached on foot. Suddenly, a lioness, that had been hidden in a thicket, charged them. All turned and raised their rifles. The game warden said to my friend, "Okay, Clark, give her your best shot."

As my friend trained his rifle upon the lioness that was coming toward them at about sixty miles an hour, he froze. He was totally unable to pull the trigger. At the last minute, the game warden fired, and the lioness slumped to the ground less than twenty feet from where they were standing. Fear rendered my friend incapable of taking decisive action. By contrast, Benaiah took the initiative, and killed the lion. In all probability, what he had done would *not* have become known had he not borne some flesh wounds to testify of the event.

The third incident illustrating Benaiah's ability to size up a situation and take appropriate action has to do with an Egyptian. This man was of impressive stature, seven and a half feet tall; and his spear, nearly twice the thickness of a 4"× 4", was probably about ten feet long. Benaiah was armed only with a rod. Once again he acted decisively. Possibly avoiding the Egyptian's lunge, he wrested the spear from his hand and then killed him with his own weapon.

Of great importance to us as we consider Benaiah's accomplishments is the fact that he did not fear failure. The training he had received in his home had developed a positive trust in God, his skills had been honed with practice, and he had developed the ability to size up a situation and take prompt action.

Bruce Larson illustrated this for us in his book *There's A Lot More To Health Than Not Being Sick*. He wrote:

When I was a small boy, I attended church every Sunday at a big Gothic Presbyterian bastion in Chicago. The preaching was powerful and the music was great. But for me, the most awesome moment in the morning service was the offertory, when twelve solemn, frock-coated ushers marched in lock step down the main aisle to receive the brass plates for collecting the offering. These men, so serious about their business of serving the Lord in this magnificent house of worship, were the business and professional leaders of Chicago.

One of the twelve ushers was a man named Frank Loesch. He was not a very imposing-looking man, but in Chicago he was a living legend, for he was the man who had stood up to Al Capone. In the prohibition years, Capone's rule was absolute. The local and state police and even the Federal Bureau of Investigation were afraid to oppose him. But single-handedly, Frank Loesch, as a Christian layman, and without any government support, organized the Chicago Crime Commission, a group of citizens who were determined to take Mr. Capone to court and put him away. During the months that the Crime Commission met, Frank Loesch's life was in constant danger. There were threats on the lives of his family and friends. But he never wavered. Ultimately he won the case against Capone and was the instrument for removing this blight from the city of Chicago.

Each Sunday at this point of the service, my father, a Chicago businessman himself, never failed to poke me and silently point to Frank Loesch with pride. Sometime I'd catch a tear in my father's eye. For my dad and for all of us this was and is what authentic living is all about. The bottom line for the Christian is to take his faith into daily life and to choose the kind of creative and risky living that will help and bless others.[5]

Frank Loesch shared a great deal in common with Benaiah. They were both men of conviction, active in doing what needed to be done, and refusing to be neutralized to the point of inefficiency by the magnitude of the tasks they undertook or the strength of the opposition. As with Frank Loesch, Benaiah achieved success without compromise or regret.

The Importance of Handling Disappointments Properly

The third point brought before us in the text concerns the importance of handling disappointments properly. As we have found, David's mighty men were divided into two separate groups of three each. "The [First] Three" constituted his "Joint Chiefs of Staff;" the second triad appears to have held special positions in the army. "The Thirty" were commanders of various divisions within David's army. While Benaiah's exploits had earned him well-deserved fame, he "did not attain to the three." He was not permitted into this "inner circle" of David's advisors. This may have been of great personal disappointment to him.

All of us face personal disappointments. We may not achieve our goal of becoming president of our company or even of receiving recognition from our peers. The way we handle such setbacks determines whether or not we become a hero to ourselves. Our circumstances are not decisive; we are decisive. We do not need to allow personal setbacks to sour our personality or grind cinders into our soul. We can do as Benaiah did and faithfully persevere with the tasks assigned to us.

Much later, after David had become king, he placed Benaiah in charge of his personal bodyguard. It was now his responsibility, along with the Cherethites and Pelethites, to guard the king's person. Why did David do this? He had found that Benaiah could be trusted! But why did David need a company of foreigners to guard his person? Apparently there were some in Israel who had not sworn allegiance to him. And murder of those in high places was not unusual. Ish-bosheth, Saul's son, had been murdered, and David could not fully trust Joab, his general, for he had murdered both Abner and Absalom, and in the future would murder Amasa. As we shall see in our next chapter, David also found it necessary to have close at hand his personal army of six hundred Gittites.

Applying the Truth

As we consider how these principles impact our lives, we have presented to us some valuable insights.

Success does not come to us automatically. It is also not to be equated with making money, owning a large home, driving a

European car, or taking a Club Med vacation to some exotic destination. Benaiah, we read, was prepared for a life of significant service because of the example that was set for him by his parents and grandparents. They had encouraged him to discipline himself and perfect his skills. In time he became known for his "mighty deeds." And these in turn paved the way for the notable "things [which] Benaiah did."

It is in the home, and from one's parents, that we see modeled for us the kind of attitudes that eventually prepare us for a fulfilling and satisfying life of accomplishment. In the home, the beliefs in which we are reared become the foundation for (1) our attitudes and (2) the goals we establish for ourselves. It is also from our parents – through their involvement in our lives, their modeling, and the instruction they give us – that we develop our strengths, are guided by principles of right and wrong, learn when to take chances, and acquire that sense of confidence which is essential to success. Wise counsel, unconditional acceptance, and encouragement are what our children both need and deserve. Their training for positions of mature responsibility can only be achieved through the development of an atmosphere in the home that makes growth possible.

There is no substitute for a godly home. We, as parents, make many mistakes in the rearing of our children. In the final analysis, however, it is what we are, and the love and encouragement and guidance we give our children, that will make the difference in their lives.

When our children are not allowed to participate in making decisions and take appropriate courses of action unaided by us, they will spend their adult years seemingly waiting for others to tell them what to do. Anger and resentment, caused by frustration and disappointment, may build inside them because of the frustration they feel. And the reason? They were not prepared in their formative years to think independently and take responsible action.

It is the proactive person who eventually enjoys success. A successful outlook on life takes time to develop. Its development comes as we encourage our children to keep on trying and not be neutralized by the fear of failure. Such an outlook will give meaning to life, invest what they do with significance, and lessen the blow of life's disappointments.

But what happens when we (or our) children face some crushing setback? What are we (or they) to do when some long-sought goal or lifelong ambition has to be relinquished? And what do we or they do when some overdue promotion or recognition is given to someone else? Benaiah, as we have noticed, "had a name, as well as the three mighty men [i.e., David's 'Joint Chiefs of Staff'] ... but he did not attain to the three."

When this kind of pressure makes its presence felt, it can result in anger: a mate may turn on us and blame us for not being more assertive or understanding or helpful, or a child who was not selected as class president or prom queen may allow some trivial incident in the home to escalate into a nasty scene. And when we face such disappointment, do we then experience a slump in our morale and a lowering of our confidence?

While popular psychology is prone to point the way to employing behavioral principles to help individuals "bounce back" from disappointment, and stress the need for some "new success" to replace the feeling of loss, such an approach fails to deal with the depth of human emotion involved. In reality, each of us must draw heavily upon our inner strength if we are to regain our emotional stability. By recognizing God's past goodness, and by placing our trust in His unchanging goodwill toward us, we and/or our children can revise our goals, and continue to serve faithfully in the place where He has placed us.

Benaiah handled disappointment manfully. He was able to place emotional distance between himself and the honor of being included in the "inner circle" of David's advisors. And because he did not give way to resentment or act irresponsibly, in time David promoted him in a different way. He was placed over David's personal bodyguard.

The Seeds of Greatness

As we take a final look at these verses, we note that Benaiah "was [nonetheless] honored among the thirty." His deeds did not pass unnoticed. It is true that he was overshadowed by the greater gifts and brilliance of David, and his accomplishments were viewed as subordinate to the works of Jashobeam, Eleazar, and Shammah, but in his personal life and service he embodied the courage, loyalty, and other virtues that inspired confidence. He was in every sense a leader of men.

Leaders differ from managers. They have the ability to separate themselves from the organization in which they work, and while remaining loyal to the principles of right and wrong, contribute significantly to the progress of the group. They model mature autonomy. Their attainment of goals – corporate as well as personal – is based upon their individuality and their independence. Managers, on the other hand, prefer to work with people, avoiding independent action. They have an effective part to play in the forward movement of their company, but often lack the ability to switch roles as Benaiah was able to do. A leader can also be an effective manager, but few managers have leadership potential.

As we sum up the truths that lie latent in these verses, we need to remind ourselves that the seeds of greatness are to be found in (1) the importance of having right attitudes about ourselves, our work, and our place in society; (2) the necessity for being proactive, and taking the initiative without becoming neutralized by the fear of failure; and (3) the need to handle disappointment maturely and not give way to resentment, or allow discouragement to destroy our confidence. Benaiah possessed these skills and abilities. As a result, he was able to enjoy success without compromise or regret.

10

The Loyalty of a Friend
(1 Chronicles 11:26-47)

The apostle Paul wrote his letters to encourage believers in their personal and spiritual growth, and to correct errors in doctrine and practice that were creeping into the different churches. He also pointed out that often, when a schism threatened to split the church, God would raise up a man who would call believers back to the truth. The resulting church "fights" were never pleasant, but they were necessary and served the purpose of bringing to the fore those whom God had appointed for positions of leadership. Paul described the process as follows: "For there must also be factions among you, in order that those who are approved may become evident among you" (1 Corinthians 11:19).

At first this seems like a strange teaching, and some will question, "Aren't Christians supposed to love one another?" And the answer is, "Yes, except where the person and work of Christ and the purity of Christian doctrine are concerned. To emphasize 'love' to the exclusion of holiness, righteousness, and truth, is to set in motion a course of action that will eventually lead to the demise of true Christianity."

In the study before us we find how ably this verse from 1 Corinthians 11 is illustrated in the Old Testament.

A Matter of Identification

We have been considering the elite corps of men who gathered about David, and Dr. William G. Blaikie, whose comments are always worth noting, summarizes the data we have covered so far.

David had an order of thirty men[1] distinguished for their valour; and besides these there were three of super-eminent merit, and another three, who were also eminent, but who did not attain to the distinction of the first three. Of the first three, the first was Jashobeam the Hachmonite, the second Eleazar, and the third Shammah. Of the second three, who were not quite equal to the first, only two are mentioned, Abishai and Benaiah; thereafter we have the names of the thirty.[2]

Of course, this leaves the question, Who was the third man in the second triad? Most writers ignore the problem posed by the omission and pass on to a cursory discussion of the thirty warriors.[3] But the question persists, and while it cannot be solved with finality, certain possibilities have been suggested. One of these is Asahel.[4] Still others, based on the fact that both Abishai (11:20) and Amasa (12:18) are referred to as *rosh* ("head" or "chief"), conclude that Amasa's name was dropped from the list on account of his alliance with Absalom in the coup that drove David from Jerusalem.[5] But other men were referred to as "head" or "chief", so this distinction is not decisive.

A possible solution to the unfortunate omission is to be found in a consideration of *the divisions* of David's armed forces: Abishai is said to have been "chief of the [second] three" and presumably the leader of "the thirty" (a position in which he could counterbalance the self-serving and unscrupulous behavior of his younger brother, Joab); and Benaiah was over the Cherethites and Pelethites – foreign mercenaries – who comprised David's bodyguard. This leaves Ittai of Gath who may well have been the third member of the trio because he was over David's private army of six hundred Gittites (note 2 Samuel 15:22 where reference is made to "all his men"). Also to be noted is the fact that the Cherethites and Pelethites are mentioned in the same context as the Gittites in 2 Samuel 15:18.[6]

Without being dogmatic or insisting on Ittai as the third "general" in the second triad, we will consider his life and leave the reader to reach his or her own conclusion. Our information about Ittai comes from 2 Samuel 15:1-23 and 18:1-5. He appears on the pages of God's Word at what was probably the darkest period of David's life. David had many children, and he was fond of them all. Absalom was the oldest and considered himself the heir-apparent to the throne. He had heard the gossip that circulated through the palace following Nathan's visit to David in which God had designated his younger brother, Solomon, as the nation's next king. Not being content to submit himself to the will of God, he determined to secure the throne for himself. Taking advantage of his father's long illness (cf. Psalms 38–41), he set himself up as a judge of the people. But instead of dispensing justice, he seized the opportunity to secure a following among the people of the northern tribes.

Sinister Events

The Planned Coup

Absalom's task was made easy for several reasons. First, to the new generation the exploits of his father, the king, were mere hearsay. They had enjoyed years of peace, and felt that the present administration was out-of-touch with the aims of the younger generation who desired a more vigorous, ostentatious administration. Second, Absalom's task was made easier because the older population had been alienated from David as a result of his unwise numbering of the people. And third, many of the godly in Israel had lost respect for David following his adultery with Bathsheba.

After four years of careful planning Absalom sensed that the time was right to institute his carefully laid plans. He obtained permission from his father to go to Hebron and there pay a vow that he claimed he had made while in exile. David gladly gave his permission, and Absalom left Jerusalem for Hebron where, in the midst of his sacrifices, he proclaimed himself king.

The Hasty Retreat

News of the activities in Hebron traveled quickly, and it wasn't long before a runner reached Jerusalem with the news of Absalom's revolt. On hearing the report, David was shocked by his son's treachery.[7] As a military leader, however, he realized that at that very moment, Absalom was marching on the city. Hebron is only nineteen miles south of Jerusalem, and so Absalom and his followers could be expected to reach the capital a short time after the runner's arrival. In agony of heart and mind David gave instructions for the city to be vacated. The report he had received had led him to believe that the defection was widespread, and he had no means of knowing how many in the city were loyal to him. Furthermore, as an old warrior, he knew that Jerusalem was too large to be garrisoned by the small force at his disposal.

Inside the palace the alarm spread rapidly as the wives and servants of David became aware of what had taken place. And they had good cause to fear. They knew that the wives and children of a deceased king became the automatic possession of the new king. Often, to remove all claimants to the throne, a new king would issue orders for all who belonged to the former king to be killed (cf. 2 Samuel 12:8; 16:20-22; 1 Kings 15:29; 2 Kings 11:1; 2 Chronicles 21:4). It is easy for us to imagine, therefore, the air of anxiety that pervaded the palace as hasty preparations were made for vacating the city.

Leaving ten women in charge of the palace, David, his family, his servants, and his bodyguard took leave the city and, turning eastward, took the road that lead to the Kidron Valley.

The Loyalty Shown

With his mind still reeling from the shock of Absalom's defection, David paused at a place called the *beth-merhak*, the "far house" – quite possibly the last house before descending into the Kidron Valley. It is here that we meet Ittai, the leader of six hundred Gittites. We do not know when Ittai and those under his command joined David, but it is reasonable to conclude that they had been with him ever since Achish, king of Gath, gave

Ziklag to David. If this view is correct, then they had participated in his inauguration when he became king over the southern tribe of Judah, and accompanied him to Jerusalem seven and a half years later after the northern tribes had anointed him king over a united Israel. There they had settled down and for the past twenty years had enjoyed a measure of peace and security. Now, however, the tide of adversity had turned against David, and they were prepared to leave the comfort of their homes and follow him into exile.

As David stood by the last house, taking note of those who had chosen to accompany him into exile, he saw Ittai with his wife and children. His generous heart was stirred, and addressing Ittai, he asked in effect, "Why are you going with us? Turn back and stay with the [new] king.... Turn back and take your brethren with you; may Yahweh show His steadfast love and faithfulness to you."

But David's gracious proposal was turned aside by Ittai, who said, "[As] Yahweh lives, and [as] my lord the king lives, surely the place where my lord the king is, there [your servant shall be], whether for death [or] whether for life" (2 Samuel 15:21).

Ittai's affirmation of loyalty is rivaled only by the well-known statement of Ruth the Moabitess when she promised to remain with her mother-in-law, Naomi (Ruth 1:16-17). From his statement we can deduce certain truths. In all probability, at the beginning, Ittai had been attracted to David, because he found in David qualities of character that he admired. And in the years that followed, he had demonstrated his loyalty to David. In the course of time, however, a gradual change came over Ittai as he became impressed with the truths he learned about David's God. Then, there must have come a day when he deliberately abandoned his former adherence to the gods of the Philistines and became a worshiper of Yahweh. His conversion was real and his life was changed forever.

David was so touched by Ittai's confession that he allowed him to pass over the Brook Kidron with all his men and their wives and children, and accompany him into exile. Then he, too, turned his back on Jerusalem, crossed the stream, climbed the Mount of Olives, and after cresting the summit, he made his way down into the Jordan River valley en route to the city of Mahanaim.[8]

The Honor Bestowed

Some scholars are of the opinion that once David had established his headquarters in Mahanaim, the city was attacked by Absalom's forces. This is possible, though no statement in Scripture supports the idea. On the other hand, as Josephus points out, when David had numbered his followers "he resolved not to tarry until Absalom attacked him, but set over his men captains of thousands, and captains of hundreds, and divided his army into three parts – the one part committed to Joab, the next to Abishai, Joab's brother, and the third to Ittai, David's companion and friend."[9]

It is more in keeping with David's proactive style to believe that he took the initiative and chose as the site of the battle the Wood of Ephraim. He was also confident of success as he gave instructions to his generals. From the biblical record we know that the battle was decisive. David's army was victorious; and Ittai, whose past loyalty had not gone unnoticed, had been rewarded by being made a general.

Ittai's promotion illustrates for us the New Testament principle that those who have been faithful over a few things, Christ will make ruler over many things (cf. Matthew 25:21, 23). From this we come to realize that *the reward of faithful service is increased responsibility.*

Timeless Lessons

The Importance of One's Conversion

Ittai was a Philistine, and the righteous in Israel may have doubted if a Philistine could ever be converted to faith in Yahweh, the God of Israel. In spite of Ittai's background and early adherence to the Philistine pantheon (with all of the pagan practices associated with their worship), his life was forever changed when he put his faith in Yahweh, the God of Israel. Initially he had been drawn to the qualities of godly manhood he saw in David, but in time he came to trust in David's God. And, as later events showed, this commitment forever changed his life. It gave him new goals. And later, in a time of crisis, the events precipitated by Absalom's rebellion only served to bring to the fore the genuineness of his beliefs.

There are many modern people like Ittai. One of them is Nikolai Alexandrenko. As his name suggests, he is a Russian. In his youth the Communist ideology of Lenin and Marx was instilled in him. He remembers his Communist teacher telling him that the Bible contained a collection of fairy tales, and that all of the evils of the world could be blamed on its teaching. And he believed her, for he had no reason to doubt her.

His high marks qualified him for entrance into the military academy in Odessa, Russia, and when war came he was commissioned as an officer in the paratroops. In two years of fighting at the front he was wounded three times before being captured by the Germans. His captors neglected to tend to his wounds and did not give him proper food, compelling him to survive on a diet of grass soup.

In 1945 the American army liberated the prison camp where he had been incarcerated, and he was given permission to return home. He feared being sent to Siberia, for the Communists expected their leaders to commit suicide rather than surrender. Along with thousands of other prisoners who refused to return to Russia he was sent to displaced persons' camp on the outskirts of Munich, Germany. There he had plenty of food to eat ... and time to think. Why had his life been spared? Why had he survived the prison camps when so many of his fellow-prisoners had died of starvation?

One day he went to start a fire in the stove only to find that someone had crammed the door of the stove full of waste paper, shutting out the oxygen. As he began clearing the blockage some words on a dirty, torn piece of paper caught his eye. They read,

"Come unto Me, all you who labor and are heavy laden, and I will give you rest." He read on. The words spoke to his deep need, and he began to feel the first faint flicker of hope. Could this be true? How could he find out more of this teaching? In his despondency he scarcely dared entertain the thought of happiness, and yet what he read spoke to his heart. Tears began to well up in his eyes and then course down his cold cheeks. Could this man Jesus really be the Son of God? And from his broken heart he cried out, "God, if You exist, help me."

A strange warmth seemed to fill Nikolai's being. Next he searched for a Bible, but without success. Later an old army comrade came to visit him, and he secured a Bible for him. Nikolai read it avidly. In time he began sharing his new faith with the other Russian prisoners. Then, miraculously, there came the opportunity to study in a Christian college in the United States. Seminary education followed. Now, with an earned doctorate, Dr. Nikolai Alexandrenko is the professor of Bible, Louisiana College, Pineville, Louisiana.

Ittai illustrates for us the life-changing effect of genuine conversion.

The Test of One's Priorities

Ittai also stood boldly for his beliefs at a time when many in Israel had turned aside to follow a self-appointed king named Absalom. His convictions were such that he was prepared to suffer the loss of all his temporal possessions, and (if need be) of life itself, in order to follow David into exile.

A contemporary "Ittai" whose priorities were likewise tested is Nora Waln. Before World War II Nora wrote a book exposing Hitler and his henchmen. The manuscript, *Reaching for the Stars*, was intercepted in the German mail and never reached the American publisher. Fearing for her life, Nora fled to London where she rewrote the book. When the book was published Heinrich Himmler took vengeance on Nora's friends and imprisoned them.

Fearing for their safety, Nora returned to Germany and offered her life for the freedom of her friends. Himmler offered to empty the whole prison if she would write another book making Hitler appear good. Nora refused, stating that she was willing to forfeit her life but not her beliefs. She expected to be executed. Instead, she was imprisoned and tortured, and after the war released.

Nora stands before us as an example of a person who was prepared to suffer rather than go against what she believed to be right.

The Reward of One's Service

As we have seen, Ittai's faithfulness resulted in increased responsibility. His single-mindedness reminds us of Marie Sklodowska. Before her marriage, Marie lived in poverty. Her passion for science was so great that she decided not to marry but devote herself to her calling. A celibate life was not what God intended for her, however, for at age twenty-six she met a young man named Pierre Curie whose love for science was as great as hers. Together these two toiled in an abandoned shed, searching for a mysterious element they believed possessed great radioactivity. Finally, after many experiments, they prepared a decigram of pure radium.

The discovery rocked the scientific world. Experts believed that here was a cure for cancer. Now, however, the Curies faced a crucial choice: should they give the formula to the world or patent the discovery and hold the rights of manufacture themselves. The former would leave them as poor as they had been before; the latter would offer hope to millions. Pierre and Marie Curie chose the former, and though they were offered many honors they never allowed these accolades to turn their heads. To the end of their lives they continued to devote themselves to alleviating the hurts of others.

It often takes a crisis to bring to the fore those of whom God approves. Ittai illustrates the truth of this New Testament principle. His example also serves to *encourage us in our quest for the truth, practice of our faith, and loyalty to the Lord and the teaching of His Word.*

135

11

When God Is At Work
(1 Chronicles 11:26–12:40)

Two statements, like complementary bookends, sum up what the chronicler has been describing for us in the unit that extends from 11:10–12:40. The first is found at the beginning of the account of David's mighty men: "Now these are the heads of the mighty men whom David had, *who gave him strong support in his kingdom, together with all Israel, to make him king, according to the word of Yahweh concerning Israel*" (11:10, emphasis added). And the second is a fulfillment of the first: "All these, being men of war, who could draw up in battle formation, came to Hebron with a perfect heart, *to make David king* over all Israel; and all the rest also of Israel were of one mind *to make David king*" (12:38, emphasis added).

The nation had come through a very dark period of its history. Saul's faulty leadership had been followed by years of civil war, and this had brought the people to the brink of ruin. Poverty stared them in the face. Their enemies were strong and warlike, and if these powers had possessed unity they could easily have overrun Israel. In the face of such opposition, how could God's purpose of a righteous king ruling over His people ever be brought to fruition? Israel's cause seemed hopeless, and God's promises made to their forefathers seemed but idle words, for the nation lacked the kind of leadership that could guide them out of their present malaise and secure for them an enduring future.

What we often ignore, because it is not obvious, is God's work behind the scenes. The darkness of the hour did not mean that He had forgotten to be gracious. James Russell Lowell emphasized what is not evident to our senses:

> Careless seems the great Avenger; history's
>   Pages but record
> One death-grapple in the darkness 'twixt
>   Old systems and the Word;
> Truth forever on the scaffold, Wrong
>   Forever on the throne–
> Yet that scaffold sways the future, and,
>   Behind the dim unknown,
> Standeth One within the shadow, keeping
>   Watch above his own.[1]

As we turn from the nation of Israel to David, and consider the vicissitudes through which he had passed, it must have seemed to him as if the Lord's promise that he would be king over God's people was a distant memory that had become shrouded in the mists of the passing years. Yet during all this time the Lord had been at work (1) preparing David so that he became the kind of leader who could restore the fortunes of Israel, and (2) building David's army until, in the end (and with permissible hyperbole), it "[was] a great army, like the army of God" (12:22).

This section brings into clear focus the kind of men whom the Lord brought to David. At first glance 11:26-47 seems to have little in common with 12:1-40. In reality, the verses before us continue the account of *David's mighty men begun in 11:10*. 11:26-47 reads like a "who's who" of his mighty warriors. It is followed by a description of those who joined David while in exile (12:1-22). And it concludes with an overview of the men of war from the different tribes who came to Hebron to make David king (12:23-40). The material may be outlined as follows:

• David's Mighty Warriors (11:26-47).

• David's Willing Supporters (12:1-22)
    Those Who Joined David in Ziklag (12:1-7)
        Those Who Joined David in the Stronghold (12:8-15)
        Those Who Joined David in the Stronghold (12:16-18)
    Those Who Joined David in Ziklag (12:19-22)

• David's Long-Awaited Enthronement (12:23-40).

David's Mighty Warriors (11:26-47)

The record of David's *wegibbore hahayalim*, "the mighty warriors," begins with Asahel, the brother of Joab. He was killed by Abner soon after David had been made king in Hebron (2 Samuel 3:18-23). The fact that mention is made of him in this context shows us that David had begun this list early in his reign.

The chronicler's list is longer than the one in 2 Samuel 23. That ends with Uriah the Hittite (cf. 11:41*a*), whereas here the names of men from the tribe of Reuben (east of the River Jordan) have been added.

As we examine this list we notice that it seems to follow a geographical order.[2] Most of those listed in verses 26-30 were from Judah; several of those mentioned in verses 31-37 were from the northern tribes; and verses 38-41*a* contain the names of those who were resident aliens. The list then closes with mention of the men from east of the River Jordan who threw in their lot with David during his "outlaw" years.

All of this stands in marked contrast to Saul's policy at this period of time. He drew his men from his own tribe of Benjamin (1 Samuel 22:7-8). By contrast, David's leadership had broad appeal.

Now the mighty men of the armies [were] Asahel the brother of Joab, Elhanan the son of Dodo of Bethlehem, Shammoth the Harorite, Helez the Pelonite, Ira the son of Ikkesh the Tekoite, Abiezer the Anathothite, Sibbecai the Hushathite, Ilai the Ahohite, Maharai the Netophathite, Heled the son of Baanah the Netophathite, Ithai the son of Ribai of Gibeah of the sons of Benjamin, Benaiah the Pirathonite, Hurai of the brooks of Gaash, Abiel the Arbathite, Azmaveth the Baharumite, Eliahba the Shaalbonite, the sons of Hashem the Gizonite, Jonathan the son of Shagee the Hararite, Ahiam the son of Sacar the Hararite, Eliphal the son of Ur, Hepher the Mecherathite, Ahijah the Pelonite, Hezro the Carmelite, Naarai the son of Ezbai, Joel the brother of Nathan, Mibhar the son of Hagri, Zelek the Ammonite, Naharai the Berothite, the armor bearer of Joab the son of Zeruiah, Ira the Ithrite, Gareb the Ithrite, Uriah the Hittite, Zabad the son of Ahlai,

Adina the son of Shiza the Reubenite, a chief of the Reubenites, and thirty with him, Hanan the son of Maacah and Joshaphat the Mithnite, Uzzia the Ashterathite, Shama and Jeiel the sons of Hotham the Aroerite, Jediael the son of Shimri and Joha his brother, the Tizite, Eliel the Mahavite and Jeribai and Joshaviah, the sons of Elnaam, and Ithmah the Moabite, Eliel and Obed and Jaasiel the Mezobaite.

So it was that, during the decade or more when David was an "outlaw," the Lord brought to him warriors who were both brave and loyal. They gathered about him because they saw in him the values they admired. His leadership gave them confidence. And it was these men whom David welded into a formidable army.

Reviewing these names may seem like a boring exercise, and we have to admit that with many of them we know little more than their name. Their contribution, however, is placed in perspective when we recall the wise words of a pious Jew named Jesus Ben Sirach. He wrote:

> ... all these were honored in their generations, and were the glory of their times. There are some of them who have left a name, so that men declare their praise. And there are some who have no memorial, who have perished as though they had never lived; ..."[3]

To a man they all performed their tasks well and were held in high esteem by those who knew them.

Most of us fall into the category of the unknown. Our names are not household words, and when we die none but our immediate family will miss us. What a comfort it is to know that He who motivated the chronicler to write this story knows all about us. We are important to Him, and in glory He will reward us according to our works (cf. 1 Corinthians 3:8*b*, 13-14; 2 Corinthians 5:10).

David's Willing Supporters (12:1-22)

Closely allied with the record of David's mighty warriors is a brief but complementary account of those who joined him before he became king over all Israel. They did not join David all at once. Different groups threw in their lot with him at different times and in different places.

These verses provide an interesting sidelight on David's leadership prior to being made king over all Israel, for dissidents came to him while he was at Ziklag (12:1-7); while he was in the stronghold, possibly the caves of Engedi or else Masada (12:8-15); while he was in another stronghold, possibly the Cave of Adullam (12:16-19); and at the time of Saul's war against the Philistines (12:19-22). The fact that David could attract the cream of Israel's warriors, and unite them into a disciplined army under captains of thousands, hundreds, and tens, speaks well of his ability.

Those who joined David in Ziklag (12:1-7). The chronicler begins his enumeration of the defections from Saul with information about those who joined David in Ziklag during the sixteen months he resided there. But why did these people defect to David? Was Saul's faulty administration the only cause? As Dr. Martin J. Selman has pointed out, "the impetus behind David's increasing support is thus shown to come from God himself."[4]

Now these are the ones who came to David at Ziklag, while he was still restricted because of Saul the son of Kish; and they were among the mighty men who helped [him] in war. They were equipped with bows, using both the right hand and the left [to sling] stones and [to shoot] arrows from the bow; [they were] Saul's kinsmen from Benjamin. The chief was Ahiezer, then Joash, the sons of Shemaah the Gibeathite; and Jeziel and Pelet, the sons of Azmaveth, and Beracah and Jehu the Anathothite, and Ishmaiah the Gibeonite, a mighty man among the thirty, and over the thirty. Then Jeremiah, Jahaziel, Johanan, Jozabad the Gederathite, Eluzai, Jerimoth, Bealiah, Shemariah, Shephatiah the Haruphite, Elkanah, Isshiah, Azarel, Joezer, Jashobeam, the Korahites, ad Joelah and Zebadiah, the sons of Jeroham of Gedor.

David's fighting force was augmented by these twenty-three seasoned soldiers. What is surprising is that they come from

Saul's own tribe of Benjamin. One of them, Ishmaiah, even became (for a time) the leader of "the Thirty."

The background to these events is found in 1 Samuel 27. These leaders were accurate marksmen using both sling and bow; and they were sufficiently perceptive to see that the future did not lie with King Saul. Furthermore, they were spiritually motivated to join David because of the Word of the Lord (originally through Samuel, and more recently perhaps through other prophets from the schools founded by Samuel). Their decision to leave Saul and join David in exile was not made lightly for at this time David was greatly misunderstood. He had been branded an outlaw, was unpopular, and considered "dangerous" (i.e., a threat to the crown), so much so that on several occasions Saul had taken his resident army and pursued David with the intention of killing him. These facts were well known to these men, for they had probably participated in one or more of these excursions. In spite of the negative things being said about David or done to him, some of them remembered his courage and skill when, at an earlier time, he had led Saul's army. They were not easily swayed by the current gossip, slander, or malicious innuendo. And so, in time, they came to David and threw in their lot with him.

Those who joined David in the stronghold (12:8–15). Though the arrival of the Benjamites in Ziklag caused a stir, they were not the first to join David. Earlier a group of Gadites from across the River Jordan had joined David when he was in one of the strongholds in the wilderness (cf. 1 Samuel 23–26). Several places are referred to as "strongholds" in the Bible, including the Cave of Adullam,[5] the caves around Engedi,[6] and Masada.[7] Engedi and Masada are closer to Gad than the Cave of Adullam.

And from the Gadites there came over to David in the stronghold in the wilderness, mighty men of valor, men trained for war, who could handle shield and spear, and whose faces were like the faces of lions, and [they were] as swift as the gazelles on the mountains. Ezer [was] the first, Obadiah the second, Eliab the third,

Mishmannah the fourth, Jeremiah the fifth, Attai the sixth, Eliel the seventh, Johanan the eighth, Elzabad the ninth, Jeremiah the tenth, Machbannai the eleventh. These of the sons of Gad were captains of the army; he who was least was equal to a hundred and the greatest to a thousand. These are the ones who crossed the Jordan in the first month when it was overflowing all its banks and they put to flight all those in the valleys, both to the east and to the west.

These Gadites were a welcome addition to David's army. The description of them is that they were fierce as lions and as swift as gazelles (cf. 12:8), and possessed of great skill. (12:14 does not refer to their rank but rather to their ability.) The least skilled could defeat a hundred men and the greatest a thousand. Evidence of their daring is provided in verse 15. They crossed the River Jordan while it was in flood. No task was deemed to be too hazardous or too difficult for them, and none dared stand before them or attempt to impede their progress to David's side (12:16).

Whether these men were conscious of the Lord's hand in their affairs, we do not know. We do know that when they came to David they strengthened his small but highly mobile and effective army.

Those who joined David in the stronghold (12:16-18). If the men from Gilead joined David at either Engedi or Masada, and Benjamites joined David when he was in the Cave of Adullam, their defections give us a glimpse of the internal dissension that plagued Saul's administration. It is evident that the northern tribes had tired of his ways, and the general dissatisfaction had spread to his own kinsmen. Discontent would have peaked following the slaughter of the priests of Nob (1 Samuel 21–22).

Then some of the sons of Benjamin and Judah came to the stronghold to David. And David went out to meet them, and answered and said to them, "If you come peacefully to me to help me, my heart shall be united with you; but if to betray me to my adversaries, since there is no wrong in my hands, may the God of our fathers look on [it] and decide." Then the Spirit came upon

Amasai, who was the chief of the thirty, [and he said,] "[We] are yours, O David, and with you, O son of Jesse! Peace, peace to you, and peace to him who helps you; indeed, your God helps you!" Then David received them and made them captains of the band.

What is recorded here is truly unique. When David went out to greet them, Amasai (possibly a variant spelling of Amasa), speaking prophetically, showed that there was a spiritual reason for their defection. His words also confirm God's stated purpose, for the Holy Spirit came upon him, (lit. "clothed" him) and guided his speech. From this we deduce the fact that there were those in Israel who, in spite of the prevailing spiritual apathy, still followed the Lord so that even a rugged soldier could speak prophetically.

Those who joined David at Ziklag (12:19-22). Next we read of seven leading Manassites who joined David shortly before the Battle of Aphek. The chronicler knew that his readers were familiar with the Battle of Aphek in which Saul and his sons had lost their lives on the slopes of Mount Gilboa. He was also aware that they knew of the forced march of David and his men when they had gone to Aphek with the Philistines. Happily for them they had been dismissed without having to fight against their kinsmen.

From Manasseh also some defected to David, when he was about to go to battle with the Philistines against Saul. But they did not help them, for the lords of the Philistines after consultation sent him away, saying, "At [the cost of] our heads he may defect to his master Saul."

The chronicler then continues by giving their names: "Adnah, Jozabad, Jediael, Michael, Jozabad, Elihu, and Zillethai, captains of thousands who belonged to Manasseh." And when David and his men returned to Ziklag and found that Amalekites had raided the Southland and looted their city, these men helped David as he and some of the others went after the invaders. Then the biblical writer sums up what had been taking place during

David's exile: "For day by day [men] came to David to help him, until there was a great army like the army of God."

But the reader may validly ask, "Why didn't these men from Manasseh join David sooner? Why did they wait until the last minute before journeying south to Ziklag?"

These are hard questions. One possible explanation may be derived from the location of the tribe of Manasseh. The territory of Manasseh looked out over the Valley of Jezreel that was to be the scene of the battle. Some Philistines were already living among the Israelites, and it is possible that they warned their Israeli friends of the coming invasion. It is also probable that leaders of Manasseh's militia were aware of the build up of Philistine forces, and knew that an invasion would not be delayed. Whatever the explanation, these men reached an expedient decision, left their homes, and joined David in Ziklag.

Of interest is the chronicler's repeated emphasis on the word "help" in verses 1-22. And verse 22 hints at the fact that the Lord's hand was at work in building David's army so that it became "like the camp (or army) of God."

David's Long-Awaited Enthronement (12:23-40)

Tribal support at Hebron (12:23-37). The biblical historian passes over David's seven-and-a-half year reign over the tribe of Judah in Hebron, and moves his readers forward to his enthronement as king over all twelve tribes. And so God's promise, that seemed to have been forgotten, eventually came to fruition.

> Now these are the numbers of the divisions equipped for war that came to David at Hebron, to turn the kingdom of Saul to him, according to the word of Yahweh. The sons of Judah who bore shield and spear [were] 6,800, equipped for war. Of the sons of Simeon, mighty men of valor for war, 7,100. Of the sons of Levi 4,600. Now Jehoiada was the leader of [the house of] Aaron, and with him were 3,700, also Zadok, a young man mighty of valor, and of his father's house twenty-two captains. And of the sons of Benjamin, Saul's kinsmen, 3,000; for until now the greatest part

of them had kept their allegiance to the house of Saul. And of the sons of Ephraim 20,800, mighty men of valor, famous men in their fathers' households. And of the half-tribe of Manasseh 18,000, who were designated by name to come and make David king. And of the sons of Issachar, men who understood the times, with knowledge of what Israel should do, their chiefs were two hundred; and all their kinsmen were at their command. Of Zebulun, there were 50,000 who went out in the army, who could draw up in battle formation with all kinds of weapons of war and helped [David] with an undivided heart. And of Naphtali [there were] 1,000 captains, and with them 37,000 with shield and spear. And of the Danites who could draw up in battle formation, [there were] 28,600. And of Asher [there were] 40,000 who went out in the army to draw up in battle formation. And from the other side of the Jordan, of the Reubenites and the Gadites and of the half-tribe of Manasseh, [there were] 120,000 with all [kinds] of weapons of war for the battle.

Verse 23 confirms 10:14. The Hebrew verb translated "turn over to" is translated "transfer" in the earlier chapter, and implies that the tribes were finally prepared to invite David to become their king. Of course, if they had been prepared to obey the revealed will of God once King Saul was dead, they would have spared themselves the misrule of Saul's son, Ish-bosheth.

The numbers of warriors that converged on Hebron is impressive. They included Levites (who were warriors even though their primary function had to do with worship, 12:26), and both of the tribes that were descended from Joseph (*viz.*, Ephraim and Manasseh, 12:30-31, 37). A comparison of the numbers from the northern tribes (12:29-37) with those from the tribe of Judah (12:1-24) tends to lead the reader to believe that the Judahites were not really loyal to David. A better explanation may be that they had already installed David as their king and so did not feature prominently in the census of those who gathered at Hebron.

The celebration of David's enthronement (12:38-40). Verses 38-40 form an apt conclusion to chapters 11 and 12. They describe the extended joy and rejoicing of those who were finally doing God's will. We also note the emphasis placed on *all* Israel.

All these, being men of war, who could draw up in battle formation, came to Hebron with a perfect heart, to make David king over all Israel; and all the rest also of Israel were of one mind to make David king. And they were there with David three days, eating and drinking; for their kinsmen had prepared for them. Moreover those who were near to them, [even] as far as Issachar and Zebulun and Naphtali, brought food on donkeys, camels, mules, and on oxen, great quantities of flour cakes, fig cakes and bunches of raisins, wine, oil, oxen and sheep. There was joy indeed in Israel.

The unparalleled three days of feasting that followed David's coronation unified the different tribes. Furthermore, we note that there was plenty of food. Probably Judahites contributed sacrificially, with others from Issachar, Zebulun, and Naphtali bringing more than their share. Apparently those who had the most were concerned about those who had the least, and so there was sufficient for everyone to eat.

Closing Thoughts

We close this chapter with two thoughts: God's Preparation of David, and God's Provision for His People.

God's Preparation of David

It is always easy to be a "Monday morning quarterback" and point out exactly what a player should or should not have done in a particular situation. It is a lot more difficult when one is on the field and huge defensemen are trying to get to you so that they can bury you in the sod (or else make a permanent impression in the Astroturf). While we acknowledge that God's preparation of David began early in his life, we cannot list all of the ways in which the Lord tempered and molded him for service.

David was the youngest of Jesse's sons, and as such was given the menial task of looking after his father's sheep. Being a shepherd was not easy (cf. Jacob's experience, Genesis 31:38-40). He had to tend and care for the sheep, lead them where they could find both grass and water, watch over those that were pregnant, look after any lambs whose mothers may have died or rejected them, and fight off wild beasts with nothing in his arsenal but a rod and a sling (cf. 1 Samuel 17:34-36). Yet these were the experiences the Lord used to mold David into the kind of leader He could use (Psalm 78:70-72).

A leader is a person who achieves "leadership status" because of his or her alertness and experience; willingness to accept responsibility; knack for getting along with people; open-mindedness; and ability to remain calm under pressure. A leader is also a person of vision, courage and integrity. He or she must also have the ability to inspire and warm the hearts of others, gaining their trust and confidence, and have the ability to explain what needs to be done in language that can be quickly grasped.

A leader must also be the servant of truth, and make the truth the focus of a common purpose. Then, he or she must have the force of character necessary to inspire others to follow with confidence. But this is not all. A leader should also possess an infectious optimism, and have the determination to persevere with a task until it is finished. This necessitates that he or she see the problem(s) as a whole, make the right decisions, and be able to choose the right personnel for the job. In other words, a leader must also be a good judge of character. And when all is said and done, a leader must be able to master and finally control the events that stand in the way of completing his or her assigned task.

The trials David endured, and the obstacles he faced, were used by God to hone David's skills and prepare him to lead His people Israel.

God's Provision for His People
Because of our preoccupation with the world of time and our senses, it is difficult for us to see clearly the Lord's involvement in our lives. A careful reading of God's Word, however,

reinforces the fact of His watchfulness, faithfulness and lovingkindness. Our problem is that we cannot always see the means He uses, though in retrospect we can see the process He has used to prepare us for service.

In his biography of R. G. LeTourneau entitled *Mover of Men and Mountains*, the writer tells the story of how LeTourneau was awarded a contract to built a road to a dam. His preparation was thorough, and, based on the geologist's report, he went ahead with construction. He did not know that there were major difficulties with the terrain that the geologist had failed to uncover. Building the road proved to be anything but routine. Every possible problem arose. As LeTourneau faced each crisis, he was surprised to note how the Lord used his earlier experiences – learned, as he put it, in the "university of hard knocks" – to enable him to solve the difficulties that now confronted him. Without such practical wisdom he would not have been able to complete the contract without losing everything he owned.

The same is true of us. Though the path we tread seems to be long and hard, we can draw comfort from the fact that the Lord is using each difficulty to make us more mature and prepare us for what lies ahead. Then, in time and when we really need it, we will be able to draw on these experiences and be saved from almost certain disaster.

12

The Ark Narrative (1)
(1 Chronicles 13:1–16:43)

The material contained in the Bible is true to life. It does not present a picture of peace that finds no place in reality. When heeded, its message does lead us through our problems to the enjoyment of the blessings God in Christ has made available to us. But first the impediments to such fellowship have to be removed. This sometimes causes us confusion. We try to do what we believe to be right, but we may do it in the wrong way. It is of encouragement to us to know that David, the "man after God's own heart," blundered in the same way we do. And, of course, there's a lot we can learn from his experience.

Before we consider the story contained in 1 Chronicles 13, we need to clarify what we mean by "right" and "wrong." In our day of moral confusion, and quite apart from the teaching of Scripture, what is right is what is morally required, and what is wrong is what is morally prohibited. In the context of the Christian faith, however, talk of right and wrong is intimately linked with the revealed will of God. For the Christian, to specify that an action is wrong is to declare that it is contrary to the will of a holy, loving, just God. To specify that an action is right is to declare that it is in keeping with the will of a holy, loving, and just God.[1] This, of course, presupposes that the believer has become familiar with the teaching of Scripture so that he or she knows what is approved or disapproved.

But the question still remains, "Can the right thing be done in the wrong way?" We'll learn more about this as we consider 1 Chronicles 13.

As we have studied David's activities following the death of King Saul, we have seen him crowned king over all Israel (1004 BC), and he has also secured a new capital (*viz.*, the city of

Jerusalem). Following this brief introduction to his reign, the chronicler introduced us to his mighty men and then indulged in a series of retrospective reviews of the ways in which the Lord brought to David's side leaders who were seasoned warriors.

Now he returns to an account of David's activities. It had long been David's desire to make the worship of the Lord of Hosts the center of his people's life. To do this, and further unify the people, he determined to bring the Ark of the Covenant from Kiriath-jearim (the "city of forests")[2] to Jerusalem – a distance of approximately eight miles. The Ark was the visible symbol of the Lord's presence. It had been neglected throughout Saul's reign (1043–1011 BC), and David did not want to allow this deplorable state of affairs to continue. So, after building a tabernacle in Jerusalem, he made plans to bring the Ark to Jerusalem. The events described by the biblical historian are not in chronological order and so must be understood as supporting a specific, thematic approach that highlights events in David's reign (13:1–29:21). For our purpose we will follow the following outline:

Bringing the Ark to Jerusalem, 13:1–16:43

From High Hopes to Hopeless Despair, 13:1-14
    Sharing the Vision, 13:1-4
        Consulting the Leaders, 13:1
        Involving the People, 13:2-5
    Implementing the Vision, 13:6-13
        Ignorance of the Law, 13:6-8
        Failure of the Plan, 13:9-13
    Rewarding the Righteous, 13:14

The *initial focus* of chapter 13 is on David, for we read that "David consulted... David said ... so David gathered ... and David went ... then David played ..." (13:1-8). This does not mean that the people were not involved. They were, but they are incidental to the events that are taking place. And apart from David's opening suggestion (13:2) and despondent conclusion (13:11-12), there is an absence of recorded dialog. Furthermore, from the mid-point of the chapter the *focus shifts* suddenly and undeniably to God.

Chapters 13:1–16:43 have as their central theme the unification of the people.

Transporting the Ark, I (13:1-14)

Sharing the vision (13:1-4). David began to unify the people by consulting the leaders (13:1). We read: "And David consulted with the captains of thousands and of hundreds, even with every leader." His good intentions and vision of a united Israel, with God in the midst of His people, were matched by his candid proposal. But when did he talk with the leaders? And when would he have had the opportunity to lay the entire matter before "all the congregation of Israel"?

The most expeditious time and place for David to share his plans with Israel's leaders would have been during the three days of feasting in Hebron following his enthronement as king over all Israel. The festive atmosphere, combined with the happiness of the people, would have made it an ideal occasion for him to lay before them his plans. These plans would have included the securing of a new capital (for Hebron was too far from the mainstream of the nation's life to be practical), and his desire to bring the Lord into the very heart of their everyday lives by moving the Ark of the Covenant to the new capital. And so David shared his vision with the leaders. They probably appreciated being consulted, for the king's actions contributed to their sense of worth and gave them the opportunity to discuss the issues. It also afforded David the chance to explain his motivation and answer any of their questions. The result was their enthusiastic support.

Next David involved the people (13:2-5).

Then David said to all the assembly of Israel, "If it seems good to you, and if it is from Yahweh our God, let us send everywhere to our kinsmen who remain in all the land of Israel, also to the priests and Levites who are with them in their cities with pasture lands, that they may meet with us; and let us bring back the Ark of our God to us, for we did not seek it in the days of Saul." Then all the assembly said that they would do so, for the thing was right in the eyes of all the people.

The people of David's time knew little about the Ark for it had remained in Kiriath-jearim ever since it had been captured by the Philistines (i.e., from about 1049–1004 BC). Even the priests and Levites were ignorant of the teaching of Scripture about it. All that was perpetuated in their tradition was a very shallow "theology" that, as we shall see, was inadequate for the occasion. And because there may be some in our day who remember relatively little about the Tabernacle and its furnishings (which included the Ark), we have chosen to include the following summary from the *New Unger's Bible Dictionary*.

The Ark of the Covenant was the only piece of furniture within the Holy of Holies. It was called the "Ark of the Covenant" (Heb. *'aron berit*, Numbers 10:33), or "Ark of the Testimony" (Heb. *'aron ha 'edut*, Exodus 25:22; etc.), from the law that was kept therein.

The Ark was made of acacia wood two and one-half cubits long, one and one-half cubits broad, and one and one-half cubits high (external dimensions) and was plated inside and out with pure gold. Running around each side was a gold border extending above the top of the Ark, so as to keep the lid from moving.

This lid was called the "mercy seat" (Exodus 25:20,22; Heb. *kapporet*, a "covering"), was the same size as the Ark itself, and was made of acacia wood covered with gold. The Ark was transported by means of two gold-covered poles run through two gold rings on each side, from which they were not to be removed (25:15) unless it might be necessary to remove them in order to cover the Ark when the Tabernacle was moved (Numbers 4:6).

Upon the lid, or Mercy Seat, or at the ends of the Ark, as in the Temple, were placed the cherubim, probably figures beaten out of gold, as was the lampstand. In shape they were probably human, with the exception of their wings, though some authorities think they were of the same complex form as the cherubim mentioned by Ezekiel (Ezekiel 1:5-14). They were no doubt the normal or full height of a man and are always spoken of as maintaining an upright position (2 Chronicles 3:13). They stood facing each other, looking down upon the Mercy Seat, with their wings forward in a brooding attitude (Exodus 25:20; cf. Deuteronomy. 32:11). The golden censer, with which the high priest once a year entered the Most Holy Place, was doubtless, set upon this lid.

Between the cherubim was the Shekinah (Heb. *shekina*, "residence"), the cloud in which Jehovah appeared above the Mercy Seat (Exodus 25:22; cf. Leviticus 16:2). It was not the cloud of incense (16:13), but the manifest appearance of the divine glory. Because Jehovah manifested His essential presence in this cloud, not only could no unclean and sinful man go before the Mercy Seat, i.e., approach the holiness of the all-holy God, but even the anointed high priest, if he went before it at his own pleasure, or without the expiatory blood of sacrifice, would expose himself to certain death.[3]

Before we leave 13:2-4 we need to consider what may be learned from David's leadership style. Having been crowned king by popular demand, it would have been easy for him to exercise his new authority by telling people what he wanted done. Instead, he enlisted the cooperation of the leaders and discussed with them his plans. This was a radical approach, for the monarchs of the surrounding nations acted more like demigods whose word was law and whose displeasure meant almost certain death. By giving the leaders the opportunity to interact with his ideas and voice any concerns they may have had, David won them to his side. It also gave him the opportunity to allay any fears they may have had and persuade them of the viability of his ideals.

Then, with the solid support of the leaders, he convened an assembly of all the people. If this convocation took place toward the end of the three days of feasting at Hebron (11:3), his presentation of his plan would have come when everyone was in high spirits. Furthermore, the people would be eager to hear firsthand what had been discussed with their leaders. And once his plans had been explained to them, their response was one of enthusiastic acceptance.

Let us note that David did not try to coerce the people into going along with his plan. Nor was he devious. He did not try to trick them or promise them something that he could not deliver. He presented to them the facts. His whole approach was a marked departure from the spirit of his times. There was no mention of "me" or "I" or "my." Instead, we notice an emphasis on "you... us ... our...." Years ago Edmond Hoyle set forth the principles of proper English usage. One of his principles was that proper literary style should always use "you" or "your" or "they" and never "we" or "us" or "our." That was until Winston Churchill came along. As we read his war time speeches we note the frequency with which he used "we" and "our," reserving "they" for the enemy or those whom he disliked.[4] And David did the same. His words created a sense of unity and harmony, and infused the people with a singleness of purpose. They felt they were in full partnership with him. And the religious leaders (priests and Levites, 13:3) were also included.

In his address to the people David made specific reference to the fact that the Ark of the Covenant had been neglected throughout Saul's administration.[5] But he did not do so in a way that would cause the people to feel this neglect was their fault. He did not use guilt to manipulate them into supporting his plans. Saul's era had witnessed the neglect of all things sacred, and David assured the people that he did not want to perpetuate the mistakes of the past, thus depriving them of God's blessing.[6]

The result of David's approach was a *unanimous decision* on the part of the people. And David was able to begin at once to implement his vision (13:5-13). The capture of Jerusalem came first, and then he began making plans to bring the Ark of the Covenant to his new capital.

> So David assembled all Israel together, from the Shihor [probably the Nile] of Egypt even to the entrance of Hamath, to bring the ark of God from Kiriath-jearim (13:5).

It would appear as if the chronicler, in writing to those who had returned from exile, was reinforcing the need for proper priorities. The people were particularly lax when it came to the worship of the Lord, and so he showed from David's experience how, by putting the Lord first, he enjoyed God's blessing.

As David made elaborate preparations for the transportation of the Ark, he may even have composed one or two new psalms for the occasion. When all was ready he sent out invitations to all the people (from Israel's southern border to those living in the far north), inviting them to join with him in this auspicious occasion.

> David and all Israel went up to Baalah, that is, to Kiriath-jearim, which belongs to Judah, to bring up from there the Ark of God, [even] Yahweh, who is enthroned above the cherubim, where His name is called. They carried the Ark of God on a new cart from the house of Abinadab, and Uzzah and Ahio drove the cart. David and all Israel were celebrating before God with all their might, even with songs and with lyres, harps, tambourines, cymbals and with trumpets (13:6-8).

David's carefully laid plans seemed to insure success, and the people were so filled with joy they danced and sang before the Lord. It seemed as if nothing could go wrong. And, in fact, all went well until they come abreast of the threshing floor of Chidon. There the cart on which the Ark had been placed may have become snagged on a protruding rock or else the oxen pulling it slipped on some soft earth. Whatever the cause, the cart began to tilt and Uzzah, fearing for the Ark's safety, reached out to steady it. At this the anger of the Lord blazed forth and Uzzah was struck dead (13:9-10).

David, who was close to the Ark, saw this and became angry. All of a sudden, and without warning, his carefully laid plans miscarried (13:11). But then, almost as quickly, his anger gave way to fear. He became afraid of God. And then his fear turned to despair and he said, "How can I bring the ark of God [home] to me?" (13:12).

As we seek to understand David's feelings of fear, anger and despair, we must first ask ourselves, What gave rise to these diverse though related emotions? All he wanted to do was honor the Lord, and now he was confronted with a corpse lying on the ground at the side of the cart. Why had this happened? What had gone wrong? Though he was unaware of it at the time, he had consistently engaged in practices that were contrary to the teaching of God's Word. For example, the Ark had been placed in a "new cart" – one that had not been used for any commercial or secular purpose. The explicit teaching of the Law of Moses, however, stated that the Ark was not to be carried in a cart but borne on the shoulders of the Levites (Exodus 25:14-15; Numbers 3:30-31; 7:9). The Law also taught that to touch the Ark was a violation of God's holiness that would result in death (Numbers 4:15). Had David been better acquainted with the Scriptures, this would not have happened.

What becomes painfully obvious to us is the fact that David and the religious leaders of his day were ignorant of portions of God's Word, for none of the priests or Levites objected to the Ark being placed on a cart. This illustrates for us the solemn truth that when the Word of God is not taught, people soon become ignorant of what the Lord requires of them (note Hosea 4:6; Amos 8:11).

David's anger at the death of Uzzah is easy to explain. Anger is generated by one or more of three things: frustration, humiliation, or rejection. In David's case, he may have suffered from all three. He was probably *frustrated* because, just when he thought his carefully laid plans were succeeding, this incident occurred and the whole procession stopped. His desire to have the Ark to reside in Jerusalem, so that the Lord would be at the center of His people's national life, was, of course, a noble one. And because he knew that this was what the Lord wanted, he could not understand why the Lord had killed Uzzah. David may also have felt *humiliated*, for the people looked to him for an explanation of what had happened, and he had none to give them. And deep inside his heart, he may have felt as if God had *rejected* him by not prospering his plans.

David's initial disappointment soon turned to despair, and that is why he asked piteously, "How can I bring the Ark of God [home] to me?" And coursing through his mind at runaway speed were other questions. Where did I go wrong? What could I have done differently? Why did Uzzah die? How could I have prevented this from happening? After all, Uzzah had done what any other person would have done under similar circumstances. And because David did not have the answers, a sense of hopelessness compounded his feelings of despair, and this further contributed to his emotional upheaval.

David, of course, would have to dismiss the people. Many of them had traveled for days to be present at this once in a lifetime event. Now, they would have to return to their homes frustrated and disappointed.

> So David did not take the ark with him to the city of David, but took it aside to the house of Obed-edom the Gittite[7] (13:13).

The reward of the righteous (13:14). Obed-edom was a Levite (26:1-4), and so could properly take care of the Ark. "Thus the Ark of God remained with the family of Obed-edom in his house three months; and Yahweh blessed the family of Obed-edom with all that he had" (13:14). He did not fear to care for the Ark; and, as Dr. Joseph Hall observed, the Almighty paid "liberally for his lodging."[8]

This experience of failure on the part of David would make an impact on those who had returned from exile. They earnestly desired God's blessing, but His mercies were not readily forthcoming. Why? What was wrong?

Something to think about

Albert Stauderman in his book *Let Me Illustrate* pointed out that biblical ignorance is widespread. He then recounted how, in a sermon one Sunday, he told an old joke about a person who was conducting a Bible class. In the course of his teaching he happened to mention "Paul's epistles." One woman raised her hand: "Who were the epistles?" she asked. Before the teacher could reply, another woman volunteered the answer: "The epistles were the wives of the apostles." Of course, that resulted in a lot of laughter. Dr. Stauderman, however, concluded his sermon illustration by saying that after church that Sunday a woman came up to him and asked, "Pastor, I didn't get the joke. If the epistles weren't the wives of the apostles, whose wives were they?"

Though this story is probably fictional, it does illustrate an important point. It forces us to ask, How widespread is biblical naiveté? The reason for David's failure can be traced to the fact that he was ignorant of the teaching of God's Word (cf. Deuteronomy 17:18-20; see also Joshua 1:8). This would be remedied during the three months the Ark resided in the house of Obed-edom.

The Philistines, of course, had been made aware of the gathering of Israelites and probably misconstrued their motive. Within a short period of time they would launch two successive attacks on Israel, but even these distractions would not prevent David from ascertaining the real reason for his failure to bring the Ark to Jerusalem. And nothing should prevent us from our study of Scripture so that we may come progressively to know and approve the good and acceptable and perfect will of God.

13

The Ark Narrative (2)
(1 Chronicles 13:1–16:43)

A book was published recently with the title *Lost Gold and Buried Treasure: A Treasure Hunters Guide to 100 Fortunes Waiting to be Found.* In it the author,[1] a captain in the U.S. Air Force Reserve, describes in detail the fabled wealth of seventeen sites in the United States. The arrangement of the material is by state (e.g., California, Nevada, Colorado) with a description of the caches of gold and jewels that were lost and now wait to be found. Of course, there have been many who have looked for these treasure troves, but without success. Nevertheless, there are always those who are lured on by the promise of sudden riches.

The Bible contains limitless wealth – not in money or precious stones, but the kind of treasure that brings satisfaction in this life and has the promise of providing untold blessing in the life to come (1 Timothy 4:8*b*). And its benefits are to be found in the most unlikely places. For example, the chapters before us treat David's desire to bring the Ark of the Lord to Jerusalem. They include his failure (ch. 13); a few subsequent events including two wars with the Philistines (ch. 14); a second attempt to bring the Ark into the capital (chs. 15:1–16:3); and the way in which he instituted the worship of the Lord (16:4ff.).

But it may well be asked, "What can we possibly learn from such a dry rehearsal of the facts?" To answer this question we must first come to a clear understanding of the text. To do this we do not have to engage in allegorism or a spiritualizing of the text before we can apply the truth to life, even though the events appear to have no relevance to us or the new millennium we have entered.

Because chapters 13–16 form a unit we will briefly review

the material covered previously. The theme is still concerned with the transfer of the Ark to Jerusalem and the worship of the Lord that David instituted. The following brief outline will bring the contents of these chapters into focus.

Bringing the Ark to Jerusalem, 13:1–16:43

Unexpected Problems	13:1-14
Unmistakable Blessings	14:1-17
Untarnished Success	15:1–16:43

We will begin with a brief review of chapter 13. As we proceed, it will readily be seen that the events in David's life yield *principles* that have application to our own time and are of encouragement to us.

Unexpected Problems (13:1-14)

A Commendable Beginning (13:1-4)

As a wise "chief executive," David began by consulting with the leaders of his people. He knew the value of involving them in the decision-making process. He had only recently been anointed King over a united Israel, and he was aware of the importance of having the leaders and the people participate in this joint venture. His goal was two-fold: (1) to have the Lord of glory at the center of His people's lives, and (2) to build unity among the previously disunited tribes.

David's consultation with the leaders and the people worked. The people agreed to his plan. And so, without having to issue commands or use persuasive tactics, he secured the willing co-operation of all involved.

It is important for us to remember that none of David's hearers had ever seen the Ark. Descriptions of it were (and still are) to be found in Exodus 25 and 37. However, in spite of the teaching ministry of Samuel, a general biblical illiteracy prevailed during the reign of Saul. And after Samuel's death, spiritual decline set in. It is unlikely, therefore, that the people knew any more about the Ark than the fact that it was a sacred object made by their forefathers some 440 years earlier. Then, about two generations previously, it had been carried into battle against the Philistines. Israel had lost the battle and the Ark had been taken to Philistia as part of the spoils of war. It had wreaked such havoc upon the Philistines that they finally returned it to Israel (1 Samuel 4:1–7:2). It was then kept in the city of Kiriath-jearim, where it stayed throughout King Saul's reign.

Some of the people may have agreed to bring the Ark to Jerusalem because they had heard stories of its power. Others may have been more inclined to go along with David and their leaders for the sake of preserving unity. They may even have agreed that the Ark would provide an important focal point around which the tribes could gather in the time of crisis. And then there were those who realized the value of uniting the political and religious forces in Israel for the greater good of the people. They were probably in the minority. Few, however, were aware of the fact that the Ark symbolized the presence of God.[2]

The National Convocation (13:5-12)

The invitation (13:5). Careful readers of the text will note the biblical writer's emphasis on "all" and "every." This was purposeful. Each person was important and, as Dr. Sara Japhet has pointed out, the leaders and the people were "full partners" with the king in this momentous event.[3]

Once consensus had been obtained, the decision was implemented (13:5). Messengers carrying the king's message were sent out in all directions. They brought David's summons to "all Israel" – from Shihor in the South,[4] to the entrance of Hamath in the north.[5] All the *'arasot*, "lands," were included (i.e., the districts of Judah and Benjamin, and all the territories occupied by the ten tribes of Israel).

The procession (13:6-10). When all was ready, David led the people to Baalah (better known as Kiriath-jearim, the "City of Forests"), to bring up from there "the Ark of God – [even]

Yahweh who dwells among (i.e., is enthroned above) the cherubs."

It may have seemed to the people living at that time that the most natural and logical way to transport the ark was on a *new* cart – one that had not been used for any personal or commercial enterprise. The Philistines had done so when they returned the Ark to Israel (1 Samuel 6:7, but it must be remembered that they were pagans). Apparently no one knew the Mosaic Law that specified that the Ark was to be carried by Levites (Numbers 4:15). Had any of the priests or Levites known of God's requirement, we may be sure that they would have reminded David about it. Had they done so, we may be sure David would have insisted that the Law be followed. This points to the danger facing them (and us) that ignorance of God's Word results in costly mistakes that could have been avoided. This incident also illustrates for us how easy it is for portions of God's Word to be so neglected that in time they are forgotten.

As we recreate in our minds the scene in Kiriath-jearim, it is easy for us to imagine the Ark being carefully loaded on to the ox cart. The procession began. Progress was slow, but the joy of the people was unmistakable. David and all the people were dancing before the Lord, playing on a variety of musical instruments, and singing His praises. But when they come abreast of the threshing floor of a man named Chidon, the oxen stumble and temporarily lose their footing. This caused the cart to tilt. A man named Uzzah, fearing that the Ark is in imminent danger of falling to the ground, instinctively reached out to steady the sacred chest. To everyone's astonishment, he was immediately struck dead (13:10). His intentions may have been good, but the results were devastating. The Ark, which was the visible evidence of God's presence, shared God's holiness and could not be profaned by human hands.

The reaction (13:11-12). Two results followed Uzzah's death: David's great joy is turned to anger,[6] then sudden fear, and finally discouragement. The text reads quite literally, "and it burned to David (i.e., David became angry), for Yahweh had broken forth (lit. broken a breach against) Uzzah; and he called that place *Perez-uzza* 'the Breach of Uzzah'.... And David feared God of that day, saying [in his disappointment], 'How shall I bring the Ark of God [home] to me?'"

But how are we to explain David's lament, "How shall I bring the Ark of God [home] to me?" Was this a selfish wish? No. David realized that the kingdom he had received had been severely weakened by Saul's bad leadership followed by seven years of civil war. Israel's neighbors were powerful and could easily crush his tiny nation. He believed that with God in their midst they would receive the power and guidance they needed. The failure of his plans constituted a severe setback!

The Result (13:13-14)

This chapter closes with some interesting statements: "And David did not turn (i.e., bring) the Ark to himself, to the city of David, but turned (i.e., brought) it aside to the house of Obed-edom the Gittite. And the Ark of God remained with the household of Obed-edom, in his house [for] three months; and Yahweh blessed the house of Obed-edom, and all that [was] to him (i.e., all that he had)."

Whereas God had vindicated His holiness in striking Uzzah dead (cf. Leviticus10:1ff.), we now read of another instance of His "breaking through," only this time it is in blessing. "And Yahweh blessed the family of Obed-edom with all that he had." In this we catch a glimpse of God's sovereignty and goodwill.[7] He is gracious and blesses those who are prepared to honor Him.

But who was Obed-edom? Levites were responsible for the care of the Ark. How then could it be given into the care of someone from Gath?

It is probable that Obed-edom was a Levite (cf. 15:18, 21, 24; 16:5, 38; 26:4ff.). He may have been from the Levitical village of Gath-rimmon near Shechem (Joshua 21:25; 1 Chronicles 6:69). Others, however, believe he was a Philistine from Gath who had become a proselyte.[8] This is unlikely. But another possibility exists. Perhaps, during a time of famine or religious persecution, Obed-edom's parents (who were Levites) may have gone to Philistia temporarily. Such a practice was not uncommon. Obed had been born there, and after their return to Judah his birth on foreign soil was remembered by the appellation, "Gittite."

Reflection on leadership issues

In spite of all that has been written on the subject of human relations, there are many in different areas of leadership who (perhaps unwittingly) follow the century-old theories of Frederick W. Taylor and Max Weber. Taylor propounded his theory of cost-efficiency that required those in authority to focus attention on a worker's economic performance. In time employees were treated like things whose sole value was the enhancement of the company's profits. And Weber asserted that employees are essentially lazy and will not work unless made to do so. As these approaches were put into practice, individuals lost value as persons and were looked upon solely as a means to achieve the ends or goals of the organization.

Nearly everyone can point to a time in their lives when they have worked in an environment where more and more was required of them and they derived less and less satisfaction from the work they did.[9] Such an approach eventually has disastrous results for both production and morale. David illustrates for us the importance of a more democratic form of leadership (cf. Luke 22:25-26). The result of his approach was glad and willing participation on the part of the people. They left their farms and places of business, journeyed to Jerusalem, and joined in the grand venture.

A second principle that emerges from our study has to do with asking counsel of the Lord. David failed to do so. Had he asked God for directions, the Lord would most assuredly have alerted him to the importance of having the Ark carried by Levites. His neglect of this simple matter proved to be very costly. Uzzah died, and the project was suddenly called off. The people must have been baffled by the sudden change in his plans. They had to make their way back to their homes (some as far away as the Nile River in the south or the southern border of Hamath in the north) without knowing why the procession had been halted.

David, of course, had a responsibility to share with them why he was putting an end to the transfer of the Ark, but he was bewildered by what had taken place and had no explanation to give them.

Uzzah's death, of course, serves as a warning to all who take upon themselves honors to which the Lord has not called them (cf. Jeremiah 14:14). There are many today who have thrust themselves into pastoral roles or who preach without having a clear understanding of the seriousness of the office they have assumed (cf. James 3:1). And others like to officiate in worship services and the celebration of the Lord's Supper, solely to be seen by members of the congregation. They do so to meet their own ego needs. To all who seek their own advantage, the fate of Uzzah serves as a solemn warning. They may not be struck dead as was Uzzah, but the Lord has shown how He views such practices and this should be warning enough.

Lastly, David feared that he had lost the blessing of the Lord. There are times in our lives when we, too, believe that the Lord is angry with us and has forgotten to be gracious. This, of course, is a matter of our perception. From the events that unfold in our next chapter we will see how the Lord blessed David in spite of his doubts and fears.

Unmistakeable Blessing (14:1-17)

David's failure to bring the Ark to Jerusalem caused him to fear that God had become his adversary. The chronicler's intent in chapter 14 is to describe the ways in which the Lord sought to reassure and bless David. He clusters events together to show how the Lord honored and provided for His servant in spite of David's misgivings. And in showing how God graciously blessed David, the writer offered encouragement to the people of his own time – returned exiles – who may have felt that God had forgotten to be gracious to them.

The blessing of friendship (14:1-2). The introduction of Hiram[10] is abrupt. His kindness to David is perceived as the beginning of the fulfillment God's promise to bless His people (cf. Isaiah 60:5; 61:6; Haggai 2:7; etc.). In all probability a treaty was established between Tyre and Israel, and as a result of this David realized that the Lord was giving his kingdom recognition beyond the borders of his own land.

The blessings of family (14:3-7). The blessings of family, and the assurance of a continuing dynasty, is overlooked by most evangelical writers[11] who are more interested in reminding their readers that David's actions were in violation of Deuteronomy 17:17. They ignore the fact that the interpretation of a biblical passage must be in accordance with the biblical writer's theme and the history of the times. They also ignore the fact that in the culture of the ancient Near East many of the marriages of the Old Testament kings were entered into to confirm treaties. It was a part of the cultural milieu.

Also worthy of note is the fact that none of the names of David's wives or daughters are given. From this it would appear as if the writer's emphasis is being placed on the establishment of David's dynasty. He appears to be contrasting the house of Saul (10:6) with that of David. Saul's house came to an end; David's was in the process of being established.

In the final analysis the Bible teaches that "children are the heritage of the Lord" (Psalm 127:3). The inclusion of David's growing family at this point in the narrative underscores one of the ways in which God was blessing him.

The blessings of victory (14:8-16). Next the biblical historian turns to David's wars with the Philistines. While living in Ziklag, David had been the vassal of Achish, king of Gath. And even when he became king of Judah in Hebron, the Philistines did not take any hostile action against him, perhaps assuming that he was still their ally. However, when he was made king over a united Israel and made Jerusalem his capital, they decided that he now constituted a threat to them. They, therefore, marched up the valley of Rephaim[12] toward Jerusalem.

As soon as David learned of the invasion, he left Jerusalem and went down to the "stronghold" (possibly the cave of Adullam). This placed him behind the Philistine lines and close to their relatively unprotected towns and cities. Not knowing where David was, the Philistines were compelled to look for him. This gave David's militia (some of whom came from north of the Valley of Jezreel) time to gather.

David had learned well the importance of asking counsel of the Lord, and when he was ready he asked God for specific directions: "Shall I go up against the Philistines, and will You give them into my hand?" (14:10*a*). The fact that David asked if he should "go up" against the Philistines indicates that he had moved out of Jerusalem, for had he remained in Jerusalem he would have "gone down" to them. The Lord responded to David's petition, "Go up, and I will give them in(to) your hand" (14:10*b*).

David and his army attacked the camp of the Philistines at a place later named Baal-perazim. He was victorious and, as the Philistines fled back to their own land, David exclaimed: "God has broken out [upon] my enemies by my hand, like the breaking [through] of waters" (14:11).

The usage of the word *perez* first occurs in 13:11. Now David uses the word to describe how the Lord "broke through" to rout the Philistines. To David, the attack and subsequent victory were as irresistible as water breaking through a dam wall. In light of what had happened, he called the place "Baal-perazim," "Lord of the break through."

The rout was so complete the Philistines did not have time to gather their possessions. They even left behind their gods that were supposed to be the guarantors of success (14:12). David ordered them gathered up and burned (Deuteronomy 7:5).

Once back in their own country, the Philistines determined not to allow David's sudden attack to be the cause of their defeat. They gathered together a new army and once again invaded the valley of Rephaim (14:13-16).

David could have presumed that, inasmuch as the strategy

employed in the first attack had worked, he would do the same game. Instead, he wisely sought guidance from the Lord. This time the Lord's instructions were entirely different. He stated emphatically,

> "You shall not go up after them; turn around (i.e., away) from them, and come to them from across the [stand of] weeping trees. And it shall be, when you hear the sound of marching in the tops of the weeping trees, then you shall go out in (i.e., to) the battle; for God has gone out before you to strike the camp of the Philistines" (14:14-15).

David obeyed the Lord implicitly. And once again he was given a significant victory. He and his men struck down the Philistines from Gibeon (possibly Geba) as far as Gezer.[13]

A Few Principles Worth Noting

First, from what is recorded in this chapter we learn *not to give way to discouragement*. The turn of events may leave us disappointed and even cause us to doubt if God is still with us or will again be gracious to us. Chapter 14 illustrates for us the different ways the Lord uses to reassure us of His blessings. There is no reason, therefore, why we should give way to discouragement. Charles Lamb wrote, "Our spirits grow gray before our hairs." And J. Francis Peak observed, "Discouragement comes to old and young alike. Things often go contrary to our dreams and plans.... The major cause of discouragement is a temporary loss of perspective. Restore proper perspective and you take fresh heart." The evidence of God's blessing restored David's perspective and enabled him to learn from the past.

Second, from David's experiences we learn *not to give way before those who try to intimidate us, but to pray for guidance, and then to take appropriate action*. On two occasions the Philistines penetrated far into the land of Judah and pitched their tents close to Bethlehem. David took prompt action. He determined not to allow the Philistines to trap him in Jerusalem.

Instead, he made his headquarters in the "stronghold" and there gathered his forces together. Then, in answer to prayer, and with the assurance of God's blessing, he boldly attacked his enemies. Each engagement was sudden, and both victories were most gratifying.

A third lesson we learn from this story has to do with presumption. *We should not presume that because a particular strategy has worked in the past, it is the only one worth using.* When the Philistines came into the land for the second time, David again went down to the "stronghold." Once again he asked God for guidance, and this time the Lord told him to circle around behind the Philistines and wait for His signal. When it came, he attacked the Philistines from the rear. And once again God gave him the victory.

Enthusiasm, and a desire to do what needs to be done, comes more easily than obedience. It is not *after* keeping God's commandments, but *in* keeping them that there is great reward. Every successful individual has learned how to obey, whom to obey, and when to obey. David's experiences in the valley of Rephaim, therefore, are worth pondering.

Untarnished Success (15:1–16:43)

The events of chapter 14 help to fill in the gap of three months between the first and second attempts to bring the Ark to Jerusalem. Though David's marriages were not all consummated during this time, nor could all of the children have been born during these ninety days (for four of his sons were the children of Bathsheba, and Solomon wasn't born for many years), the chronicler included them in the record to show to his readers who had recently returned from exile how gracious God can be, and to assure them of the continuation of the Davidic dynasty.

With chapter 15 we realize that the death of Uzzah had had a beneficial effect. It had awakened a new study in the Law and had also given the people a new respect for the awesomeness of their God. In this respect what happened on the first attempt to bring the Ark to Jerusalem is analogous to the situation in many of our churches. People call Christ "Lord, Lord" but do not do what He says (cf. Luke 6:46). True reverence is the product of our relationship with Him, the conviction that we are indeed worshiping Him in spirit and in truth, and that to the best of our ability and with the enabling power of the Holy Spirit we will obey His Word.

Answering the Critics (15:1a)

In answer to those who denounce David's polygamy[14] and offer in support of their accusations the undeniable evils of an oriental harem, the biblical writer makes mention of the fact that David built houses in Jerusalem. Hiram had already built him a palace and so *he* had no need of other residences. It seems obvious, therefore, that each of his wives had her own house.

Accommodation for the Ark (15:1b)

David also prepared a place for the Ark of God. Because the Ark had been housed in a Tabernacle throughout Israel's wilderness wanderings, David prepared a tent for it in Jerusalem. And though the text does not say so, we may be sure that he also composed several psalms (e.g., Psalm 15) to be sung by the Levites as they brought up the Ark from the house of Obed-edom (with Psalm 24 possibly being sung as the Ark entered the gates of Jerusalem).

Assembling the People (15:2-28)

David then sent word to all the people, the priests and Levites, to come to Jerusalem. When they were all gathered he announced to them the reason for their former failure to bring up the Ark from Kiriath-jearim. They had been disobedient to the Word of the Lord. "Then David said, 'None [should] carry the Ark of God except the Levites, for Yahweh has chosen [them] to carry the Ark of God, and to minister to Him forever.'" Following this brief statement, and with the heads of the priestly and Levitical houses before him, he instructed them to consecrate themselves by setting themselves apart to the Lord for the task of bringing the Ark to Jerusalem. Outwardly such consecration involved washing their clothes (Exodus 19:10-14), avoiding defilement (Leviticus 11:44), and, for a time, refraining from sexual intercourse (Exodus 19:15).

When everything was ready, David, together with the elders of Israel and the captains went down to the house of Obed-edom (15:25). The Levites placed poles through the rings in the side of the Ark so that they could carry it according to the Law. To insure that no new sin was the occasion of God's displeasure, seven bulls and seven rams are sacrificed (cf. Leviticus 1; 3).

David was clothed with a robe of fine linen and wore over the top of it a linen ephod. Then leading the procession, and to the accompaniment of singers and music from a variety of different instruments, "all Israel" brought up the Ark to Jerusalem.[15]

Verse 29 makes mention of Michal, King Saul's daughter. In his youth, David had married her,[16] and there was a time when she really loved him. As she grew older, however, more and more of her father's disposition began to dominate her personality, and by the time David brought the Ark up to Jerusalem she was completely consumed by her selfish desires and had no Godward aspirations. As she looked out of a window and saw her husband dancing before the Ark, contempt rose in her heart, for in her eyes his actions were unbecoming a king. Instead of this being her supreme moment when she took her place by his side, she revealed by her attitude that her heart had become like stone. She was spiritually dead.

It is tragic to think of a couple unable to share in the really important things of life. Alas, it was so for David and Michal. To despise David for his devotion to the Lord was to despise the Object of his devotion. Had Michal borne David an heir, she would most probably have been made his queen. Instead, God punished her by withholding children from her (cf. 2 Samuel 6:23).

The Ark was carried to its resting-place to the accompaniment of the musical instruments, and with the Levites singing praises to the Lord. As it was placed in the tent that David has pitched for it, the music died away. David then offered burnt offerings and peace offerings (Leviticus 1; 3). He then turned to bless the people. As God's representative[17] he had the power to do so. He then gave to each person a loaf of bread, a portion of meat, and a raisin cake (16:1-3). None went hungry.

Arrangement for the Ark (16:4-43)
Verses 4 through 42 deal with David's plans to insure the care of the Ark and the continuous praise of the Lord. The psalm the Levites sang (16:7-36) consisted (with slight variations) of Psalms 105:1-15; 96:1-13; and 106:1, 47-48. Though in the Psalter they are listed anonymously, their arrangement on this occasion lends support to the belief that they may have come from the pen of David.

Prominence in the Levites' choral praise was given to the Abrahamic Covenant (16:16-18; cf. Genesis 12:2-3; 13:14-17; 15:13-21; 17:7-8; 22:16-18; and 26:24-25).[18] Though uttered centuries before David's time, the promise was still in effect and readers of Chronicles, who had recently returned to Judah from captivity in Babylonia, would be heartened by the reminder of what God had pledged. They would also remember their nation's history and receive fresh incentive from the fact that the Lord had always looked after His people.

Asaph and his relatives were left in Jerusalem to take care of the Ark while Zadok and Abiathar remained at the high place in Gibeon where many in Israel had formerly worshiped.

Finally, with 16:43, the long digression of 16:4-42 comes to a close. The people returned to their homes happy, and David returned to the palace to bless his household.

It is through the gates of thanksgiving
    That we enter the courts of praise;
Our thanks for the little bounties
    That compass us all our days

Shall bring us to greater blessings,
  And lead us to larger ways.

O Lord of the manifold mercies,
  As we number them one by one,
From the least of Thy loving-kindness
  To the uttermost gift of Thy Son,
Lead us on from selfish gladness
  To the marvelous things Thou hast done.

As we offer our small rejoicing
  For the love that surrounds our days,
All the wonderful works of Thy goodness
  Shall open before our gaze;
Through the gates of narrow thanksgiving
  We shall enter Thy courts of praise.

Annie Johnson Flint.[19]

14

Good Intentions and God's Blessings
(1 Chronicles 17:1-27)

There is a problem that faces nearly all of us in our study of Bible history. It is the tendency to read back into a story facts that, at a particular point in time, are not in evidence. For example, we know that David was a great king. The mistake we make is in reading his later success into the early events of his reign. When we commit this kind of error, we tend to overlook his very real humanity with its fears and feelings of insecurity. Is there confirmation of this in the biblical text? Yes, there is. In chapter 14, verse 2, we read that, though crowned king over Israel, David was acutely aware of the powerful enemies that surrounded the nation, and these minimized his sense of security. He also had enemies within Israel who were loyal to the memory of King Saul. They wished to see the Saulide dynasty continue. It took time, therefore, for David to become aware of the fact that God had indeed established his kingdom.

But even then, after twice defeating the Philistines, David was still concerned about his dynasty. Would it continue, or would it come to an end like Saul's? He could only hope that the mercies of God would extend to his children's children, and that no usurper would arise, kill off all claimants to the throne, and bring his dynasty to an end. And so, even though David now had a growing family and could anticipate the continuation of his line, as far as he was concerned nothing was certain.

In this chapter we will read of God's continued favor toward His servant, so much so that He entered into a special covenant with him.

There are numerous covenants in the Bible. A few examples of the Lord's "administrative" covenants are: the one He made with Adam before the Fall (cf. Genesis 1:28-29 with 2:15-17);

His covenant with Noah after the Flood (Genesis 9:1-17); and His covenant with the Israelites at Mount Sinai (Exodus 19–20).

God also entered into other covenants. For example, God made a covenant with Abraham that was later confirmed to Isaac and Jacob. In this covenant He promised (1) that the land of Canaan would be given to Abraham and his descendants for an inheritance; (2) that Abraham would have an heir through whom His purposes would be fulfilled; and (3) that this covenant would involve personal, national and universal blessing (Genesis 12:1-3; 13:14-17; 15:1-7, 18-21; 17:1-8. Cf. 13:2; 23:6; 24:35).

The covenant God made with Abraham became the foundation of three other Covenants: the Palestinian covenant that reaffirmed Israel's right to the land (cf. Deuteronomy 29:1–30:20); the Davidic covenant that promised a descendant of the line of David who would sit on his throne (2 Samuel 7:8-17); and the New Covenant by means of which blessing would come to all people (Jeremiah 31:31-34). Each of these covenants was built upon God's promise to Abraham.

This chapter lends itself to the following outline:

The Davidic Covenant

The Proposal (17:1-2)

The Promise (17:3-15)
    God's Response (17:3-6)
    God's Reminder (17:7-10*a*)
    God's Plan (17:10*b*-14)
    Conclusion (17:15)

The Prayer (17:16-27)
    David's Praise (17:16-22)
    David's Petition (17:23-27)

This is one of the most significant chapters in the Bible. A proper understanding of it explains why the Jews are central in God's program of the ages.

The Proposal (17:1-2)

At the time of our story David's wars were over. His people were happy and recovering some of the prosperity they had lost during the reign of King Saul. And God's blessing rested upon David's activities. As the king reflected upon recent events, his heart was filled with gratitude to the Lord for all that He had done for him. Perhaps these reflections coincided with a dinner to which his longtime friend, Nathan, had been invited. As David reminisced about God's faithfulness, he may have gestured toward the munificence of his palace, as he said to Nathan: "Behold, I am living in the house of cedar, and the Ark of the Covenant of Yahweh, [is] under curtains" (17:1).

David and Nathan had been friends from their youth, and it is possible that they had often spoken of their desire to one day be involved in building the Temple. Now that David was king, and the Lord had blessed him, he had the leisure as well as the means to accomplish this task.

Nathan knew what was in his friend's heart. He was also familiar with God's word through Moses that the Lord would place His name in a particular city in Canaan (Deuteronomy 12: 10-11; etc.). It was easy for him, now that the Ark was safely ensconced in Jerusalem to conclude that Jerusalem was the place God had chosen, and so he responded to David with words of encouragement: "Do all that [is] in your heart" (17:2).

The Promise (17:3-15)

God's response (17:3-6). God's spokesmen, however, are not infallible. When speaking in His name (e.g., "Thus says the Lord …") they are, but not when engaged in normal conversation. On this occasion, and during the night, the Lord said to Nathan:

> "Go; say to David my servant, 'Thus says Yahweh, You shall not build a [lit. the] house for me to dwell in; for I have not dwelt in a house from the day that I brought up Israel [out of Egypt] to this day, but I have gone from tent to tent and from tabernacle [to tabernacle]. When [lit. Where in all] I have walked among all Israel

have I ever spoken a word with one of the judges of Israel (whom I commanded to feed my people), saying: "Why have you not built Me a house of cedars?"'"

There is something noteworthy about Nathan's prompt fulfillment of God's command. He obeyed at once. He was not concerned about saving face. In Old Testament times God's true prophets were so focused on His honor and glory that selfish pride and personal considerations were excluded from their lives.

On arriving at the palace, Nathan must have knocked so as to attract the attention of the night watchman. When he came to the door he told him he had a message for the king. Anyone else might have been turned away, but Nathan was known to be God's messenger and so he was allowed entrance.

David, of course, was then aroused and told that Nathan wished to see him. At the same time the court secretary was probably awakened and told that his services may be needed. The meeting probably took place in an antechamber, and God's full message was then recounted to the king.

As we take a close look at the Lord's words through Nathan we find that they shed light on His character. He is not a punitive deity. The manner in which He said "No" to David is both gracious and loving. At no time did David feel rejected or humiliated, for God gave him specific reasons for His decision. We may paraphrase His words as follows: "David, I appreciate what you want to do for me, but in reality I have no need of a Temple. I have been content with a tent or a tabernacle for lo these many years. And I have something far more important on My mind."

God's reminder (17:7-10a). Then, by way of assuring David of the special place he had in His plan and purpose for His people, the Lord entered into a covenant with him. As He did so He again referred to David as His "servant." There is no higher accolade than to be called a "servant of God," and the repetition of this title in this passage is designed to reinforce His unconditional regard for David. He then went on to remind David of his place in the theocratic kingdom. Speaking through Nathan, He said:

> "And now this is what you shall say to David, My servant, 'Thus says Yahweh of Hosts, I took you from the pasture, from [following] after the sheep, to be leader over My people Israel; and I have been with you everywhere you have walked; and I have cut off all your enemies from before you; and I have made for you a name like the name of the great ones who [are] in the earth. And I will put (i.e., prepare) a place for My people Israel, and I will plant them [lit. he], and they [lit. he] shall dwell in their [lit. his] place, and they [lit. he] shall not be troubled anymore; nor will the sons of wickedness waste them [lit. him], as at the first; [as happened] from the day that I appointed judges over My people Israel.'"

David's place in the kingdom was to fulfill God's purposes. The repeated emphasis on "I have …" (17:7-8*a*) culminated in His promise "I will …" (17:8*b*-10*a*), and united David's past God-given achievements with his future God-given attainments.

God's plan (17:10b-14). All that the Lord purposed to do was now confirmed to David in a gracious, unconditional covenant.

> "And I will humble all your enemies; and I declare to you that Yahweh shall build a house for you; and it shall be (i.e., come to pass), when your days have been fulfilled to go to your fathers, that I will raise up your seed after you, who shall be of your sons, and I will establish his kingdom. He shall build Me a house, and I shall establish his throne forever. I shall become to him a Father, and he shall be to me a son."

First, God pledged to establish David's kingdom. The emphasis on "forever" is unmistakable. It is surprising to note, therefore, how many learned writers go to elaborate lengths to try and prove that God didn't mean "forever" when He said "forever." They are quick to point out that a king no longer sat on David's throne after the people of Judah were carried away captive to Babylonia.

Now it is a fundamental rule of biblical interpretation that words spoken to a person or group are to be understood by us in the same way they were understood by those to whom they were first addressed. *The Open Bible* contains the following note:

> In this covenant David is promised three things: (1) a land forever (v.10); (2) an unending Dynasty (vv.11, 16); and (3) an ever lasting kingdom (vv.13, 16). The birth of Solomon, David's son who is to succeed him, is predicted (v. 12). His particular role is to establish the throne of the Davidic Kingdom forever (v. 12). His throne continues, though his seed is cursed in the person of Jeconiah (Coniah), who was the king under whom the nation was carried captive to Babylon. Jeremiah prophesies that no one whose genealogical descent could be traced back to David through Jeconiah and Solomon would ever sit on David's throne. Joseph, the legal, but not physical, father of Jesus traces his lineage to David through Jeconiah (Matthew 1:1-17). David, however, had another son, Nathan. His line was not cursed. Mary, the physical mother of Jesus, traces her lineage back to David through Nathan. Notice the care and the extent to which God goes to keep His word and to preserve its truthfulness. The virgin birth was absolutely essential, not only to assure the sinless character of Jesus but also to fulfill the Davidic covenant. Jesus receives his "blood right" to David's throne through His earthly mother, Mary, and His "legal right" to David's throne through His adoptive earthly father, Joseph. The virgin birth guarantees that one of David's line will sit on David's throne and rule forever, while at the same time preserving intact the curse and restriction on the line of descent through Jeconiah.

This is confirmed in a note by Dr. Charles C. Ryrie in the *Ryrie Study Bible.*

> This great covenant that God graciously made with David included the following provisions: (1) David would have a son who would succeed him and establish his kingdom (v. 12); (2) that son (Solomon), rather than David, would build the Temple (v. 13b); (3) though David's sins justified chastening, God's *lovingkindness* (Hebrew, *hesed*, "steadfast love" ...) would be forever (vv. 14-

15); (4) David's house, kingdom, and throne would be established forever (v. 16). The covenant did not guarantee uninterrupted rule by David's family (and, in fact, the Babylonian Exile interrupted it), but it did promise that the right to rule would always remain with David's dynasty. Jesus Christ is the ultimate fulfillment of these promises (Luke 1:31-33) and, although at this present time He is not ruling from the throne of David (Hebrews 12:2), at His second coming He will assume this throne.

Of special importance is the fact that a descendant of David, as yet unborn, would build the Temple. And each successive king of David's line would enjoy the unique privilege of being God's adoptive son. Disobedience would be punished, but the transgression of Israel's king(s) would not abrogate, cancel out or annul God's word. And to all who claim that this covenant was conditional and temporary, or to be understood "spiritually" and not literally, Gabriel's words to Mary in Luke 1:31-33 provide a powerful corrective.

Conclusion (17:15). Nathan faithfully relayed to David the vision God had given him. He left nothing out. His words were clear and unambiguous.

The Prayer (17:16-27)

David's response was one of humble belief. He was aware of the great honor God had given him. And, as if in answer to those who argue for a limited, temporary covenant, David accepted everything Nathan had told him at face value. God's words brought comfort to his heart, for they promised David an enduring dynasty. His glad embrace of God's promise is evident in his prayer.

David's praise (17:16-22). With a heart full of gratitude David left the palace and walked through the darkened streets of the city. A small retinue followed him. Anyone seeing him must have wondered what someone dressed more for bed than a walk about town was doing out of doors at that hour.

David made his way to the tent that housed the Ark of the Covenant. There, sitting before the Ark, he began his praise with two rhetorical questions: "Who am I, O Yahweh God?" and "What is my house?" This was a most unusual beginning and showed his humble recognition of his unworthiness. He was the youngest member of his father's family and came from one of the smallest villages in Israel. The Lord's choice of him and his elevation to the throne of His people left David in awe God's lovingkindness. And the Lord's assurance of a continuing dynasty (when other kingdoms experienced frequent coups with a corresponding change in the royal line) caused him to feel honored beyond anything he deserved.

These thoughts led David to affirm, "There is no one like You, O Yahweh, and apart from You there is no [one worthy of the name of] God" (17:20). The Lord is not only unique, He is without a rival. And David, with his heart overflowing with wonder, went on to ask, "And what one nation in the earth [is] as Your people Israel, whom God has brought out to ransom to Himself for a people, to make (lit. put) for Yourself a great and fearful name, to drive out the nations from before Your people Israel, whom You have ransomed out of Egypt. And, You have chosen (lit. given) Your people Israel for Yourself, for a people forever, and You, O Yahweh, have become God to them" (17:21-22).

An interesting issue is David's usage of the word "forever" in verse 22. If his dynasty was temporary (as some theologians affirm), then God's choice of Israel may also be said to be of limited duration. In Romans 9–11, however, the apostle Paul specifically stated that the Jewish nation is still the people of God even though for a time they have been removed from the place of blessing due to their unbelief. And in portions of the Bible that describe events during the Tribulation and Millennium, it is evident that the Lord still has a place for His covenant people.

David's petition (17:23-27). Whenever a promise is made in the Bible there is invariably some indication of its acceptance. For example, in the New Testament, when the Lord Jesus said, "Come to Me all you who are weary and heavy-laden, and I will give you rest" (Matthew 11:28), His words contain an undeniable promise. To benefit from this open offer, a person must take Him at His word and come to Him. Only then can the promise become effective.

So it was that David prayed, "And now, O Yahweh … do as You have spoken." What was it that the Lord had spoken through Nathan? It concerned David's house (dynasty) and the promise that it would be established forever (17:23). David then continued,

"And now, O Yahweh, the word that You have spoken as to Your servant, and as to his house, let it even be established forever, as You have spoken; let it even be established, and Your name be great forever, saying, 'Yahweh of Hosts, [is] God to [lit. of] Israel; and the house of Your servant David shall be established before You; for You, O my God, have uncovered the ear of Your servant, to build a house for him; therefore, Your servant has found to pray before You. And now, O Yahweh, you [are] God Himself, and You spoke of Your servant this goodness; and now, You have been pleased to bless the house of Your servant, to be forever before You; for You, O Yahweh, have blessed; yea, it is blessed forever!'"

A literal rendering of the Hebrew text makes difficult reading, yet its message is clear. An integral part of David's petition was that God's name be magnified as a result of His actions. David was concerned for God's honor, and he desired that both his "house" and also the house of Israel bring glory to His name. This was more than a pious end to a prayer. It reflected the desire of his heart as well as the focal point of his life.

More Than We Deserve

In our last chapter we took note of the way in which God blessed David by giving him a friend in Hiram, increasing his family, and enabling him to defeat the Philistines. In this chapter we read more of the same. The covenant the Lord established with David was a gracious one. And its far-reaching ramifications boggled his mind.

It does each of us good to remember where we were mentally and emotionally, spiritually and relationally at the time we came to know Christ personally. Then, as we look back on the way in which the Lord has led us, we are given a new appreciation of how graciously he has dealt with us in bringing us to where we are now.

When the Lord sent Nathan to David it was to remind him that he had once been a lonely shepherd. Solely by the grace of God he was now king over a united Israel. Many years had intervened between his anointing by Samuel and his being crowned king over the twelve tribes of Israel, and even though he had faced many vicissitudes the Lord had brought him safely through them all.

Further examples of this gracious reminder are to be found in Psalms 66 and 89. These admonitions should encourage us to persevere through our discouragements (cf. Psalm 44:1ff.).

A Matter of God's Timing

David's desire to build the Temple was a noble one. His timing, however, was premature. God knew of the wars that would soon break out. These would prevent David from pursuing his goal, and so in sending Nathan to him He declined his offer.

New believers often become frustrated when God doesn't answer their prayers. It is a hard lesson for them to learn that when God says "No" is always for their good. When speaking to some college students, Billy Graham told of some of his prayers that God did not answer. With commendable frankness he shared with them that during his late teens and early twenties he had a succession of girlfriends. Each time he imagined himself "in love" and prayed that the Lord would work in the heart of the young girl so that she would consent to become his wife. And each time God said "No." Later he met Ruth Bell – the person who did become his wife. When reminiscing on these early friendships, Dr. Graham stated that he was profoundly thankful the Lord did not answer him, for each of these girlfriends would have negated (and perhaps completely ruined) his ministry.

Ruth Harms Calkin, in her excellent book *Tell Me Again Lord, I Forget*, has written a poem in which she thanks God for saying "No" to her.

Lord, day after day I thank You
For saying yes.
But when have I genuinely thanked You
For saying no?

Yet I shudder to think
Of the possible smears
The cumulative blots on my life
Had You not been sufficiently wise
To say an *unalterable* no.

So thank You for saying no
When my wants list with things
Far exceeded my longing for You.
When I asked for a stone
Foolishly certain I asked for bread
Thank You for saying no.

....

Thank You for saying no
When the temptation that enticed me
Would have bound me beyond escape.

Thank You for saying no
When I asked You to leave me alone.

....

Lord, my awe increases
When I see the wisdom
Of Your divine no.

The Importance of Thanksgiving

A heart of gratitude needs cultivating. It has been observed that "A thankless person seldom does a thankful deed." Parents know the difficulty of training their children to say "Thank you." It seems as if gratitude and thankfulness develop relatively late in their young lives. And if they are not taught it diligently by us, they probably will never learn it and will grow to adulthood thinking that the world owes them a living. Developing a thankful spirit is important, for if a person isn't thankful for what he or she has, that person isn't likely to be thankful for what he or she is going to get. As we grow older, the attitude of the thankless person sours the disposition, and as selfishness takes over it squeezes out of life all appreciation for better things.

Helen Keller could have spent her life complaining about her misfortunes. Instead she said, "There are three things I thank God for every day of my life: thanks that He has vouchsafed me knowledge of His works; deep thanks that he has set in my darkness the lamp of faith; [and] deep, deepest thanks that I have another life to look forward to – a life joyous with light and flowers and heavenly song." And on another occasion she remarked, "I thank God for my handicaps; for through them, I have found myself, my work, and my God."

Dr. John Henry Jowett was a contemporary of Helen Keller. With genuine insight into human nature, he wrote: "Life without thankfulness is devoid of love and passion. Hope without thankfulness is lacking in fine perception. Faith that lacks thankfulness lacks strength and fortitude. Every virtue divorced from thankfulness is maimed and limps along [life's highway]."

Let us never forget that God is honored by His people's praise (Psalm 50:23).

15

God-Given Success
(1 Chronicles 18:1–20:8)

The people of Judah, for whom the books of Chronicles were written, had been enslaved in Babylonia (605–536 BC). They had returned to their homeland to find Jerusalem in ruins and their towns and villages in dire need of repair. Their fields and vineyards were thick with weeds, and a tremendous amount of work was required to clear the land of thorns and thistles before the first seeds of a new crop could be sown.

To add to their difficulties, Bedouin from the desert as well as marauders from Philistia, Moab, Syria (also called Aram), Edom, and Ammon constantly invaded their land, plundered their crops, drove off their cattle, and captured their wives and children to be sold as slaves.

It was to encourage these discouraged people that the chronicler penned this selective history of God's past dealings with their nation. He wanted to remind them of the Lord's faithfulness to them. To do so, he illustrated His goodness to their forefathers by describing His past involvement in the life of the nation. And, to underscore God's faithfulness, he described briefly and concisely the gracious covenant the Lord had made with David. Now, he records equally as briefly the notable victories He gave His servant.

Chapters 18 to 20 are not hard to outline. Their purpose is to underscore God's commitment to His promise to "humble all David's enemies" (17:10). Most of the wars the chronicler recounts took place within a relatively short period of time. It seems as if the Lord had no sooner assured David of a continuing dynasty than the devil set about trying to thwart His plan by destroying the nation and its king. Psalm 83 gives the context of Judah's oppression and the people's need.

The main (and most obvious) "seams" of the story revolve around repetitious thoughts or ideas. For example, in chapter 18 we take note of the fact that "Yahweh preserved David wherever he went" (18:6, 13). Similarly in chapter 19 (which forms a subdivision within the account of David's wars), the repetitious ideas have to do with "going out" and "coming in (or returning)." In verses 2 and 5 we note that "David sent [out] messengers ..." from Jerusalem to Rabbah followed by a statement "and [they] returned." Likewise in verses 8 and 15 "David sent Joab ..." and later "Joab went (i.e., returned) to Jerusalem." Then, in 20:1 and 3 we observe that "Joab led out the armed forces." Just before the fall of Rabbah, David was summoned to join the army. He did so, and this section concludes with the statement "then David and all the people returned to Jerusalem."

Here is the outline we will follow:

David's Wars (18:1–20:8)
Victory Over the Philistines (18:1)
Victory Over the Moabites (18:2)
Victory Over the Syrians (18:3-6)
    Digression: The Spoils of War (18:7-11)
Victory Over the Edomites (18:12-13)
    Digression: Summary of David's Reign (18:14)
    Digression: David's Cabinet (18:15-17)
Victory Over the Ammonites (19:1–20:3)
    Shameful Treatment of David's Ambassadors (19:1-5)
    Hasty Alliance with David's Enemies (19:6-19)
    Digression: Victory Over the Syrians (19:16-19)
    Inevitable Success (20:1-3)
Victory Over the Philistines (20:4-8)

David's Wars (18:1–20:8)

The connection between the previous chapter and this new section is often overlooked. Without pomp or ceremony the Lord had lifted David above the dull routine of rebuilding the nation and entered into a solemn covenant with him. The uniqueness of this event is clearly seen when we consider how seldom this had happened in the past. David now enjoyed the same kind of status that Adam, Noah and Abraham had received. But as far as David was concerned, he passed from his peaceful contemplation of the Temple to the invasion of the land by Israel's enemies and the horrors of war.

Victory Over the Philistines (18:1)
"Now after this it came about that David defeated the Philistines and subdued them and took Gath and its towns from the hand of the Philistines." We may be sure that the Philistines were the aggressors, for David did not provoke wars, and we know that on two previous occasions the Philistines had been the ones to attack Israel. This receives further, tacit confirmation from the writings of Moses. Moses in Deuteronomy 20:1ff. had given Israel specific instructions on how they were to wage war. There is no indication that anything like this happened on this occasion, and so we have reinforced in our thinking the strong probability that the Philistines were the first to enter the field of battle. All that the chronicler records is that David defeated them and took Gath with the towns that surrounded this leading city of the pentapolis.

Achish, king of Gath, had been David's protector and friend during his "outlaw" years. We may be sure that David would not willingly have taken up arms against his former benefactor. It is possible, therefore, that Achish had died and that another king, who now sat on the throne, had assumed the hereditary title.

Victory Over the Moabites (18:2)
After defeating the Philistines, David's other wars take place in Transjordan.[1] The first nation to be mentioned is Moab.[2] Earlier in his life, when David was being persecuted by King Saul, the king of Moab had offered a secure asylum for David's parents. It surprises us to read that David now takes up arms against

them. What precipitated these hostilities? We do not know. All we are told is that "he defeated Moab, and the Moabites became servants to David, bringing tribute."

Later Jewish writers speculated that the Moabites had treacherously murdered David's parents, and that it was to punish this crime that the attack was made. Such a view is unlikely. It is more probable that some reprehensible action on their part, or possible breach of an existing treaty, or some other violation of an existing law code, required that stern measures be taken to preserve Israel's sovereignty.

David's army is victorious and the Moabites are completely subdued. They are then required to pay an annual tribute.

Victory Over the Syrians (18:3-6)

With David's victories to the west and east, Hadadezer, king of Zobah,[3] decides to take action and stake his claim in the north.[4] Hadadezer was originally from Beth-Rehob (2 Samuel 8:3) in southern Lebanon. At some time in the past he had established himself in Zobah, where he ruled an empire of small Syrian (or Aramean) states.[5]

David must have been aware of Hadadezer's hegemony and of the threat his control of trade from the Tigris-Euphrates Valley would pose to Israel, for he took immediate action to safeguard his people's right to peace and safety. So it is that we read:

> David also defeated Hadadezer king of Zobah [as far as] Hamath, as he went to the Euphrates River to establish his rule. David took from him 1,000 chariots and 7,000 horsemen and 20,000 foot soldiers, and David hamstrung all the chariot horses, but reserved [enough] of them for 100 chariots.

> When the Syrians (or Arameans) of Damascus came to help Hadadezer king of Zobah, David killed 22,000 of them. Then David put [garrisons] among the Syrians of Damascus; and the Syrians became servants to David, bringing tribute.

Psalm 9 expresses David's thankfulness to the Lord for the help He gave Him. David's prayer that the name of the wicked would perish forever would seem to have been answered, for apart from the biblical record Hadadezer and Zobah are virtually unknown.

This section concludes with a summary statement: "And Yahweh helped David wherever he went." That divine help was needed may be deduced from the fact that the Syrians had chariots as well as cavalry, and that during the fighting in the north Edom invaded the south. Apparently there was a well-established coalition intent on preventing David's further rise in power. Joab and Abishai were sent to meet this new challenge, leaving David with fewer soldiers (all of whom were infantry) to face the combined forces of Zobah and Damascus.

Digression: The Spoils of War (18:7-11)

From the regions thus subdued, David brought a vast amount of gold and bronze to Jerusalem. His portion of the spoils of war was set aside for the Temple that he believed his yet-to-be-born son would build.

Further evidence of God's blessing is to be seen in the recognition given David by Tou, king of Hamath,[6] who sent his son to David with gifts. This token of homage seems to indicate that a peace treaty was entered into at this time.

David never failed to honor the Lord for His goodness to him, and though denied the opportunity of building the Temple, he nonetheless prepared for its embellishment by dedicating to the Lord his portion of the spoils of war, together with the gold, silver and bronze that were his part of peace treaties. The bronze was later used by Solomon to make the huge laver, pillars, and other Temple utensils (cf. 2 Chronicles 5:1 and 26:26-27).

This example of David's generosity would be of particular significance to the Jewish remnant that had returned from Babylonia. They had neglected the rebuilding of the Second Temple until the time of Haggai (Haggai 1:1–2:23). Yet they desired God's blessing, and complained when they did not receive it. David's actions show that he put the Lord first in everything (cf. Matthew 6:33).

Verse 11 makes mention of David's victories over the Ammonites.[7] We have yet to read about this war, and it is possible that the Ammonites are mentioned here so as to provide a more complete list of David's victories.

The reference to the Amalekites may echo David's rout of them before he became king in Hebron (1 Samuel 30).

It should not escape our attention that David is now referred to as "King David" (18:10-11). Not only is he increasingly being recognized by other monarchs as someone to whom respect was due, but also his favor was being sought. And as his empire expanded, Israel became a power to be reckoned with in the Near East.

Victory Over the Edomites (18:12-13)

A brief report of Israel's war with the Edomites[8] to the south concludes this section. "Moreover Abishai the son of Zeruiah defeated 18,000 Edomites in the Valley of Salt. Then he put garrisons in Edom, and all the Edomites became servants to David."

This section ends with a further statement by the chronicler to the effect that "the Lord helped David wherever he went." None of David's victories came easily. His experience of hardship corrects the impression held by many today that if the Lord is with us, then our lives should be free from adversity; and that if we have to face repeated difficulty this indicates that there must be some sin in our life. Strength of character is not developed by a life of ease, and those who propagate such falsehood should remember that the Lord Jesus promised His followers trials and difficulties, opposition and even martyrdom (cf. John 16:33).

Summary of David's Reign (18:14)

"So David reigned over all Israel; and he administered justice (*mispat*[9]) and righteousness (*sedeq*[10]) for all his people." He did what was just and right. He was impartial and faithfully administered the Law. And his people were happy.

Digression: David's Cabinet (18:15-17)

With the expansion of David's empire it became necessary for him to have reliable officials in the different areas of government. "Joab the son of Zeruiah [was] over the army, and Jehoshaphat the son of Ahilud [was] recorder; and Zadok the son of Ahitub and Abimelech the son of Abiathar [were] priests, and Shavsha [was] secretary; and Benaiah the son of Jehoiada [was] over the Cherethites and the Pelethites, and the sons of David [were] chiefs at the king's side."[11]

His "cabinet" was broken down into "departments:" Joab was general over the army; Jehoshaphat was the recorder (probably "secretary of state"); Shavsha was the secretary (possibly responsible for royal correspondence and recording the king's decisions); the priesthood was shared by Zadok and Abiathar; and Benaiah was over David's bodyguard made up of Cretan and Philistine mercenaries.

William J. Deane provides us with a summary of chapter 18. He shows how, in his wars, David was more gracious in his treatment of Israel's enemies than the Law required. According to Moses in Deuteronomy 20:12-18,

> if a foreign city refused to surrender when summoned, and was taken by siege or by assault, all the males were to be put to death, the women and children led into captivity, and the place was to be sacked; but if the city appertained to any of the seven Canaanite peoples, the whole population, male and female, was to be put to the sword.

Regarded then as the executor of the Divine vengeance and the enforcer of the stern Mosaic Law, David erred on the side of mercy. He punished ... only those taken with arms in the hands ... and of these one large portion was spared.... No charge of cruelty could be laid against one who carried out, and that leniently, the law and custom which were universally recognized as binding.

The wars of chapter 18 were followed by another, having very serious consequences, and leading to various campaigns. It was no lust of conquest that led to these results. Israel's wars were either thrust upon them by wanton attacks, or were undertaken to secure their independence; and conquered regions were retained for safety sake and to insure the fruits of victory. Israel's amicable relations with the Phoenicians, whom they left in undisturbed possession of maritime cities and their strip of seaboard, sufficiently prove the non-aggressive character of their policy.[12]

Victory Over the Ammonites (19:1–20:3)

"And it happened after this, that Nahash the king of the sons of Ammon died, and his son reigned in his place" (19:1). The friendship between David and Nahash may date back to David's "outlaw" years, when he was a fugitive from King Saul, and their common enmity toward Saul may have brought them together (cf. 1 Samuel 11; 14:47).

Shameful treatment of David's ambassadors (19:1-5). "And David said, 'I will show kindness (*hesed*) to Hanun the son of Nahash, because his father showed kindness (*hesed*[13]) to me.' So David sent messengers to console him concerning his father." Such messages, whether of sympathy or congratulations (as when Hiram sent his ambassadors to David), were customary in those days, even as they are today. And though there is no record of Nahash having granted David and his men sanctuary, there is evidence of a treaty (implied by the word *hesed*) that was quite possibly entered into at the time David became king in Hebron.

David's kindness, however, was rejected. The Ammonites had heard about the treatment meted out to their allies, the Moabites, and though they had ignored the (probable) provocation on the part of Moab, they now viewed the visit of David's ambassadors with suspicion.

And David's servants came into the land of the sons of Ammon to Hanun to console him. But the princes of the sons of Ammon said to Hanun, "Do you think that David is honoring your father, in that he has sent comforters to you? Have not his servants come to you to search and to overthrow and to spy out the land?" So Hanun took David's servants and shaved them and cut off their garments in the middle as far as their hips, and sent them away. Then [certain persons] went and told David about the men. And he sent to meet them, for the men were greatly humiliated. And the king said, "Stay at Jericho until your beards grow, and [then] return."

The arrival of David's ambassadors would have been an ideal time for Hanun to reaffirm the treaty with David (or, if he was unaware of the existence of one, negotiate a new one). Instead he seizes David's ambassadors and, according to the text of 2 Samuel, shaves off half their beards and cuts off the lower part of their long garments, exposing their genitals. Then he sends them back to King David.

Given the Near Eastern culture where a man's beard is sacred, Hanun's actions constitute one of the worst insults that could ever be paid to anyone. And to expose these ambassadors to further public humiliation by cutting off their clothing was to invite retribution. Furthermore, let us not forget that to insult a monarch's representatives was the equivalent of insulting the monarch himself. Seen in this light, Hanun's actions were not only rash but also ill-advised and invited retaliation.

Hanun's brother, Shobi,[14] must have known of these actions, and it is possible that he sent clothing to David's ambassadors. This may explain why, when word reaches David of what has happened, the text contains no mention of any clothing being sent, but only his instructions to them to wait in Jericho until their beards have re-grown.

Hasty alliance with David's enemies (19:6-19). When the sons of Ammon see that they have made themselves odious to David, Hanun and the sons of Ammon send 1,000 talents of silver (an amount in excess of $2,000,000) to hire mercenaries with chariots and horsemen from Mesopotamia, from Aram-maacah and from Zobah. In all they were able to hire 32,000 chariots, together with the king of Maacah and his people. These mercenaries came and camped before Medeba. And the sons of Ammon gathered together from their cities and came to battle. When David heard of it he sent Joab and all the army, together with the mighty men, to do battle with the Ammonites.

Again we encounter purposeful repetition on the part of the chronicler. Verses 6, 10, 16, and 19 all carry forward the story with the statement "When So-and-so saw that..." Apparently in Ammon saner heads at last prevailed and the new king and his advisors were made to realize that, by their actions, they had made themselves "stink"[15] in the nostrils of the people of Israel.

"But what," we may ask, "caused the unwise counsel that was given to Hanun?" Fear. Fear attributes to a person, place or thing two special attributes: the power to do us harm, and the power to take away our ability to function independently. Plainly Hanun's advisors feared the rising power of Israel, and believed that David had the power both to do them harm and to take away their ability to function autonomously. They *reacted* to the delegation from Israel and gave unwise counsel to the new king. Then, when they realized their mistake, instead of having Hanun go humbly to David and ask for his forgiveness, they compounded their error by hiring Syrian mercenaries from Hadadezer.

Apparently Hadadezer was anxious to avenge his earlier defeat at David's hands, and so, breaking whatever agreement he had made with David, he recruited soldiers from Zobah and compelled his vassals to come to Ammon's aid. These warriors were then dispatched to Medeba,[16] a city close to Rabbah.

Rabbah was a well-fortified city, about twenty miles east of the River Jordan, on the banks of the southern of the two streams which, when united, form the River Jabbok. A traveler to that region describes what he saw:

> For picturesqueness of situation, I know of no ruins to compare with Ammon. The most striking feature is the citadel, which formerly contained not merely the garrison, but an upper town, and covered an extensive area. The lofty plateau on which it was situated is triangular in shape; two sides were formed by the valleys

which diverge from the apex, where they are divided by a low neck, and thence separating fall into the valley of the Jabbok which forms the base of the triangle, and contained the lower town. Climbing up the citadel we can trace remains of a moat, and crossing it find ourselves in a maze of ruins. The massive walls— the lower parts of which still remain, and which, rising from the precipitous sides of the cliff, rendered any attempt at scaling impossible.[17]

The large army of Syrian mercenaries bivouaced in an open field before Medeba,[18] where they awaited the commencement of the battle. Joab was unaware of their presence and took up his position facing the city of Rabbah. On the day of the battle, the Ammonites came out of their city and drew up in front of the gates of the citadel. Joab and his men prepared to attack them frontally when all of a sudden they were made aware of the large Syrian force closing in behind them. They found themselves sandwiched between two hostile armies. Joab quickly divided his forces into two parts and, giving one to his brother Abishai, led the other in an attack on the Syrian mercenaries. The biblical historian describes what took place:

The sons of Ammon came out and drew up in battle array at the entrance of the city, and the kings who had come were by themselves in the field. Now when Joab saw that the battle was set against him in front and in the rear, he selected from all the choice men of Israel and they arrayed themselves against the Syrians [or Arameans]. But the remainder of the people he placed in the hand of Abishai his brother; and they arrayed themselves against the sons of Ammon. He said, "If the Syrians are too strong for me, then you shall help me; but if the sons of Ammon are too strong for you, then I will help you. Be strong, and let us show ourselves courageous for the sake of our people and for the cities of our God; and may Yahweh do what is good in His sight."

So Joab and the people who were with him drew near to the battle against the Syrians, and they fled before him. When the sons of Ammon saw that the Syrians fled, they also fled before Abishai his brother and entered the city. Then Joab came to Jerusalem (19:10-15).

Joab's strategy worked. He was victorious and the Syrians fled in haste from the field of battle. He returned to Jerusalem (possibly to report to David) while a portion of the army remained outside Rabbah and subjected the inhabitants to a siege.

Digression: Victory Over the Syrians (19:16-19). Joab's success against the Syrians had been partial. They had only withdrawn to reorganize their forces. They had no intention of giving up, and a second battle was required to end the Ammonite-Syrian coalition.

> When the Syrians saw that they had been defeated by Israel, they sent messengers and brought out the Syrians who were beyond the River, with Shophach the commander of the army of Hadadezer leading them. When it was told David, he gathered all Israel together and crossed the Jordan, and came upon them and drew up in formation against them. And when David drew up in battle array against the Syrians, they fought against him. The Syrians fled before Israel, and David killed of the Syrians 7,000 charioteers and 40,000 foot soldiers, and put to death Shophach the commander of the army. So when the servants of Hadadezer saw that they were defeated by Israel, they made peace with David and served him. Thus the Syrians were not willing to help the sons of Ammon anymore (19:16-19).

This time David was made aware of the Syrian advance as it moved south. Instead of waiting for the Syrians to invade Israel, he mustered all of his forces and attacked them at Helam, a place 30 miles east of the Sea of Galilee and considerably north of the territory of Ammon.

Before the battle took place, Syrian morale was high. They believed that they were in a very strong position, and had even secured the services of a wise general named Shophach. Drs. Chaim Herzog and Mordechai Gichon describe the events:

> David rushed his army to meet his foe in the Edrei gap, some twelve miles of traversable ground between the deep gorge of the Yarmuk River and the natural barrier of the Trachona, a vast area of petrified blocks. Here the Byzantines withstood the Muslim armies between

AD 334 and 336 and it was through this area that the British moved against the Vichy French in 1941. The armies [of David and Shobach] clashed at Helam. The Israelite victory was complete, and all the Aramean kingdoms from Zobah southwards accepted Israel domination.[19]

The battle was decisive, and the dead bodies of the charioteers and infantry were strewn over a wide area. The Ammonite-Syrian alliance was broken, and the Syrians had learned an important lesson: They will not again help the Ammonites.

Inevitable Success (20:1-3). The war against Syria being over, Joab could now devote his attention to taking the seemingly impregnable fortress of Rabbah. In time the long siege came to an end. The capital fell and its citizens were assigned forced labor.

Then it happened in the spring, at the time when kings go out [to battle], that Joab led out the army and ravaged the land of the sons of Ammon, and came and besieged Rabbah. But David stayed at Jerusalem. And Joab struck Rabbah and overthrew it. David took the crown of their king from his head, and he found it to weigh a talent of gold, and there was a precious stone in it; and it was placed on David's head. And he brought out the spoil of the city, a very great amount. He brought out the people who [were] in it, and cut [them, i.e., put them to forced labor] with saws and with sharp instruments and with axes. And thus David did to all the cities of the sons of Ammon. Then David and all the people returned [to] Jerusalem.

The conquering heroes were given a warm welcome as they walked into Jerusalem, and it is possible that Psalm 20 was sung to honor their victory.

Victory Over the Philistines (20:4-8)

The account of David's wars is brought to a conclusion with three "snapshots" of three separate Philistine engagements.

And it was after this, that there was war again with the Philistines in Gezer; then Sibbechai the Hushathite struck (i.e., killed) Sippai, one of the children of the giant, and they were humbled (i.e., subdued). And there was war (lit. a battle) again with the Philistines, and Elhanan the son of Jair killed Lahmi, the brother of Goliath the Gittite, the wood (i.e., shaft) of his spear [was] like a weaver's beam. Again there was a battle (i.e., war) at Gath, and a man of [great] stature was there and his fingers and toes were six and six, twenty-four (i.e., six fingers on each hand and six toes on each foot); and he also had been born to the giant. When he taunted Israel, Jonathan the son of Shimea, David's brother, struck (i.e., killed) him. These were descended from the giants in Gath, and they fell by the hand of David and by the hand of his servants.

The significant point to be noted is that each of these accounts involved a man of considerable size, and the subtle emphasis of the chronicler is that in these wars David's men were the real heroes.

Timely Lessons

The change from David's worship of the Lord in chapter 17 to the wars of this section underscores for us the fact that life's transitions are often abrupt. And while we would like to linger in the place of peace and tranquility, there are battles that must be fought and victories that must be won. So it is that, as we read David's psalms with these chapters in mind, we realize that the Lord can bring blessing in the midst of the stresses of life.

It is also instructive to note that these wars occupy a relatively small portion of God's Word. If a contemporary historian were writing of these events we would expect a major treatise replete with commands, written correspondence, and details of each engagement. Perhaps additional details were given in *The Book of the Wars of the Lord* and *The Book of Jashar*. Here the facts are sparse and in some instances information has to be supplied from other Scriptures (e.g., Psalms 44 and 60). Though spiritual struggles are necessary, and we need to be reminded of them lest we mistakenly believe that the Christian life is one of continual ease, yet they are only a part of life. The real issues involve the development of character and trust in the Lord.

This fact was brought home to me recently. I was talking to a friend whose wife has cancer. She has come out of remission and is not doing well. Chemotherapy and radiotherapy have been halted. His response to my inquiry about her health, was, "We do not know what is going to happen, but we're using this time to learn more about trusting the Lord."

On earlier occasions David seems to have been content with driving out invaders (e.g., 14:8-17). Now he presses his advantage into their territory and places the aggressors under tribute. His actions emphasize the need to insure that our spiritual victories are made permanent. If not, then we will find ourselves fighting the same battles again and again.

As a result of the victories won by David and his men, the people of Israel entered a period of prosperity previously unknown. And with David administering justice, the people enjoyed greater happiness than ever before.

16

God's Wrath, God's Mercy
(1 Chronicles 21:1–22:1)

The chronicler has been writing to encourage God's people with the assurance of God's faithfulness. They were experiencing hard times. They had entered into a covenant with the Lord (Nehemiah 10) to abstain from intermarriage with non-Israelites, refrain from planting crops during the sabbatical year, remit all debts every seven years, and maintain the Temple by bringing their tithes to the Lord.[1] They had sinned against the Lord by breaking this covenant in every particular, with the result that the Lord had withdrawn His hand of blessing from them.

In writing to encourage his people, God's historian used an illustration from the life of King David. He had recently shown how, during his reign, David had been beset by enemies on all sides. Each battle had been hard-fought, but the Lord had given him the victory so that, when the fighting was over, God's people were in a stronger position than before. Formerly hostile nations were now Israel's vassals.

With peace David was free to devote his energies to preparing for the building of the Temple. His primary concern, however, was the fear that some of the nations that surrounded Israel might band together, launch an attack, and in this way try to regain their independence. To ascertain the nation's strength, David ordered that a census be taken.

The material in this section may be outlined as follows:

The Power of Satan (21:1)
The Sin of a Believer (21:2-6)
The Punishment of God (21:7-14)
The Propitiation of Sin (21:15-27)
The Place of Worship (21:28–22:1)

Other outlines have been suggested by different commentators, and the reader is encouraged to become familiar with them.

The Power of Satan (21:1)

The writer begins his recounting of events in a startling way. "And Satan stood up against Israel and moved David to number Israel." The style of language reminds us of Job 1:6-12. It is as if Satan had appeared before the Lord in heaven and brought an accusation against Israel. Their sins were obvious. No one could deny them. Would God be just in punishing them or would He compromise His holiness and turn a blind eye to their offenses?

Satan is mentioned directly only three times in the Old Testament (cf. Job 1–2; Zechariah 3:1-2; and here). Of course, he was also active in the Garden of Eden (Genesis 3 where he took possession of the body of a serpent [cf. Revelation 12:9; 20:2]) as he has been throughout history. However, only in this Old Testament passage does the word *Satan* appear as a proper name. Elsewhere it is accompanied by the definite article and means "the adversary" or "the opponent."

In 2 Samuel 24:1 Satan is not mentioned directly, but his activity lies latent in the word "incited." And God permitted him to move David to number the people.

Some writers have suggested that pride motivated David to take the census. They claim he wanted to know how great was the nation over which he ruled.[2] But the immediate context is against such a view. The recent wars coupled with the inveterate hostility of Israel's enemies made continual vigilance a necessity. It would be natural for him to want to know the number of fighting men he could call on should a crisis arise. The only way to find out this information was to take a census.

The Sin of a Believer (21:2-6)

The Bible contains numerous illustrations of census-taking (cf. Numbers 1:3, 45; 26:2; see also Exodus 38:25-28; Numbers 3:14-39 and 40-41; 26:52-55; Nehemiah 7:4-5; 1 Chronicles 23:2ff.; etc.). Taking a census was not in and of itself wrong. A requirement, however, was a special half-shekel tax (Exodus 30:11-16). It would appear as if David was ignorant of this requirement, for there is no mention of this money being collected.

When David commanded Joab and the elders of the people to "Go, number Israel, even from Beersheba to Dan; and bring [a report] to me, that I may know their number" (21:2), Joab voiced strenuous objection. It is possible that, had the remonstrance come from the leaders, David would have listened. Joab, however, had been engaged in a power struggle with David for many years. He had sided with Absalom in seeking to have the young prince recalled from exile (2 Samuel 14) and within a few years would side (against David's wishes!) with Adonijah and seek to make the young prince king (1 Kings 1:5-7). The army was under Joab's control. Had it not been for the faithful Ittai and his band of 600 Gittites, and the loyalty of Benaiah who was over David's bodyguard, Joab might have staged a coup and placed the crown on the head of one of David's easy-to-manage sons. He could then be the power behind the throne.

Joab's objection to taking the census was couched in pious terms, but this did not mean that Joab cared one whit about spiritual matters. He knew from past experience that such issues weighed heavily with David, and so he said, "May Yahweh add to (i.e., multiply) His people a hundred times; are not, O my lord king, all of them servants to my lord? Why does my lord seek this [knowledge]? Why will he become the cause of guilt to Israel?" (21:3).

Whatever may have been the import of his last statement, it was lost on David. Joab had murdered Abner when he was about to unite the northern tribes under David (2 Samuel 3:27-30); and had also killed Absalom when David had given specific orders that Absalom's life should be spared (2 Samuel 18:5ff.); and he had murdered Amasa when David had placed him over the army (2 Samuel 20:4-5, 9-10). Joab could no longer be trusted. And had he not been such a powerful man, David may have tried to remove him from office.

It took Joab ten months to take the census (21:5-6); and in all this time, as David waited for the results, he did not realize that he had done wrong.

After almost a year, when Joab reported back to David, he stated that there were 1,100,000 fighting men in Israel. Did he inflate his actual figure to cover the tribe of Benjamin? We cannot be sure. Scholars have noted the apparent discrepancy between 21:5 and 2 Samuel 24:9. Dr. Charles C. Ryrie, in his valuable study Bible, offers a plausible explanation to account for the difference. He writes:

> The 800,000 from Israel in 2 Sam. 24:9 may not have included the 300,000 listed in 1 Chron. 27, which would make the total (as here) 1,100,000. The 470,000 in Judah may not have included the 30,000 of 2 Samuel 6:1, which would bring the total (as here) to 500,000. Or perhaps the Chronicles figure represents a round number.[3]

Whatever the explanation, the apparent discrepancy can easily be explained.

The Punishment of God (21:7-14)

We live at a time in history when men and women who believe in a Supreme Being (*viz.*, God) are prone to emphasize His love, but ignore His other attributes. They ignore the fact that the Bible tells us that He is angry with sinners every day (Psalm 7:11), and that all our thoughts and deeds come under His scrutiny (Psalm 90:8; Mark 4:22), and will eventuate in either our reward or punishment (2 Corinthians 5:10).

In the passage before us we read that the people of Israel had sinned and had incurred God's displeasure (2 Samuel 24:1). God permitted Satan to tempt David into numbering them. David did so, and because he failed to obtain the half-shekel tax, he was the catalyst that brought God's judgment on the nation (21:7).

We do not know how David became aware of his error. Recreating what took place is difficult. It may be that David became aware of the enormity of his sin while reading the writings of Moses (Deuteronomy 17:18-20). Whatever the cause his response was to immediately ask God for His forgiveness: "I have sinned, exceedingly," he said, "in that I have done this thing; and now, cause I pray [You] the iniquity of your servant to pass, for I have acted very foolishly" (21:8).

In response to David's prayer, the Lord sent Gad to David.

"Go; and speak to David, saying, 'Thus says Yahweh, three [things] I am offering you; choose for yourself one of them, that I may do to you.... Either three years of famine; or three months to be swept before your adversaries, even to be overtaken [by] the sword of your enemies; or three days, [punished by] the sword of Yahweh, even pestilence in the land, and the angel of Yahweh destroying in all the borders of Israel. And now consider what I shall bring back to Him who sent me word" (21:10-12).

David knew God to be more gracious and merciful than his enemies, and wisely chose the third option. He said to Gad, "I am in a great distress; let me fall into the hand of Yahweh, for very many [are] His mercies; but do not let me fall into the hand of man" (21:13). Two important emphases are evident in the Hebrew text. They are indicated by the position of words within the sentence. David's response reads quite literally, "Distress [is] to me great." He had no idea that the census would result in such calamity, and his heart is crushed at the thought of the suffering his action would bring upon his people. He was also unaware of God's purpose to punish Israel and so took the blame upon himself. The second emphasis is in the last part of his reply, "but into the hand of man let me not fall." His trust in the Lord, even in judgment, was implicit.

The Propitiation for Sin (21:15-27)

God's punishment was not long delayed. Probably at dawn the next day the plague began (21:7). It was nationwide (i.e., from Beersheba to Dan) and by mid-afternoon on the first day the destroying angel had reached Jerusalem. In the providence of God the progress of destruction was halted at the threshing floor of Ornan[4] the Jebusite. The fact that God caused the plague to stop confirms the observation of Dr. J. G. McConville who stated that "despite the severity of the punishment there is a sense in which the real subject [of this chapter] is [God's] mercy."[5]

And God sent an angel to Jerusalem to destroy it; and while destroying [perhaps in the area around the city], Yahweh saw, and repented about the evil, and said to the angel who was destroying [the people], "Enough! Now let drop your hand." And the angel of Yahweh was standing by the grain floor of Ornan the Jebusite (21:15).

At this time the Lord enabled David and the elders to see the angel with his drawn sword in his hand. They all put on sackcloth as a sign of mourning, fell to their knees and bowed their faces to the ground (21:16). And David said to the Lord,

"Did not I,[6] I say to number the people? Yes, [it is] I myself who sinned, and indeed have done evil; but these, the flock (i.e., the people), what have they done? O Yahweh, my God, I pray You, let Your hand be on me and on my father's house, but not on Your people, to be plagued" (21:17).

David apparently had no idea that the destruction had begun already, and it is interesting to note that he took full responsibility for his sin. He asked only that he be punished and his people spared.[7]

At this point, the Angel of the Lord spoke to Gad and told him to tell David to rise up an altar to the Lord on the threshing-floor of Ornan (21:18). In obedience, David climbed the hill to the place where Ornan and his sons had been threshing wheat.

And David came to Ornan, and Ornan looked and saw David, and went out of the threshing-floor and bowed down to David, [with his] face to the ground. And David said to Ornan, "Give me the site of the threshing-floor, that I may build an altar to Yahweh [on it]; for full money (i.e., for the full price) give it to me, that the plague be restrained from the people."

And Ornan said to David, "Take [it] for yourself and do, my

lord the king, the good (i.e., what is good) in his (i.e., your) eyes; see, I give the oxen and the threshing tools for wood [for] the burnt offerings, and the wheat for the food offering. I give it all."

And King David said to Ornan, "No, for I will surely buy [it] with full money (i.e., for the full price[8]); for I will not offer that which [is] yours to Yahweh, so as to offer a burnt offering without cost." And David gave to Ornan for the place six hundred shekels in gold weight[9] (21:21-25).

A threshing-floor was invariably a flat, hard-beaten area on high ground outside a town or village on which the sheaves of grain were threshed (Isaiah 21:10; Jeremiah 51:33; Micah 4:12). On this surface the sheaves were spread out and sometimes beaten with flails, but more commonly oxen were driven over it. The oxen were either yoked side by side and driven around over the grain, or were yoked to a "drag" (a heavy board or a block of wood) with stones or pieces of iron fastened to the lower surface to make it rough. It was dragged over the grain to separate the kernel from the husk. Then, in the afternoon, when a cool breeze would blow, it was thrown up into the air. The heavier kernel would fall to the ground while the husks would be blown to the end of the threshing-floor where a fire would be burning.

Having bought the threshing-floor, David then built an altar on it. He also slaughtered the oxen and placed them on it. The Lord signified His acceptance of the sacrifice by sending down fire from heaven to consume the offering. After this the plague was stayed.

Originally David had agreed that the punishment should last for three days. God demonstrated His mercy by limiting it to about nine hours. Even so, 70,000 men of Israel died.

The Place of Worship (21:28–22:1)
This brief section is bounded by two statements: "When David saw ..." (21:28) and "then David said ..." (22:1). When fire came down from heaven and consumed the sacrifice, David knew that the Lord had accepted his sacrifice. He then offered other

sacrifices on the threshing-floor of Ornan. These were most likely thank offerings in gratitude for the plague having been stayed.

The writer then adds a "theological postscript." The Tabernacle of Moses was at that time at Gibeon. David, however, seemed to have become aware of the fact that Ornan's threshing-floor was to be the site of the Lord's Temple. That is why he exclaimed, "This [is] the house of Yahweh God, and this [is] the altar for burnt offering for Israel" (22:1).

And so a series of events that could have been extremely deleterious became an occasion for the furtherance of David's plan for the Temple. He now owned the threshing-floor upon which his son would one day build the Temple.

Is God Immutable?

This chapter gives us insights into the nature of God. He is just and righteous and must punish sin (Habakkuk 1:13), yet in grace He gives sinners time to repent. What sometimes causes confusion to readers of the Bible is the fact that, on occasion, God is represented as changing His mind (21:15). And if He does appear to change His mind, how can He be all-knowing (i.e., omniscient)?

This facet of Christian theology falls under the category of God's "immutability" (James 1:17; cf. Psalms 33:11 and 102:25-27). On the one hand, and from our finite perspective, it appears as if God does change His mind (Genesis 6:6); but on the other hand, where there is repentance He sovereignly lifts the punishment (James 2:13b). Such change is evidently a part of His decree. This is illustrated for us in the book of Jonah. Jonah was commissioned to go to Nineveh and pronounce the judgment of God on the city and its people. When the people turned from their evil deeds, God relented and did not punish them (Jonah 3:10).

God's goodness to David and the people of Jerusalem demonstrated that He is gracious and compassionate, slow to anger and abundant in lovingkindness (Jonah 4:2b). And He deals with us in the same way. Peter tells us that He is longsuffering, not willing that any should perish (2 Peter 3:9; cf. Paul's rhetorical question in Romans 2:4, and Christ's own words in John 9:39*a*). No one should treat sin lightly (Matthew 12:36). Our actions have consequences (2 Peter 2:9). Some people's sins are punished in this life as a warning to others, and some will only be punished in the life to come (2 Timothy 5:24), but the Lord will bring each one of us before His judgment seat and we will have to account for our deeds, whether they have been good or evil (Ecclesiastes 12:14; Hebrews 9:27). It is a fearful thing to fall unrepentant and unforgiven into the hands of the living God.

17

Final Preparations
(1 Chronicles 22:1–29:30)

When the Apostle Paul gave instructions to the church in Corinth on the way in which they should conduct their worship services, he stated that everything should be done decently and in order (1 Corinthians 14:40). In these closing chapters of 1 Chronicles it is easy for us to become lost in the long lists of names, and overlook some of the principles that lie latent in these pages. At no time did David want any of his plans for the Temple to detract from the prime focus of every believing Israelite, namely, the worship of the Lord. And we do not want the long lists of names to obscure what we can learn from this portion of God's Word. David wanted the munificence of the Temple to bear testimony to the greatness of God, and that is why his planning was so precise.

These chapters contain three addresses by King David (22:2-19; 28:1-21; and 29:1-9). And, as we found previously (21:20–22:1), it serves to identify the site on which the Temple would be built. Here is the outline we will follow:

Preparation for Building the Temple (22:1–29:30)

The Charge to Build the Temple (22:1-19)
  Initial Preparations (22:1-5)
  Charge to Solomon (22:6-16)
  Charge to the Leaders of the People (22:17-19)

Those Who Are to Minister in the Temple (23:1–26:32)
  Duties of the Levites (23:1-32)
  Duties of the Priests (24:1-31)
  Singers in the Temple (25:1-31)
  Temple Guards (26:1-32)

Organization of the Leaders of the Nation (27:1-34)

David's Final Words of Admonition (28:1–29:30)
    Charge to the People (28:1-19)
    Charge to Solomon (28:20-21)
    Charge to All Israel (29:1-25)
    Conclusion (29:26-30)

At first glance this data is daunting. As the pieces fall into place, however, we shall see how the information flows so that each group, and each person within the group, was fully aware of the duties that had been assigned to them.

The Charge to Build the Temple (22:1-19)

Initial Preparations (22:1-5)

David, having identified the site of the future Temple (22:1), began his initial preparations for the building of the House of the Lord. He selected workers from among Israel's resident aliens (22:2), and provided them with diverse materials (22:3-4). His goal was expressed in verse 5: "And David said, 'My son, Solomon, [is] a youth and tender, and the house to be built to Yahweh [is] to be made exceedingly great, for fame and for beauty to all the land; I pray You, let me prepare for it.' And David prepared in abundance before his death."

The question, however, arises, "How did David know what kind of preparations to make?" According to 28:11-12 the Lord had revealed to him the plan of the Temple (cf. the Tabernacle, Exodus 25:40). As Dr. Warren W. Wiersbe has pointed out, "When you are going to do something for the Lord on earth, be sure you get the plans from heaven."[1]

It is impossible for us to place a value on all that David had set aside for the construction and embellishment of the Temple. All we can say is that he intended it to be the most magnificent building in the ancient Near East at that time.

Charge to Solomon (22:6-16)

At the time David spoke to Solomon, the young lad, now in his late teens, had been crowned king over Israel and had begun a co-regency with his father. In stating things "for the record," David first reviewed the past (22:6-10). Of importance was the fact that, when David expressed his desire to Nathan to build the Temple, Solomon had not yet been born.

> And David said to Solomon, his son, "As for me, it was in my heart to build a house to the name of Yahweh my God; but the word of Yahweh [was] against me, saying, 'Blood in abundance you have shed, and you have made (i.e., waged) great battles; you shall not build a house to My name, for you have shed much blood to (i.e., on) the earth before Me. Behold, a son shall be born to you; he shall be a man of rest, and I will give to him rest from all his enemies all around, for Solomon shall be his name; and peace and quietness I will give to Israel in his days; he shall build a house to My name.'"

David plainly admitted that he had been a man of war. The times demanded it. Solomon (*Selomoh*, from the same root as *salom*, "peace"), however, would enjoy tranquility all his days, and he would build the Temple for the Lord. Other nations had built temples to their gods, and some of these edifices were very impressive. Their deities were invariably rapacious and warlike, and often demanded human sacrifices. It was fitting that the place of worship erected to the true God should honor Him as a God of peace, not war.

David also admonished Solomon to trust the Lord and obey Him. The task of building the Temple would be a daunting one, and there were problems in laying the foundation and in construction that needed to be overcome. David believed, however, that as Solomon trusted the Lord, He would give him the wisdom and discretion he would need.

David then outlined the preparations he had made:

> "And behold, in my affliction, I have prepared for the House of Yahweh a hundred thousand talents of gold, a million talents of

silver; and of bronze and of iron there is no weighing (i.e., a quantity beyond the ability to weigh), for it is in abundance; and wood and stones I have prepared, and you shall add to them. And there [are] workers with you, masons and carvers in stone, and of wood, and every skillful man for every work.

With verse 16 David began to repeat himself. Like an old man he now spoke in generalities. So vast was the store that he had laid up that it boggled the mind, and artisans were ready to be put to work. Nothing, therefore, should hinder Solomon from carrying out this important assignment.

Charge to the Leaders (22:17-19)

David then encouraged the leaders of the people to help Solomon. Their motivation should be gratitude for all that the Lord has done for them:

"Is not Yahweh your God with you? And (i.e., Yes) [He] has given rest to you all around, for He has given into my hand the dwellers of the land, and has subdued the land before Yahweh and before His people."

Once again we note that David's (seemingly) negative opening statement is in reality a Hebraism making a positive assertion. Then he spurred them to action with words designed to focus their hearts and minds on the task at hand:

"Now give your heart and your soul to seek Yahweh your God, and rise up and build the sanctuary of Yahweh God, to bring the Ark of the Covenant of Yahweh, and the vessels of the holiness of God, to the house that will be built to the name of Yahweh."

As a good leader, David was able to communicate what he wanted done in clear, concise terms. No one was in doubt as to what he wanted done. It remained for him to explain where everyone fitted into the overall plan.

Those Who Are to Minister in the Temple (23:1–26:32)

In much the same way that this book opened with a long list of names, so it closes. At the beginning the chronicler was intent on establishing the royal line of David. Now he records the names of those families who were to serve in the Temple.

We may outline the contents of these chapters as follows:

Organization of the Levitical Houses (23:1-32)
 Enumeration of the Levites (23:1-6)
 Organization of the Gershonites (23:7-11)
 Organization of the Kohathites (23:12-20)
 Organization of the Merarites (23:21-23)
 Duties of the Levites (23:24-32)

Organization of the Priests (24:1-31)
 Divisions of the Sons of Aaron (24:1-19)
 Organization of the Kohathites (24:20-25)
 Organization of the Merarites (24:26-31)

Organization of the Musicians (25:1-31)
Organization of the Gatekeepers (26:1-19)
Organization of the Temple Treasuries (26:20-28)
Organization of the Officers Outside the Temple (26:29-32)

It will be observed that what David did set a precedent for everything being done decently and in order. According to 28:13 and 19, David's plan for the efficient functioning of the Temple had been given to him by God.

It will also be noted that the duties of the priests and Levites revolved around twenty-four courses. Each individual performed his assigned duties for two weeks a year. The rest of the time was devoted to ministering to the people in the tribes where they lived. A major part of their time was to be spent teaching them the Word of God.

The work of the Temple included gatekeepers who protected the Temple and its treasures.

All necessary aspects of the work were covered. There was something for each person to do. No job was unimportant, and with the diversity of their gifts, each person could receive a measure of fulfillment from his service.

The Leaders of the Nation (27:1-34)

Nor did David ignore the civil government of his people. In chapter 27 we have the responsibilities assigned to different individuals:

> The Twelve Captains of Israel (27:1-15)
> The Leaders of the Twelve Tribes (27:16-24)
> The Royal Officers (27:25-32)
> The Royal Counselors (27:32-34)

The army was organized into twelve units with an efficient chain-of-command. Each adult male served for one month a year, and the twelve units could be combined quickly in case of emergency.

There is no indication that David had any formal taxation in Israel. Crown expenditure was met by "income" from crown property. In 27:25-32 we have detailed for us the officers who administered these estates and other assets on behalf of the king. He wisely divested himself of all responsibilities that would detract from his duties to his people.

Finally, David had his personal counselors (or advisors). These trusted individuals were consulted on matters of state. The result was that the nation was well governed, and the people prospered.

David's Final Admonition (28:1–29:30)

Charge to the People (28:1-8)

In these verses we have David's second address to all the people. In them, and after a brief introduction (28:1-2*a*), he made it clear that Solomon was to be the builder of the Temple (28:2*b*-10).

Then he handed to Solomon the plans for the Temple (28:11-19), and concluded with an exhortation (28:20-21).

In structure and content this speech was closely related to chapter 22, although there are differences.[2] The similarities should not surprise us, for the subject matter is the same.

David then affirmed that the tribe of Judah had been chosen by God to be the royal tribe (Genesis 24:8-12). In this way he legitimized his dynasty (28:4-7). Such knowledge precluded the possibility of rivals who might try to set someone else on the throne after his death.

Then David charged the officers and all the people to obey God's commands (28:8), for he knew that only by doing so would the nation continue to enjoy God's blessing.

Charge to Solomon (28:9-19)

David had previously charged Solomon with the task of building the Temple (22:6-16). This had been done in the presence of the leaders of the people. Now he repeated the charge in the hearing of all the people. His purpose in doing so was to insure that none challenge Solomon's youthful authority.

"And you, Solomon, my son, know the God of your father, and serve Him with a perfect (i.e., whole) heart, and with a willing mind; for Yahweh searches out all hearts, and He understands every intent of the thoughts. If you seek Him, He will be found by you; but if you forsake Him, He will reject you forever. See, now, for Yahweh has chosen you to build a house for the sanctuary; be strong (i.e., courageous) and act."

Then David gave to his son the plan (lit. pattern) of the porch [of the Temple], and its houses (i.e., buildings), and its treasures (i.e., storehouses), and its upper rooms, and its innermost rooms, and the house (i.e., room) for the mercy seat; and the pattern (i.e., plan) of all that was with him by the Spirit (or, in his mind), for the courts of the house of Yahweh, and for all the rooms all around, for the treasures (i.e., storehouses) of the house of God, and for the treasures (i.e., storehouses) for the dedicated things; and for the divisions of the priests and the Levites and for all the work of the service of the house of Yahweh, and for all the vessels of service in the house of Yahweh; for the gold, by the weight of the gold, and for all the vessels of service; for the all vessels of silver by weight, for all vessels of service; and [by] weight for the golden lampstands, and their golden lamps, with the weight of each lampstand and its lamps; and the weight of silver for the silver lampstands, with the weight of each lampstand and its lamps according to the use of each lampstand; and the gold [by] weight for the tables of showbread, for each table; and silver for the tables of silver; and the forks (i.e., flesh-hooks), and the bowls and the cups (or pitchers), [of] pure gold; and for the basins of gold by weight for each basin; and for the basins of silver by weight for each basin; and for the altar of incense refined gold by weight; and for the patterns (i.e., model) of the chariot, [even] the gold cherubs [that] spread out their wings and cover the Ark of the Covenant of Yahweh.

"All [was] in writing from the hand of Yahweh; He caused me to understand all the works of the pattern (i.e., plan)."

Now none could dispute Solomon's authority.

Of particular encouragement to earnest readers of the Bible is David's statement, "If you seek Him, He will be found by you." So often people offer excuses for not coming to Christ. "I've done terrible things, how can a holy God receive me?" "I have no assurance that I'm one of the elect. Surely I would have some inner assurance – some feeling – if I was numbered among the chosen." "I tried this 'religious stuff' as a child, and it didn't work. Ever since I've determined to live the best way I know how. In the end God will have to accept or reject me on the basis of my merits." And so we could go on. Here, David stated explicitly that if a person truly set out to seek the Lord, He would be found by him or her.

A small problem arises with the word *ru'ah* in verse 12. It can mean "mind" or "spirit" or "Spirit." Some translators believe that it means "mind" (i.e., "all that David had in mind"). Others with equal assurance are convinced the word should be translated "spirit" (i.e., "all that David determined in his spirit"). Still others are convinced the reference is to the Holy Spirit. We may be sure that for a godly man like David, his mind would be in harmony with the Spirit of God. In the end, 28:19 would seem to resolve the debate. "All this," David said, "Yahweh made me understand in writing by His hand upon me, namely, all the details of the plan" (cf. 2 Peter 1:21).[3]

Verses 13-19 mention the duties of the priests and Levites. Their duties will not be suspended once the Temple has been built. After this David listed each of the sacred vessels that Solomon was to have made. The amount of gold and silver to be expended on each (or, where appropriate, bronze or iron) indicated how awe-inspiring the end product would be.

In conclusion, David exhorts Solomon to

> Be strong and courageous, and act; do not fear nor be dismayed, for Yahweh God, my God, is with you. He will not fail you nor forsake you until all the work for the service of the house of Yahweh is finished. Now behold, there are the divisions of the priests and the Levites for all the service of the house of God, and every willing man of any skill will be with you in all the work for all kinds of service. The officials also and all the people will be entirely at your command (28:20-21).

The Provision for the Temple (29:1-25)

The concluding aspects of David's reign bring to a close his story. The chronicler recorded the provision he made for the Temple (29:1-5); the contribution of the people (29:6-9); David's final prayer of thanksgiving (29:10-19); the second coronation of Solomon, followed by his accession to the throne (29:20-25); and David's death (29:26-30).

In order for the people to feel that they have had a part in the building and embellishment of the Temple, David appealed to them for their support. He encouraged them to give of their means. All offer willingly so that an impressive amount of gold, silver, brass and iron is donated to the Temple. Their willing identification with him in this project impressed the aged king with their sincerity. Raising his hands over the assembled throng, he led them in a prayer of praise:

Blessed are You, O Yahweh, God of Israel our father, forever and ever. Yours, O Yahweh, is the greatness and the power and the glory and the victory and the majesty, indeed everything that is in the heavens and the earth; Yours is the dominion, O Yahweh, and You exalt Yourself as head over all. Both riches and honor come from You, and You rule over all, and in Your hand is power and might; and it lies in Your hand to make great and to strengthen everyone. Now therefore, our God, we thank You, and praise Your glorious name. But who am I and who are my people that we should be able to offer as generously as this? For all things come from You, and from Your hand we have given You. For we are sojourners before You, and tenants, as all our fathers were; our days on the earth are like a shadow, and there is no hope. O Yahweh, our God, all this abundance that we have provided to build You a house for Your holy name, it is from Your hand, and all is Yours. Since I know, O my God, that You try the heart and delight in uprightness, I, in the integrity of my heart, have willingly offered all these things; so now with joy I have seen Your people, who are present here, make their offerings willingly to You. O Yahweh, the God of Abraham, Isaac and Israel, our fathers, preserve this forever in the intentions of the heart of Your people, and direct their heart to You; and give to my son Solomon a perfect heart to keep Your commandments, Your testimonies and Your statutes, and to do them all, and to build the temple, for which I have made provision.

The next day they offered sacrifices to the Lord (29:21-22). Then they crowned Solomon king a second time, and they anointed him as ruler on Yahweh's behalf. Then all the officials, the mighty men, and also the sons of David pledged their allegiance to him.

Conclusion (29:26-30)

With all of this accomplished, David was able to die a happy man. The biblical historian sums up his reign for us:

Now David the son of Jesse reigned over all Israel. The period that he reigned over Israel was forty years; he reigned in Hebron seven years and in Jerusalem thirty-three years. Then he died in a ripe old age, full of days, riches and honor; and his son Solomon reigned in his place."

It is common in our day for writers to emphasize David's failings, and to try and "cut him down to size" – our size. But this is not the testimony of Scripture. Long life is a gift of God, and David lived to a "ripe old age." He had lived a full life. In addition, in the Old Testament wealth was often a sign of God's favor. In spite of David's donation to the Temple, he was nonetheless rich. And he was held in the highest esteem by his people (i.e., he was "full ... of honor").

And so the first book of Chronicles comes to an end. David died, but the work of God continued, and in Second Chronicles the inspired historian will tell us about those who succeeded David on the throne.

References

Introduction

[1]Bibliographic details for these commentaries are as follows:

E. L. Curtis and A. A. Madsen, *A Critical and Exegetical Commentary on the Books of Chronicles,* International Critical Commentary, Edinburgh: Clark, 1910;

J. M. Myers, *1 Chronicles: Introduction, Translation and Notes* and *2 Chronicles: Introduction, Translation and Notes*, The Anchor Bible, Garden City, NY: Doubleday, 1965.

J. G. McConville, *I and II Chronicles*, Daily Study Bible, Philadelphia: Westminster, 1984.

M. J. Selman, *1 Chronicles: An Introduction and Commentary* and *2 Chronicles: An Introduction and Commentary,* Tyndale Old Testament Commentaries, Leicester, UK: InterVarsity, 1994.

J. A. Thompson, *1, 2 Chronicles*, New American Commentary, Nashville: Broadman and Holman, 1994.

M. Wilcock, *The Message of Chronicles*, The Bible Speaks Today, Leicester, UK: InterVarsity, 1987.

[2]*The Talmud*, Baba Bathra, 15a. R. H. Pfeiffer, however, in his *Introduction to the Old Testament* (New York: Harper & Brothers, 1948), 782-811, argues for a date of composition much later than the time of Ezra. M. F. Unger in an *Introductory Guide to the Old Testament* (Grand Rapids: Zondervan, 1970), 407-09, ably refutes his views.

[3]The authorship of Chronicles is discussed in all introductory studies and critical commentaries. Examples of the former include B. S. Childs, *Introduction to the Old Testament as Scripture* (Philadelphia: Fortress, 1979), 643-47; R. K. Harrison, *Introduction to the Old Testament* (Grand Rapids: Eerdmans, 1969), 1169-71; and J. A. Soggin, *Introduction to the Old Testament*, 3d ed., (Louisville, KY: Westminster/John Knox, 1989), 483-88. In addition to the commentaries mentioned earlier in this chapter, issues of authorship are discussed by R. Braun, *1 Chronicles*, Word Biblical Commentary (Waco, TX: Word, 1986), xxiii-iv; and S. Japhet, *I & II Chronicles*, Old Testament Library (Louisville, KY: Westminster/John Knox, 1993), 23-27. It is important for the lay student of God's Word to realize that negative issues have been answered by conservative scholars (cf. Archer, *Survey of Old Testament Introduction*, 390; Harrison, *Introduction to the Old Testament*, 1157; B. K. Waltke, in

New Perspectives on the Old Testament, ed. J. B. Payne (Waco, TX: Word, 1970), 212-39.

Here are a few representative journal articles: W. F. Albright, for example, was convinced of Ezra's authorship (see *Journal of Biblical Literature* 40 [1921], 104-24; *idem, Biblical Archaeologist* 9, 1 [1946] 15). S. Japhet, *Vetus Testamentum* 18 (1968), 332-72, sought to refute Ezra's involvement as compiler. See also M. Throntveit, *Vetus Testamentum* 32 (1982), 201-16, and D. N. Freedman, *Catholic Biblical Quarterly* 23 (1961), 436-42.

[4]See Archer, *Survey of Old Testament Introduction*, 391-92.

[5]Cf. E. J. Young, *An Introduction to the Old Testament* (Grand Rapids: Eerdmans, 1949), 414.

[6]See D. N. Freedman, *Catholic Biblical Quarterly* 23 (1961), 436-41; J. D. Newsome, Jr., *Journal of Biblical Literature* 94 (1975), 201-17. When compared with Samuel-Kings, Ezra omitted information not pertinent to his purpose. Here is a brief summary of the most significant omissions: The life of Samuel (1 Samuel 1–7); Saul's reign (1 Samuel 8–15); David's exile (1 Samuel 16–30); David's conflict with Abner and Ish-bosheth (2 Samuel 1–4); David's dual acts of adultery and murder (2 Samuel 11-12); Absalom's rebellion (2 Samuel 13–20); Adonijah's attempts to seize the throne (1 Kings 1–2); Solomon's marriage to Pharaoh's daughter (1 Kings 3); Solomon's royal palace (1 Kings 7); Solomon's wives and enemies (1 Kings 11); Events in the Northern Kingdom (1 Kings 12–2 Kings 17); Abijah's sinful character (1 Kings 15:3-5); Jehosophat's campaign with Jehoram (2 Kings 3); Hezekiah's payment of tribute to Sennacherib (2 Kings 18:7-8, 13-16); Jehoahaz' evil character (2 Kings 23:32); Jehoiakim's rebellion (2 Kings 23:35; 24:1-4); the siege of Jerusalem and Zedekiah's captivity (2 Kings 25:1-7, 18-21); Gedaliah's appointment and death (2 Kings 25:12, 23-26); and Jehoiachin's release from prison (2 Kings 25:27-30).

[7]Data found in the Books of Chronicles that is not found in Samuel–Kings (or appears in a different form): The genealogies (I:1–9); David's mighty men (I:12); David's preparations for the building of the Temple (I:22); David's organization of both Temple and civil workers (I:23–27); the loyalty of the Levites to Rehoboam (II:11); Rehoboam's fortifications and family (II:11); Asa's peaceful reign, covenant, and sin (II:14:1; 15:1-15, 19; 16:7-10); Jehosophat's fortifications, reforms, "Bible teaching" ministry of the Levites, warning by Jehu, et cetera

(II:17–20); Jehoram's slaughter of his brothers (II:21); Jehoiada's death (II:24:15-16); Joash's sins (II:24:3, 17-19); Zechariah's martyrdom (II:24); Hazael's defeat of Judah (II:24); Amaziah's mercenaries and sins (II:25); Uzziah's army and fortifications (II:26); Jotham's defeat of the Ammonites (II:27); Ahaz's punishment by Edomites and Philistines (II:28); Hezekiah's reforms (II:29–31); Manasseh's captivity, repentance, and return (II:33); Josiah's early reforms (II:34); the decree of Cyrus (II:36:22-23).

[8]The persistent disobedience of the Hebrews to God's revealed will had eventually resulted in the fulfillment of Deuteronomy 28:15-68. The conquest of Jerusalem by Nebuchadnezzar had ushered in a period of Jewish history that would be known as "the times of the Gentiles" (Luke 21:24). This era began in 587 B.C. and will continue until the coming of Christ at the end of the age.

[9]Such a view differs from C. C. Torrey's *The Chronicler's History of Israel* (New Haven, CT: Yale University Press, 1954), x, xix, xxxi-xxxii; *idem, American Journal of Semitic Languages and Literatures* 25 (1908-09), 157-73, 200, who sees the Books of Chronicles as an anti-Samaritan polemic. Torrey also believes that Chronicles-Ezra-Nehemiah were originally one book, and that Nehemiah was the author. He also differs from the theory proposed by R. H. Pfeiffer who saw in Chronicles a compilation of data intended as pro-Levitical propaganda (see his *Introduction to the Old Testament*, 782-811).

[10]Cf. G. L. Archer, *A Survey of Old Testament Introduction*, rev. ed. (Chicago: Moody, 1994), 75-81.

1. An Unexpected Oasis (1 Chronicles 1:1–9:44)

[1]S. Japhet, in *I and II Chronicles*, Old Testament Library (Louisville, KY: Westminster, 1993), 109, writes: "Jabez is mentioned in 2.55 as a place-name. Although from a literary point of view there is no connection [between Jabez' name and the town of the same name], these two passages may, in the present genealogical framework, be somehow related to the 'Ephrathite' element within Judah."

[2]*The New International Dictionary of Old Testament Theology and Exegesis*, ed. by W. A. VanGemeren, 5 vols. (Grand Rapids: Zondervan, 1996), II:577-87.

[3]C. R. Swindoll favors this interpretation. See "Missions, Motivation ... and Me," Sermon #220, Evangelical Free Church of Fullerton, California (June 13, 1976); and "Jabez, Jehovah, and George!" Sermon

#480, Evangelical Free Church of Fullerton, California (June 21, 1981).

[4]Helen Keller, *The Story of My Life* (New York: Dutton, 1956, 166pp.; *idem, Teacher, Anne Sullivan Macy* (Garden City, NY: Doubleday, 1955), 247pp.

[5]E. M. Bounds, *Preacher and Prayer* (Grand Rapids: Zondervan, n.d.), 99.

[6]Little is available on John Hyde's life. The following books can be read with profit: B. W. Miller, *Praying Hyde* (Grand Rapids: Zondervan, 1943), 132pp.; and F. A. McGaw, *Praying Hyde* (Philadelphia: Sunday School Times, 1923), 64pp.

2. Saul's Nemesis (1 Chronicles 10:1-14)

[1]Hesiod, *The Homeric Hymns and Homerica*, trans. By H. G. Evelyn-White, Loeb Classical Library (Cambridge, MA: Harvard University Press, 1964), 95 ("Theogony," line 223).

[2]H. T. Peck, ed., *Harper's Dictionary of Classical Literature and Antiquities* (New York: Cooper Square, 1965), 1086; and C. B. Avery, *New Century Handbook of Greek Mythology and Legend* (New York: Appleton-Century-Crofts, 1972), 369.

[3]D. N. Freedman, *Catholic Biblical Quarterly* 23 (1961), 436-42.

[4]Y. Aharoni, M. Avi-Yonah, eds., *The Macmillan Bible Atlas*, completely revised 3d ed. by A. F. Rainey, and Z. Safrai, (New York: Macmillan, 1993), 68-69. Hereafter cited by title. For a discussion of Philistia and the Philistines, see C. R. Conder, *The Bible and the East* (Edinburgh: W. Blackwood, 1896), 25-27, 32, 110, 117-21, 147; *idem, Palestine* (London: G. Philip, 1889), 35-36, 40. The value of Conder's works lies in the fact that he mapped out the lands of the Bible *before* they were thrust into the 20th century. His descriptions of the places where biblical events took place are of the utmost value. Up-to-date archaeological data can easily be obtained from other sources.

[5]*Macmillan Bible Atlas,* 212, 230. See C. R. Conder's excellent description of the valley and the events that took place on that plain in his *Tent Work in Palestine*, 2 vols. (London: R. Bentley, 1878), I:110-35.

[6]*Macmillan Bible Atlas*, 95.

[7]E. Robinson, *Biblical Researches in Palestine*, 3 vols. (London: J. Murray, 1856), II:316-17, 325; III:336-37; W. M. Thomson, *The Land and the Book*, 3 vols., (New York: Harper and Brothers, 1886), I:324; II:173-75, 177,198-200,208-10; III:579. See also C. Herzog and M. Gichon, *Battles of the Bible* (New York: Random, 1978), 72-74, and

R. Gale, *Great Battles of Biblical History* (London: Hutchinson, 1968), 40-43.

[8]J. M. Myers, *I Chronicles*, Anchor Bible (Garden City, NY: Doubleday, 1965), 78. Used by permission.

[9]W. Manchester, *American Caesar* (Boston: Little, Brown, 1978), 250.

[10]D. Zeligs, *Psychoanalysis and the Bible* (New York: Bloch, 1974), 121-59, makes much of Saul's emotional instability, low self-esteem and castration complex. She believes his self-inflicted death was his punishment of himself for his aggressive wishes. Though at times insightful, her opinions should be read with caution. A different approach was taken by J. S. Baxter in *Mark These Men* (London: Marshall, Morgan and Scott, 1955), 23-36. Baxter has some wise observations on the text, but obliquely side-steps important interpretative issues.

[11]J. G. McConville, *I and II Chronicles*, Daily Study Bible (Philadelphia: Westminster, 1984), 15. See also S. Zalewski, *Vetus Testamentum* 39 (1989), 449-67.

[12]Some of the people of Dan had migrated to Laish, cf. Judges 18.

[13]It seems probable that these tribes received help from the east. Abner placed Ish-bosheth on the throne in Mahanaim, thus continuing the Saulide dynasty (2 Samuel 2:8). It is probable that, over time, Abner brought relief to the Israelites living in Ashur, Jezreel, Ephraim, and Benjamin by expelling the Philistines (2 Samuel 2:9, for this is the only way Ish-bosheth could have ruled over them). Though Ish-bosheth reigned over the tribes east of the River Jordan for about five years, he reigned over the tribes west of the Jordan for only two years – making a reign of seven years in all, and approximating the length of David's reign in Hebron).

[14]No mention is made of David ousting the Philistines from the land of Israel after he became king over all Israel, and so it is possible that they did not take permanent possession of the Valley of the Esdraelon or any Israelite cities.

[15]W. Rudolph, *Vetus Testamentum* 4 (1954), 401-09; W. F. Albright, *Archaeology and the Religion of Israel* (London: Penguin, 1954), 74-75, 106, 220.

[16]Cf. C. F. Pfeiffer, *The Biblical World* (Grand Rapids: Baker, 1966), 143-44.

[17]*Macmillan Bible Atlas*, 87.

[18]Cf. M. J. Selman, *1 Chronicles*, Tyndale Old Testament Commentaries (Downers Grove, IL: InterVarsity, 1994), 136.

[19]I have dealt with this aspect of Saul's personality in *The Books of Samuel* (Neptune, NJ: Loizeaux, 1994), 108-326.

[20]R. L. Harris, G. L. Archer, Jr., and B. K. Waltke, eds., *Theological Wordbook of the Old Testament*, 2 vol. (Chicago: Moody, 1980), #1230a (I:519-20).

[21]*Macmillan Bible Atlas*, 75-76, 96.

3. Finally ... God's Word Fulfilled (1 Chronicles 11:1-9).

[1]*Aesop's Fables* (New York: Sears, n.d.), 61.

[2]Robinson, *Biblical Researches*, II:431-46; M. Avi-Yonah, *The Holy Land* (Grand Rapids: Baker,1972), 13, 16-18, 54, 96, 128, 224.

[3]W. M. Taylor, *David: King of Israel* (Grand Rapids: Baker, 1961), 201.

[4]See *Theological Wordbook of the Old Testament*, II:764 (#1910).

[5]*New International Dictionary of Old Testament Theology and Exegesis*, II:946 (#4864); R. C. Steiner, *Bulletin of the American Schools of Oriental Research* 140 (1989), 15-23.

[6]B. L. Montgomery, *The Path to Leadership* (London: Collins, 1961), 9-10.

[7]See J. P. Newman, *From Dan to Beersheba: A Description of the Wonderful Land*, rev. ed. (New York: Hunt and Eaton, 1892), 485pp.

[8]An excellent, readable resume of these events is to be found in G. F. Owen's *Abraham to the Middle East Crisis* (London: Pickering & Inglis, 1957), 45-55. At the time of the conquest of Canaan, Jerusalem had obtained preeminence among the south-Canaanitish city-states. Adonizedek had been defeated and slain by the Israelites under Joshua, and the city had been burned. The Jebusites rebuilt the city and in a later battle with the Benjamites, successfully defended it.

[9]Josephus, *Antiquities of the Jews*, VII:3:1.

[10]The key to the problem lies in the usage of the word *sinnor* (cf. W. Gesenius, *A Hebrew and English Lexicon of the Old Testament*, trans. E. Robinson, eds. F. Brown, S. R. Driver and C. A. Briggs (Oxford: Clarendon, 1962), 857*b* (hereafter cited as Brown, Driver and Briggs). Further information is to be found in Robinson, *Biblical Researches,* I:323ff.; III:243-45.

Recent scholars have rejected this view. Cf. K. M. Kenyon, *The Bible and Recent Archaeology*, rev. by P. R. S. Moorey (Atlanta: John

Knox, 1987), 92. She claims that this shaft was not built for one hundred years after the time of David. It should be noted however that the Oxford professor made a similar claim regarding the Garden Tomb and "Gordon's Calvary." She reversed her opinion before her death. It is possible, therefore, that some objective archaeologist will arise to give to the world a definitive answer to this problem. Though L. Wood, in his *Survey of Israel's History*, 266, note 22, does not advance evidence for his views, he does state that "Since the Jebusites *already had* a slanting tunnel to the Spring of Gihon, it may have been this tunnel that David's men employed" (emphasis added).

Most biblical historians bypass the capture of Jerusalem without citing how the city was taken (e.g., J. Bright, *A History of Israel*, ed., [Philadelphia: Westminster, 1981], 198; and M. Noth, *The History of Israel*, 2d ed., [London: Black, 1965], 188). It is to the credit of W. C. Kaiser, Jr., that he takes a fresh look at the meaning of *sinnor*, and though he disagrees with the position taken in this book, his material is worthy of consideration (see his *A History of Israel* [Nashville: Broadman & Holman, 1998] 244).

[11]The word always appears with the article.

[12]Consider, for example, the teaching of Scripture concerning Christ. It was predicted that He would be a descendant of King David (cf. 2 Samuel 7:12-16 and Matthew 1:1). God, speaking through Isaiah said that He would be born of a virgin (cf. Isaiah 7:14 and Matthew 1:23). The Old Testament prophets predicted that a forerunner would announce His arrival (cf. Isaiah 40:3 and Malachi 3:1 with Matthew 3:3). And so we could go on. In every instance God's Word was fulfilled literally even though hundreds of years separated the prediction from the fulfillment. Two thousand years ago an announcement was made to Mary (see Luke 1:30-33). We still wait for the full realization of this promise, but when it comes to pass it will be exactly in accordance with all that Mary understood by Gabriel's words.

4. David's Mighty Men (1) (1 Chronicles 11:10)

[1]See his autobiography *To Hell and Back* (New York: MJF Books, 1977), 274pp.

[2]Data can be gleaned from R. O. Corvin's *David and His Mighty Men* (Freeport, NY: Books for Libraries, 1970), 175pp.; B. Mazar, *Vetus Testamentum* 13 (1963), 311-20; H. G. M. Williamson,

Oudtestamentische Studien 21 (1981), 164-76; N. Na'aman, *Vetus Testamentum* 38 (1988), 71-79; D. G. Schley, *Vetus Testamentum* 40 (1990), 321-26.

[3]W. G. Blaikie, *The First Book of Samuel* (Minneapolis: Klock and Klock, 1978), 339.

[4]*Macmillan Bible Atlas*, 145.

[5]*Macmillan Bible Atlas*, 94.

[6]Gale, *Great Battles of Biblical History*, 42-44; Herzog and Gichon, *Battles of the Bible*, 72-74.

[7]*Macmillan Bible Atlas*, 95.

[8]*Macmillan Bible Atlas*, 98, 112-13.

[9]Corvin, *David and His Mighty Men*, 36.

[10]See the writer's *Nehemiah and the Dynamics of Effective Leadership* (Neptune, NJ: Loizeaux, 1976), 189pp.

5. David's Mighty Men (2) (1 Chronicles 11:12-14)

[1]No mention is made of the Disruption of 1843 in the *New International Dictionary of the Christian Church*, ed. J. D. Douglas (Grand Rapids: Zondervan, 1974), or in the *Westminster Dictionary of Church History*, ed. J. C. Brauer (Philadelphia: Westminster,1971).

[2]P. Tournier, *The Naming of Persons* (New York: Harper and Row, 1975), 3-30.

[3]P. Tournier, *The Strong and the Weak* (Philadelphia: Westminster, 1963), 57.

[4]P. Tournier, *The Meaning of Persons* (New York: Harper and Row, 1957), 50.

[5]*Ibid.*, 80.

[6]Reported in *The Plain Dealer* (Cleveland, OH: February 15, 1977).
[7]*Ibid.*

[8]*Macmillan Bible Atlas*, 100. See also Blaikie, *Second Samuel*, 338ff.
[9]Blaikie, *Second Samuel*, 338ff.

[10]Many older commentators believe that Eleazar's hand became covered with the blood of his enemies. As the blood congealed his sword became "stuck" to his hand (cf. Corvin, *David and His Mighty Men*, 50). They overlook the explicit statement that his hand became "weary." Muscles taxed to their limit first stiffen, and then harden in a painful spasm.

[11]Address at Harrow School, October 29, 1941.

[12]See F. Houghton's *Amy Carmichael of Dohnavur* (London:

S.P.C.K., 1953), 3-53.

[13]His story is told in W. Y. Fullerton's *F. B. Meyer: A Biography* (Harrisburg, PA: Christian Alliance, n.d.).

[14]J. Perry, *Sgt. York: His Life, Legend and Legacy* (Nashville: Broadman & Holman1997), 349pp.

[15]C. E. Macartney, *The Making of a Minister* (Great Neck, NY: Channel, 1961), 184ff.

6. David's Mighty Men (3) (1 Chronicles 11:14)

[1]Cypress trees are common along the Pacific coast of California. They grow well in deep, dry, sandy loam, or airy sheltered sites. Their wood is of a very fine texture, and is extremely durable. In ancient Egypt, cypress wood was used to make the coffins of the Pharaohs, and some of them, that are 4,000 years old, can be seen in museums today. Cf. G. B. Gudworth, *Forest Trees of the Pacific Slope* (New York: Dover, 1967), 158-59; *Encyclopedia Britannica*, 11th ed. (1910), VII:693-94.

[2]Second Samuel 23:9 states that on a former occasion the Philistines' purpose was to do battle. That was when we read about Eleazar. In 23:11 there is no mention of a battle. It may well be that on this occasion a raiding party came to plunder the crops and rob the villagers.

[3]Most commentators agree that the scribe copying an old manuscript of Chronicles inadvertently omitted part of the information about Shammah. We are compelled, therefore, to consult the text of 2 Samuel 23 for data to complete the first triad of David's mighty men. Cf. Selman, *1 Chronicles*, 142.

[4]The name "Shammah" appears in different forms. For example, one of David's brothers named "Shanurah," is called "Shimeah, Shimea, Shimei, and Shimma in 1 Samuel 16:9; 2 Samuel 13:3 and 21:21; and 1 Chronicles 2:13. The *Zondervan Pictorial Encyclopedia of the Bible* (1975), V:374 identifies Shammah of 2 Samuel 23:11ff. with Shamhuth of 1 Chronicles 27:8.

[5]R. R. Carkhuff and B. G. Berenson, *Beyond Counseling and Therapy* (New York: Holt, Reinhart and Winston, 1967), 218-19. (Emphasis in the original.)

[6]King Saul followed the first two steps of this process in his attempt to neutralize David. At first he promoted him, then he attempted to kill him. He never changed and David remained a powerful force in the kingdom.

[7]There are many biographies on the life and labors of Martin Luther.

The one I have used in preparation of this chapter is R. H. Bainton's *Here I Stand* (Nashville: Abingdon, 1950), 121-90.

[8]Hollywood made a movie about Gordon's governorship of the Sudan entitled *Khartoum*. It stars Charlton Heston and Lawrence Olivier, and captures the power of Gordon's personality as well as portraying the formidable forces arraigned against him.

[9]H. W. Gordon, *Events in the Life of Charles George Gordon* (London: Kegan Paul, Trench, 1886), 324-408.

[10]This process has been explained in the author's books *Always a Winner* (Ventura, CA: Gospel Light, 1977), 160pp., and *Dynamic Personal Bible Study* (Neptune, NJ: Loizeaux, 1981), 139-48.

7. The Marks of Friendship (1 Chronicles 11:15-19)

[1]H. Black, *Friendship* (Chicago: Revell, 1903), 26.

[2]R. W. Emerson, *Friendship: Two Essays* (New York: Putnam, 1909), 61.

[3]G. Inrig, *Quality Friendship* (Chicago: Moody, 1981), 223pp.

[4]The best book on this subject is D. E. Hiebert's *Personalities Around Paul* (Chicago: Moody, 1973), 270pp. Other treatments can be traced through *The Minister's Library*, (Neptune, NJ: Loizeaux, 1984-86), 2 vols.

[5]Blaikie, *Second Samuel*, 344-45.

[6]One of the major problems facing archaeologists working in this part of the Holy Land is their daily need of water. Water is normally brought in by truck. David and his men had no such conveyances. His needs, as well as the needs of his wives and the six hundred men and their families (besides animals), was considerable. Each person would need at least a gallon of drinking water a day, with more required for washing and cooking. The dry summer months (which form the backdrop of our story) were extremely difficult ones for all concerned.

[7]*Macmillan Bible Atlas*, 73, 100.

[8]*Macmillan Bible Atlas*, 119, 140.

[9]*Psychology Today*, 13 (October 1979), 12.

[10]E. Kennedy, *U. S. News and World Report* (September 26, 1983), 71.

[11]C. N. Strait, *Quote* (June 1, 1982), 257.

[12]The "well by the gate" cannot now be identified with certainty (see Robinson, *Biblical Researches*, I:473). C. Ritter in *Comparative Geography of Palestine* ... (New York: Greenwood, 1968), III:340-41

relates how certain Roman Catholic monks draw water from "David's Well." This well is three-quarters of a mile north of Bethlehem and cannot be the one referred to in either 2 Samuel 23 or 1 Chronicles 11.

[13]D. Reisman, *The Lonely Crowd* (New Haven, CT: Yale University Press, 1970), 9-26. Though somewhat dated, Reisman's observations are important.

[14]Aristotle, *Nicomachean Ethics*, VIII:3:ix.

[15]Cicero, *De Amicitia*, XX.

8. The Power Within (1 Chronicles 11:20-21)

[1]Quoted in H. H. Johnston, *Livingstone and the Exploration of Central Africa* (London: Philip and Son, 1891), 147f.

[2]E. Bulwer-Lytton, *The Last Days of Pompeii* (New York: Dodd, Mead, 1946), 356pp.

[3] The writer of Chronicles gives the order of birth. In 2 Samuel 23:18 and 24 Zeruiah's sons are listed in the order of their prominence with Asahel being the youngest.

[4]The Hebrew text has "the spear." The reference is to Saul's spear, which was stuck in the ground near where the king lay. In Abishai's mind he may have felt that there was irony as well as poetic justice if Saul should be killed with his own spear.

[5]Cf. C. J. Barber and J. D. Carter, *Always a Winner* (Ventura, CA: Gospel Light, 1977), 137-48.

[6]Various views have been offered to explain what took place. They have been summarized by J. Mauchline in *1 and 2 Samuel* (Grand Rapids: Eerdmans, 1982), 205f.

[7] To have sexual intercourse with the wife or concubine of a king was tantamount to laying claim to the throne. This is what Absalom did in 2 Samuel 16:20ff., intimating by his act that he had the power to take his father's throne. Adonijah did essentially the same thing when he asked for Abishag to be given to him as his wife (1 Kings 2:13ff.). It was *after* this act that Ish-bosheth was too weak to punish (2 Samuel 3:6-8), that Abner represented himself to David as the *de facto* lord of the northern tribes. Cf. Mauchline, *1 and 2 Samuel*, 208ff. See also H. W. Hertzberg, *I and II Samuel*. Old Testament Library (Philadelphia: Westminster, 1964), 254-58.

9. Success, Without Compromise or Regret (1 Chronicles 11:22-25)

[1]Quoted in *U. S. News and World Report* (July 21, 1975), 18.

[2]*U. S. News and World Report*, (April 22, 1985), 44.

[3]*Ibid.*, 68.

[4]R. C. Stedman, *Discovery Papers* (November 4, 1973), 1-2.

[5]B. Larson, *There's a Lot More to Health Than Not Being Sick* (Waco, TX: Word, 1981), 74.

10. The Loyalty of a Friend (1 Chronicles 11:26-47)

[1]In reality thirty-seven (2 Samuel 23:39b), though this number varied from time to time. To "The Thirty" must be added the names of the men in the first and second triads, with either Joab or David (who are not mentioned in the list) completing the number.

[2]Blaikie, *Second Samuel*, 345.

[3]This is particularly true of the Book(s) of Chronicles. It is so often treated as an afterthought and this may account for the fact that commentators pay scant attention to details. It is necessary, therefore, to consult expositions of the Book(s) of Samuel in hope of finding information. Unfortunately, here, too, our search is frustrated by deliberate avoidance. E.g., A. A. Anderson, *2 Samuel*, Word Biblical Commentary (Dallas, TX: Word, 1989), 277; J. G. Baldwin, *1 & 2 Samuel*, Tyndale Old Testament Commentaries (Downers Grove, IL: InterVarsity, 1988), 294; Mauchline, *1 and 2 Samuel*, New Century Bible (Greenwood, NC: Attic, 1971), 319.

[4]H. P. Smith, who proposes to rearrange the text, believes Asahel was the third man (see *A Critical and Exegetical Commentary on the Books of Samuel*, International Critical Commentary [New York: Scribner's, 1902], 386-87. He is followed by Hertzberg, *I & II Samuel*, 406-07.

[5]Cf. Blaikie, *Second Book of Samuel*, 345.

[6]Little has been written on Ittai. For a brief, devotional study, see the author's *God Has the Answer ...* (Grand Rapids: Baker, 1974), 32-40.

[7]Matthew Henry has said that a person who "aims at the crown, aims at the head that wears it." David knew that his son intended to take his life.

[8]*Macmillan Bible Atlas, 108-09.*

[9]Josephus, *Antiquities of the Jews*, VII:x:1.

11. When God Is At Work (1 Chronicles 11:26–12:40)

[1] J. R. Lowell, *The Complete Poetical Works of James Russell Lowell*, ed. H. C. Scudder (Boston: Houghton, Mifflin, 1925), 67.

[2] *Macmillan Bible Atlas*, 94.

[3] Apocrypha, *Ecclesiasticus*, 44:7-9.

[4] Selwyn, *1 Chronicles*, 145.

[5] *Macmillan Bible Atlas*, 92, 119, 140. For a description, see Conder, *Tent Work in Palestine*, II:156; Robinson, *Biblical Researches*, I:481-82; G. A. Smith, *Historical Geography of the Holy Land*, 25th ed., (London: Hodder & Stoughton, 1931), 224-25; and Thomson, *The Land and the Book*, I:330, 332-35, 358; II:48-49.

[6] *Macmillan Bible Atlas*, 92. For a description, see Conder, *Tent Work in Palestine*, II:134; Robinson, *Biblical Researches*, I:500, 504, 506, 508; Smith, *Historical Geography*, 93, 259, 265-66, 277, 504ff., 593; and Thomson, *The Land and the Book*, I:312-14, 316-20, 423-35; III:534.

[7] *Macmillan Bible Atlas*, 92. For a description, see Conder, *Tent Work in Palestine*, II:149; Smith, *Historical Geography*, 93,137, 256, 269, 299; and Thomson, *The Land and the Book*, I: 292-95; III:586

12. The Ark Narrative (1) (1 Chronicles 13:1–16:43)

[1] J. M. Stowell, III, in *Perilous Pursuits* (Chicago: Moody, 1994), 13-81 enlarges on this theme. See also R. K. Harrison, ed., *Encyclopedia of Biblical and Christian Ethics*, rev. ed. (Nashville: Nelson, 1992), 354-56.

[2] *Macmillan Bible Atlas*, 73, 140. See Robinson, *Biblical Researches*, II:11; III:157; and Thomson, *The Land and the Book*, II:61-65.

[3] *New Unger's Bible Dictionary*, 1245. For additional information, see J. Strong, *The Tabernacle of Israel in the Desert* (1888); W. S. Caldecott, *The Tabernacle: Its History and Structure* (1904); S. Ridout, *Lectures on the Tabernacle* (1952); R. H. Mount, Jr., *The Law Prophesied* (1963); A. H. Hillyard, *The Tabernacle in the Wilderness* (1965); M. L. G. Guillebaud, *Evangelical Quarterly* 31 (1959), 90-96; J. Blenkinsopp, *Journal of Biblical Literature* 88 (1969), 143-56; H. W. Soltau, *The Holy Vessels and Furniture of the Tabernacle* (1970); S. F. Olford, *The Tabernacle* (1971); L. T. Talbot, *Christ in the Tabernacle* (1978); G. H. Dolman and M. Rainsford, *The Tabernacle* (1982); H. W. Soltau, *The Tabernacle, the Priesthood, and the Offerings* (1985).

[4] Two statements, chosen at random, illustrate this point: "Do not let

us speak of darker days; let *us* speak rather of sterner days. These are not dark days: These are great days – the greatest days our country has ever lived; and *we* must all thank God that *we* have been allowed, each of *us* according to *our* stations, to play a part in making these days memorable in the history of *our* race." And "*We* kept on doing *our* best, *we* kept on improving. *We* profited by *our* mistakes and *our* experiences. *We* turned misfortune to good account." (Emphasis added.)

[5]It is difficult to reconcile the different accounts of the length of Saul's reign. The reign of Ish-bosheth, Saul's son, clouds the issues. Without being dogmatic, it would appear as if the Saulide dynasty (i.e., Saul and Ish-bosheth) lasted from 1043 to 1011 B.C. However, through these years are assigned to the Saulide dynasty, there was at least one period of time when there was no one to sit on Saul's throne.

[6]See Selwyn, *I Chronicles,* 36-37.

[7]Obed-edom is thought by many to have been a foreigner, probably a Philistine. However, he may have been born in Gath while his parents were living there temporarily. We do know that on other occasions Hebrews sought refuge in Philistia (e.g., David, 1 Samuel 21:10-15; and the unnamed woman in Elisha's time, 2 Kings 8:1-3)

[8]J. Hall, *Contemplations on the Historical Passages of the Old and New Testaments* (London: Society for the Promoting of Christian Knowledge, n.d.), 214.

13. The Ark Narrative (2) (1 Chronicles 13:1–16:43)

[1]K. D. Randle. His book was published in 1995 by M. Evans, New York.

[2]R. De Vaux, *Ancient Israel: Its Life and Institutions*, trans. J. McHugh (New York: McGraw-Hill, 1961), 297-302.

[3]Japhet, *Ideology*, 416-27.

[4]*Macmillan Bible Atlas*, 115. In earlier times Israel's southern border had been referred to as the "brook of Egypt," possibly the *Wadi el-Arish*. See S. Japhet, *Journal of Biblical Literature* 98 (1979), 208ff.

[5] *Macmillan Bible Atlas*, 104-05, 148. See also S. Japhet, *Journal of Biblical Literature* 98 (1979), 209.

[6]See Brown, Driver and Briggs, eds., *Hebrew Lexicon*, 354.

[7]Verse 14 has a triple use of the Hebrew *bayit*, "to bless." Obed-edom's family, and house, and household are included in God's blessing.

[8]Cf . Harrison, *Introduction to the Old Testament*, 1166.

[9]See the work by C. J. Barber and G. H. Strauss, *Leadership: The Dynamics of Success* (Greenville, SC: Attic, 1982), 126pp. Note especially ch. 2 on "The Causes of Institutional Decline."

[10]W. F. Albright dates Hiram's reign from c. 969-936 BC (see his *Archaeology and the Religion of Israel*, 40). This is done to accommodate 1 Kings 5:1 where Hiram sends materials to Solomon to build the Temple. But "Hiram" could have been a titular title like "Pharaoh." See also A. R. Green, *The Word of the Lord Shall Go Forth*, eds. C. L. Meyers and M. O'Connor (Winona Lake, IN: Eisenbrauns, 1983), 373-97.

[11]One of the foundational principles of biblical interpretation is that the student of the Word proceed from an *observation* of the teaching of the text to its *interpretation*. Only after this is he or she free to engage in *application*. Those who are anxious to skewer David for his polygamy jump from observation to application and fail to interpret his actions in light of the customs of the times.

[12]*Macmillan Bible Atlas*, 73, 100.

[13]*Macmillan Bible Atlas*, 100.

[14]Polygamy was not God's original plan for a man and a woman. I have explained God's design for marriage in *Your Marriage Can Last a Lifetime* (Nashville: Nelson, 1989), 17-29.

[15]Two rather obscure words are found in the narrative: *Alamoth* and *Sheminith*. *Alamoth* may be derived from *'alamot,* "girls," and so could apply specifically to songs sung by them. *Sheminith* may mean songs sung by men.

[16]For a study of Michal, see *You Can Have a Happy Marriage* (Nashville: Nelson, 1990), 77-91.

[17]From the Garden of Eden (cf. Genesis 1:26-28) to the present God has chosen to have His representatives rule on His behalf. In the course of time His theocratic representatives occupied the offices of prophet or priest or king (see J. D. Pentecost, *Things to Come* [Grand Rapids: Zondervan, 1964], 433-66). It was appropriate for David, as king, to bless the people in the name of the Lord.

[18] *Ibid.*, 65-94.

[19] *Annie Johnson Flint's Best-Loved Poems* (Grand Rapids: Zondervan, 1962), 104.

15. God-Given Success (1 Chronicles 18:1–20:8)

[1]*Macmillan Bible Atlas*, 101-04. For information about the Moabites, see *Peoples of the Old Testament World*, eds. A. J. Hoerth, G. L. Mattingly, and E. M. Yamauchi (Grand Rapids: Baker, 1994), 317-33; and *Peoples of Old Testament Times*, ed. D. J. Wiseman (Oxford: Clarendon, 1973), 229-258.

[2]Thomson, *The Land and the Book*, III:638-41, 643-45, 654-56, 658-63, 666-68.

[3]*Ibid.*, 363-65.

[4]Literally, "place his hand." This symbolized his control of the land. Though it cannot be decided with finality if the "he" of 18:3 refers to David or Hadadezer, the latter is most likely. If the reference is to Hadadezer, then the threat to Israel involved cutting off access to the trade route between the Persian Gulf and the Mediterranean.

[5]*Macmillan Bible Atlas,* 109-10.

[6]*Ibid.*, 104-05, 115. Tou's name is spelled Toi in 2 Samuel 10. Hamath is about 120 miles north of Damascus.

[7]For a description of these ancient people, see *Peoples of the Old Testament World*, 293-316.

[8]*Macmillan Bible Atlas*, 103*b*, 137. See also *Peoples of the Old Testament World*, 335-47.

[9]*New International Dictionary of Old Testament Theology and Exegesis*, 4:837-46.

[10]*Ibid.*, 3:744-59.

[11]Cf. G. W. Ahlstrom, *Royal Administration and National Religion in Ancient Palestine* (Leiden: Brill, 1982), 27-31.

[12]W. J. Deane, *David: His Life and Times* (London: Nisbet, n.d.), 124.

[13]*Hesed* is capable of a variety of meanings depending on the context (e.g., "loyalty, faithfulness, goodness," etc.), see *New International Dictionary of Old Testament Theology and Exegesis*, 2:211-18.

[14]Cf. 2 Samuel 17:27.

[15]The word is used elsewhere of decaying animal or vegetable matter (cf. Exodus 7:18; 8:14; 16:20).

[16]Thomson, *The Land and the Book*, 636-39, 641, 644, 652.

[17]L. Oliphant, *The Land of Gilead* (Edinburgh: Blackwood, 1880), 259f.

[18]*Macmillan Bible Atlas*, 101.

[19]C. Herzog and M. Gichon, *Battles of the Bible* (New York: Random, 1978), 83.

16. God's Wrath, God's Mercy (1 Chronicles 21:1–22:1)

[1]See *Nehemiah and the Dynamics of Effective Leadership*, 139-47.

[2]A recent example is C. R. Swindoll, *David: A Man of Passion and Destiny* (Dallas, TX: Word, 1997), 274.

[3]C. E. Ryrie, *Ryrie Study Bible* (1995), 655.

[4]Referred to as Arunah (or Oranah) in 2 Samuel 24:16.

[5]McConville, *I & II Chronicles*, 72.

[6]These words do not imply doubt, but rather are a Hebraism implying "It's my fault." The repeated use of the pronoun "I" further emphasizes his feeling of guilt.

[7]As has been noted before, commentators are quick to indict David for his "sinful census," but nearly all ignore the fact of Israel's sin (2 Samuel 24:1). David did sin, and upon confession was forgiven.

[8]Scholars who have compared this passage with the text of 2 Samuel 24:24 have noted what appears to be an insurmountable difficulty – one that they believe shows the Bible to contain errors. In reality the solution is quite simple. The amount David paid *for the whole property* was about 240 ounces of gold. This secured the land on which the future Temple would be built. The text of 2 Samuel 24 records only the purchase of the threshing floor.

[9]The amount given Ornan was about 240 ounces of gold, and included the property on which the future Temple would be built.

17. Final Preparations (1 Chronicles 22:1–29:30)

[1]W. W. Wiersbe, *Wiersbe's Expository Outlines on the Old Testament* (Wheaton, IL: Victor, 1993), 264.

[2]Braun, *1 Chronicles*, 267.

[3]Verse 11 refers to the "plan" (*tabnit*) that David gave to Solomon. The usage of this word recalls the Tabernacle (cf. Exodus 25:9, 40), where the same word is used. It seems clear that in David's mind the Temple was to be a continuation of the Tabernacle.

Subject Index

Persons Index